The Poetics of Transgenerational Trauma

The Poetics of Transgenerational Trauma

Meera Atkinson

BLOOMSBURY ACADEMIC
NEW YORK • LONDON • OXFORD • NEW DELHI • SYDNEY

BLOOMSBURY ACADEMIC
Bloomsbury Publishing Inc
1385 Broadway, New York, NY 10018, USA
50 Bedford Square, London, WC1B 3DP, UK

BLOOMSBURY, BLOOMSBURY ACADEMIC and the Diana logo
are trademarks of Bloomsbury Publishing Plc

First published in the United States 2017
Paperback edition first published 2019

Cover design: Liron Gilenberg/ironicitalics.com
Cover image © Getty Images

Names: Atkinson, Meera, author.
Title: The poetics of transgenerational trauma / Meera Atkinson.
Description: New York: Bloomsbury Academic, 2017. | Includes bibliographical
references and index.
Identifi ers: LCCN 2016050062 (print) | LCCN 2017009959 (ebook) |
ISBN 9781501330872 (hardcover: alk. paper) | ISBN 9781501330889 (ePub) |
ISBN 9781501330896 (ePDF)
Subjects: LCSH: Psychic trauma in literature. | Intergenerational
communication in literature. | Psychic trauma–Patients–Family
relationships. | Families–Psychological aspects.
Classifi cation: LCC PN56.P914 A85 2017 (print) | LCC PN56.P914 (ebook) | DDC
809/.93353–dc23
LC record available at https://lccn.loc.gov/2016050062

ISBN: HB: 978-1-5013-3087-2
PB: 978-1-5013-4911-9
ePub: 978-1-5013-3088-9
ePDF: 978-1-5013-3089-6

Typeset by Deanta Global Publishing Services, Chennai, India

To find out more about our authors and books visit
www.bloomsbury.com and sign up for our newsletters.

Then a tongue

rears up to speak into the silence,
memory turns and blocks the door of sleep,
draws out temper into a wire that streams

names of lost relatives.

—Robert Adamson, from the poem "Ballad of the Word Trauma"

Contents

Foreword

At the very moment that I am writing this foreword to Meera Atkinson's profoundly affecting and brilliantly conceived book, women across the United States (and beyond) are taking to social media to share the details of their personal encounters with male sexual aggressors. These experiences, many of them long buried (although not necessarily repressed), are reemerging, coagulating, and gathering heat in the light of Republican presidential candidate Donald Trump's lurid musings—"hot mike" and otherwise—over his own sexually predatory behavior. And suddenly something that may have happened, say, twenty or thirty years ago feels viscerally in the present. Memories rise up in this moment of electoral danger, maybe still half-shivering but with the renewed urgency of gender politics. Women's voices reverberate across an already charged public atmosphere, forcefully speaking back against sexual intimidation, assault, and patriarchal power. Foregrounding not just a personal but an *extra*-personal effrontery, this collective registering of women's voices asserts something more, something projective, something perhaps even transhistorical and transgenerational: not me/not what happened to our mothers and grandmothers/not us/not our daughters and our daughter's daughters/not again/not ever.

Stop.

How to give voice to trauma that is gendered, raced, etc., in acts of public testimony? How best to transmit, to finesse, to share? How to find each other, to receive, to listen? How to acknowledge the aesthetic and ethical stakes raised in such voicings and account for the pertinent demands that they make on the past, present, and future? How to achieve some sense of reckoning, of transformation? How to turn these testimonies of trauma into resonating machines that become generative without lapsing into something that can be too hastily discounted or recuperated, too blatantly voyeuristic, too hemmed in by those humdrum pathways that can often terminate at culturally prescribed roles for victim and victimizer? Daring to offer up evocative and scrupulously conceptualized responses to challenges like these (and many more besides) are among the standout achievements of *The Poetics of Transgenerational Trauma*.

It is impossible, I think, to enter into this work and, by its finish, not be shaken into a fresh set of critical tonalities attuned to how previous postures of embodied receptivity become unstuck in the tremulous vibrancy that resounds between trauma's wordings and worldings. Atkinson's writerly voice not only serves as a reader-friendly guide through various forms of traumatic testimonies—drawn from an astounding array of literary genres: fiction, Indigenous writing, graphic memoir, *l'écriture féminine*, and other modes—but also deftly navigates some notoriously treacherous theoretical waters (within and across trauma studies, literary theory, feminist theory, queer theory, postcolonial studies, affect studies, critical animal studies, critical race studies, environmentalist discourses, philosophy, and more).

It is perhaps no accident then, that "transmission" and "poetics" are two of the key animating concepts of this book. They serve as the crucial bywords by which trauma studies and affect studies can productively intersect and extend through one another, picking up on premises and further fulfilling the promises raised by Atkinson in her 2013 book *Traumatic Affect* (coedited with Michael Richardson). The "trans" of transmission and transgeneration addresses the virtual traversing of affective capacities and incapacities between bodies: nothing mystical nor otherworldly, just the thoroughly ordinary way that feelings often come to adhere, getting handed down (and up and over), living on in matter and atmospheres, always more and other-than-human. Hence, the role of poetics and Atkinson's emphasis on the literary—as the evocation and activation of these vital forces that exist/persist/insist/resist in and about bodies, in the shimmerings and shudderings and stutterings of their enunciation into language (understood in its broadest sense). There is much to gain in discovering how distinctive literary genres wrestle with their unique tellings of transgenerational trauma, and Atkinson has gifted us with a capacious critical methodology for unfolding these lessons into the everyday.

By the time this foreword is published, the matter of Donald Trump's presidential candidacy will have been resolved, but the operations at the root of it won't likely have been dissolved. What realities and injustices might eventuate should such a man win office? There is no way of knowing precisely what shape or scope such traumas might take in the future. Thankfully, the conceptual formulations and affective formations that Meera Atkinson conveys so convincingly across the pages of this book travel a considerable distance in advancing the poetic strategies and tactics that can transform how we imagine coming out on trauma's other side.

Gregory J. Seigworth
Coeditor of *The Affect Theory Reader* and
Capacious: Journal for Emerging Affect Inquiry
Millersville University
October 18, 2016

Acknowledgments

Anna Gibbs and Magdalena Zolkos provided steadfast guidance and offered enthusiastic support from the very beginning, and throughout much of this research. Their scholarship and solidarity was critical to the writing of this book, and I extend a heartfelt thank you to them both. I am indebted to the Writing and Society Research Centre at Western Sydney University, and I thank all those there who offered contributions along the way, especially Kay Are for an early golden suggestion that helped shape this work. And I thank the Association for the Study of Australian Literature for supporting this research with seed funding. I owe hearty thanks to Marion May Campbell and Dominique Hecq for their astute comments and suggestions, Julianne Schultz, editor of *Griffith Review*, for her early backing of this project, and Katrina Schlunke for her big-hearted mentoring in the world of academia. I am grateful for the assistance of Deborah Staines, and for welcome leads offered by Teja Brooks Pribac. I am also most appreciative of Jen Webb's discerning reading and feedback. This work has benefitted from Gregory Seigworth's generous collegiality and suggestions proffered at a crucial stage, and I extend warm thanks for his further contribution of a most affirming and insightful Foreword. Elaine Swan's friendship and support in navigating the waters has proved indispensable over the time in which this book was written and prepared for publication, and I also thank my online network of intellectual womenfolk for their company and for the welcome blend of high- and low-culture discourse that punctuated my working days throughout the duration of this project. A very special thanks is in order in recognition of the all-round, tireless camaraderie of Michael Richardson, my colleague and coeditor of *Traumatic Affect* (2013), whose friendship, encouragement, and close reading of this work has been invaluable, to say the least. It was Michael, too, who introduced me to editor Haaris Naqvi, helping this book find a home at Bloomsbury Academic. I thank Haaris and the team at Bloomsbury for their assistance in getting this book to print. Deepest gratitude goes out to my partner, Gregory Atkinson, for his spirited and practical support of this project, and for accompanying me through the years of this book's making.

I would like to acknowledge previous publications in which parts of this book appeared in different forms. Chapter 1 includes material from the article "Strange Body Bedfellows: *Écriture Féminine* and the Poetics of Trans-trauma" (2014) in *TEXT: Journal of Writing and Writing Courses*, vol. 18, no. 1. Sections in Chapter 3 appear in the essay "On *Carpentaria*" (2015), commissioned by *Griffith Review* for the Copyright Agency Reading Australia Program. And an edited version of Chapter 4 was published as "Transgenerational Trauma and Cyclical Haunting in Pat Barker's *Regeneration Trilogy*" (2015) in *Cultural Studies Review: Interventions*, vol. 21, no. 4.

I am most grateful to the following publishers for granting permission to reprint. An earlier and alternate version of Chapter 3 was published as "Channeling the Spectre and Translating Phantoms: Hauntology and the Spooked Text" (2013) in *Traumatic Affect*, a collection I coedited with Michael Richardson, Cambridge Scholars Publishing, Cambridge, UK. Thanks are also due to those who have permitted me to use material as epigraphs. Robert Adamson and Black Inc. kindly approved my use of an excerpt from Adamson's poem "The Ballad of the Word Trauma" published in *Net Needle* (2015). The University of Chicago Press also generously permitted my use of an excerpt from Nicolas Abraham's essay, "The Phantom of Hamlet or The Sixth Act: Preceded by the Intermission of 'Truth'," in *The Shell and the Kernel: Renewals of Psychoanalysis* (1994) as an epigraph in the conclusion.

Finally, I want to acknowledge all those who bear the most punishing brunt of transgenerational trauma transmissions. I salute those workers, in all manner of fields and functions, on the ground and at the front lines, who come to their aid. And I pay tribute to those writers and artists of varying persuasions who testify by way of creative practice to those operations, and thank most especially those whose work I explore. I have tried to honor their courage and match their dedication through the course of writing this book.

Introduction: Trauma, Affect, and Testimonies of Transmission

Seventy-nine women were killed by violence in Australia alone in 2015 (Destroy the Joint 2016), the majority by partners or ex-partners. That's more than one violent death per week. And the World Health Organization has announced suicide as the leading cause of death for young women aged 15–19 the world over, linking this disconcerting finding to "gender discrimination" (Valenti 2015). Yet despite some political rhetoric acknowledging the sexism and misogyny that give rise to epidemics of violence against women and children, there is no direct correlation made to the traumatic and traumatizing social organization that breeds underlying attitudes and behaviors. These deaths and the mental and emotional states that motivate them are treated as aberrations in an otherwise healthy society. Rosie Batty became a tireless domestic violence campaigner and the 2015 Australian of the Year after her 11-year-old son Luke was beaten to death with a cricket bat by his father at a sporting event in 2014. Batty has declared that family violence calls for a response akin to terrorism:

> We see whenever there is the slight threat of terrorism it's amazing how funding can be found to combat that where seemingly there was no funding before: let's start calling family violence terrorism and then maybe we can start to see funding flowing to this area. (Scarr 2015)

Clearly, terrorism is political and politicized in a way these murders are not. Votes are not won or lost on whether women and children unknown to us are safe from untimely and violent death. The new age of global terrorism, we understand, affects us all. It is unpredictable, and might strike any one of us down in myriad horrific ways and random situations. But relational violence, we imagine, is someone else's problem, unless it's not. We'd rather these crimes not occur, but generally speaking most people don't feel directly threatened by them. This is a dangerous miscalculation.

Our collective denial around the social effects of familial trauma is supported by an elaborate system of slanted communications and representations. For example, the media routinely reports the murder of women and children by men in the context of family violence with quotes assuring the public that the perpetrator was a pillar of the community, a loving husband and father, who "snapped" or suffered mental illness. Granted, mental illness is often a factor, and is often closely linked to traumatic events, but this kind of reporting does not address the question of why, if mental illness were the sole cause, women aren't committing these violent crimes in the same numbers as men. There are other kinds of violence stemming from social structures of power and privilege, but they are less likely to be framed with a focus on, and sympathy toward, the perpetrator, and they are less likely to involve a glossing over of the social conditions within which the unfortunate event has taken place.

Though these crimes are publically discussed as epidemics warranting urgent attention and action, they are rarely acknowledged as intrinsically linked to a broader patterning rooted in patriarchy. They are most commonly cast as tragedies, implying both that they are exceptional events and that they are unavoidable. They are neither, though they are, within the context of patriarchal social structures, inevitable. Even maternal infanticide—the horrific murders of children by disturbed women like Andrea Yates and Susan Smith—can be seen as a consequence of these social structures. Mental illness is obviously a factor, but as Adrienne Rich (1976) and Jane Gallop (1988) point out, murderous maternal anger is a symptom of a "darker, deeper violence that systematically constitutes motherhood as a patriarchal institution" (Gallop 1988: 2). These deplorable crimes are examples of "violence by and to the mother" (2). Why and how is it, then, that attention is so routinely diverted from the operations surrounding and generating such "tragedies"? And what is necessary to break this trance?

There is a profound problem posed by these questions that *The Poetics of Transgenerational Trauma* in part seeks to address: How is it that certain traumatic acts and transmissions are understood as discrete events disconnected from the structural realities of social organization? And what can literature do to help disrupt the spell of denial and naturalization, to challenge the common tendency to cast some traumas as personal plights that would more accurately be positioned within cultural operations we all inhabit? Trauma is gendered, raced, classed, economized, and otherwise shaped by relations of power, privilege, and disadvantage. Despite this, family violence is still commonly represented as an ahistorical anomaly, a fundamentally individual catastrophe rather than a social one.

Troubling and daunting social realities have beset the first decades of the twenty-first century: legally dubious warfare, global terrorism, financial crisis, human-induced climate change, new addictions (internet, gaming, etc.), neocolonialism, and increased family and intimate partner violence. While traumas involving large-scale or historical violence are widely represented in literary trauma theory, familial trauma has had less attention. This book contributes to the emerging field of feminist trauma theory in exploring the transmission of trauma across generations and its literary testimony, revealing crucial operations at the dynamic intersection of affect and trauma between subject, text, and society. I propose this literary testimony constitutes a feminist experiment and encounter, offering new understandings of the political significance of the literary testimonies of familial trauma within the context of broader society. By interpreting a diverse range of literary works, I theorize an experimental writing capable of illuminating the ways in which trauma is transmitted affectively across generations, and between subjects, families, and societies at large. These works and my reading of them confront systematic denial of trauma as a cultural operation. Intervening on debates around trauma transmission and the nature of the literature that exposes it, this book asserts that such works stand as vital political accounts, cultural critique, and political action.

In disciplinary terms, trauma straddles the fence between clinical "trauma studies" on one side and cultural "trauma theory" on the other. It is paradoxical, then, that though I align this work with the latter I take my starting point from the former. It was the discovery of the term "chronic trauma," coined by Judith Herman (1997), that first piqued my interest in an exploration of familial trauma and the subsequent writing of it. Herman depicts chronically traumatized individuals as isolated subjects who experience acute aloneness and a social alienation and disconnection that "pervades every relationship, from the most intimate familial bonds to the most abstract affiliations of religion and community" (37). This, for me, raised the question of the role of writing as a form of communication capable of transfiguring debilitating isolation. I was also drawn to an exploration of the ways writing familial trauma addresses social connections and disconnections. Testimony, as a particular mode of communication, came into focus during the second half of the twentieth century, and as *The Future of Testimony: Interdisciplinary Perspectives on Witnessing* (Kilby and Rowland 2014) makes clear, its relevance in the twenty-first century highlights witnessing in an increasingly technologized and globalized environment. These piquings of interest naturally led to consideration of transgenerational transmissions, since familial trauma tends to run in multigenerational cycles, and it does not do so in a vacuum: social connections, disconnections, and historical contexts are contributing factors.

The Poetics of Transgenerational Trauma examines the ways in which literary testimony communicates affective and relational contagion, illuminating transmissive cycles of trauma that are grounded in structural social organization and have consequences across generations. I use the term "transgenerational trauma" to describe both intergenerational trauma transmissions, and multigenerational transmissions, as occurring outside specific family units. As such, my understanding of transgenerational trauma focuses on familial trauma, though it is by no means limited to it. It is because my investigation involves consideration of the relationship between familial, intergenerational, and multigenerational trauma, and trauma as a social phenomenon, that I primarily use the term "transgenerational" rather than "intergenerational" or "multigenerational," which might suggest traumatic transmissions as limited to a specific familial lineage (in my view such compartmentalization of trauma is impossible). *The Poetics of Transgenerational Trauma* examines the ways literature elucidates the processes of transmission and the cultural conditions that give rise to it.

I pause here to highlight my interdisciplinary approach, lest an expectation of traditional literary criticism lead to disappointment. My survey of selected texts is not one of exhaustive textual analysis that seeks to identify the formal properties of each text in terms of classical literary studies. Instead, I read the texts as portals for cultural critique and in a broadly interpretative spirit that foregrounds those aspects that relate to transgenerational trauma.

The clarification, then, is that my engagement is less concerned with the technical workings of the texts or with a forensic analysis and more concerned with the cultural realities addressed within the works and the ways in which writing reveals them. I believe this methodology is necessary for consideration of the complexities of trauma transmission and writings inspired by them.

Trauma refers to experience that occurs too quickly or suddenly to be processed, that alters brain function and other aspects of subjectivity, returning in delayed symptomology, which may or may not appear pathological. Some posttraumatic symptoms are not only accepted as normal, but are socially rewarded, while others are pathologized and stigmatized. The forefathers of psychoanalysis laid the fundamental groundwork for trauma studies and trauma theory, with an understanding of trauma as a psychic experience of an event that results in "permanent disturbances of the manner in which the energy operates" (Freud 1974: 315). Sigmund Freud's perception of trauma evolved over the course of his career and across much of this thought. Freud famously abandoned his early seduction theory, which stated that hysterical patients continued to suffer from the effects of sexual assaults that occurred in childhood, and this is still seen by many, particularly feminist theorists and survivors of child sexual assault, as a betrayal. However, other aspects of his work, including his notion of *Nachträglichkeit*, translated from German as deferred action, or afterwardness, prove productive for my conceptualization of phylogenetic heritage and its writings.

In *Nachträglichkeit*, it is not simply that a trauma or traumas that took place in the past return in the present. The word describes the way an impossible event—one not consciously registered due to its shock or speed—is registered with disproportionate affective discharge, by a subsequent, and often seemingly trivial, or at least not necessarily traumatic, experience. Trauma is related to an overwhelming or sudden experience, and it is characterized by a delayed response that features involuntary and often repetitive disturbing phenomena, such as nightmares and flashbacks, and symptomology that includes depressive and anxiety disorders, suicidal ideation, and addictions. Far from being a simple upsetting memory of an event located in the past, trauma involves a complex psychic operation that challenges the notion of a distinct psychic past and present.

The implications of what this means for testimony have been explored by leading trauma theorists such as Cathy Caruth, whose focus on literary testimony is underpinned by her view of trauma as "always the story of a wound that cries out, that addresses us in the attempt to tell us of a reality or truth that is not otherwise available" (1996: 4). Shoshana Felman echoes this vision of literature as "an alignment between witnesses" (1995: 14). These views are at odds with Ruth Leys's (2000, 2007) preoccupation with intention and signification and her cognitivist inclination regarding affect and emotion.

Leys has critiqued post-Holocaust theorists like Dori Laub, writing from a psychoanalytic position, and literary trauma theorists Felman and Caruth at length. While it is not my intention to weigh in on the debate or to engage in academic score settling, a targeted review of certain key sticking points is useful for teasing out the understanding of trauma that is elaborated upon in this book. For example, Leys objects to what she calls Caruth's "literalist version of history as chronicle, conceived as a nonsubjective, nonnarrative, and nonrepresentational method of memorializing the past" (2000: 273), because what concerns Leys most is individual accountability. Leys sees Caruth's post-structuralist leanings as constructing an ethically shaky understanding of trauma that grants perpetrators a proverbial get-out-of-jail-free-card. While Caruth and Felman don't explicitly figure transmission as occurring at the nexus of trauma and affect in the way I do, they do gesture toward some kind of transmissive operation. There are crucial questions to do with ethics in the theoretical arguments in play. These are not questions easily addressed, but I am obliged to speak, however briefly, to Leys's criticisms and offer some explanation of my position in order to frame the ideas in this book in relation to influential works in the field of trauma theory.

I am aligned with Caruth's view of trauma, but I stop short of claiming that the poetics of transgenerational trauma operates entirely independent of authorial agency, intention, or interpretation. I do maintain that a writer can testify significantly, linguistically, and affectively to aspects of transgenerational trauma and its transmissions that elude those meditative functions and direct expression in language. Leys's focus on responsibility and indignation at what she sees as a conflation of victim and perpetrator informs her critique of Caruth's conception of trauma. Leys later extends these same preoccupations and objections to affect theorists who theorize the autonomous or virtual potentials of affect. I respond to those criticisms in Chapter 4. For now, I want to acknowledge some validity to Leys's point that "trauma does not present itself as a literal or material truth," but as a "psychical or 'historical truth'" (282). Leys takes Caruth to task for expanding her model to include transmission, homing in on Caruth's suggestion that "one individual is understood as capable of haunting later generations—as if ghosts of the pasts could speak to those living in the present, contagiously contaminating them" (284). Leys's moral outrage in defending the victims of extreme and historical trauma is expressed as theoretically rigorous evaluation. Accusing Caruth of a logic that would turn "the executioners of the Jews into victims and the 'cries' of Jews into testimony to the trauma suffered by the Nazis" (297), Leys herself collapses into the literalism for which she reproaches Caruth. Sustained by catching Caruth out on analytical detail, Leys fails to acknowledge the enormity, and importance, of Caruth's vision.

Viewing trauma as a social force does not amount to promoting an equivalence of traumatic experience between "victim" and "perpetrator," an absolution of responsibility for those enacting violent crimes, or a negation of the gravity of genocide in general or the Holocaust in particular. Caruth is concerned not just with individual testimony but also with trauma at a social and political level, and one of my areas of concentration is the way trauma repeats/reoccurs at those levels. Underlying these explorations is a sense that a more sophisticated understanding of the stratums of trauma might contribute to breaking the cycles of perpetration and victimhood that continue with devastating consequences in ever-new manifestations. It is not that the Nazis can, or should, be thought of as victims of the Holocaust—clearly Nazi war criminals and those who colluded with them can never be held to have suffered the persecutions and tortures of the genocidal trauma European Jews experienced. But if we take the long view, we might consider that Nazism had its roots in trauma, which partly informed its rampant anti-Semitic affective transmissions and found such deadly collective expression in the "ethnic cleansing" agenda of the fascistic Third Reich.

Acknowledging that a traumatic national condition was necessary for Hitler (himself the product of an abusive childhood) and Nazism to have taken root does not amount to a condoning of it, or to a pardoning of the crimes committed. It is even possible that traumatic numbing, in combination with the discursive production of a certain kind of historically specific subject, was the foundation for what Hannah Arendt famously termed "the banality of evil" (1963). And so it goes on. We hope never again, and yet the world watches on as Israel blockades and routinely conducts brutal military operations in Gaza and Palestinians blow up busloads of Jews. The Syrian crisis scatters millions of refugees around the globe; many arrive at closed borders. In West Papua New Guinea, the Indonesian government continues what activists refer to as "slow motion genocide" decade after decade as other nations, including Australia, its closest neighbor, turn the other cheek (Elmslie and Webb-Gannon 2013). And racists and misogynists are emboldened by Trump's victory, while we wait to see just how much damage his Presidency will leave in its wake. At some point, each crisis ends (or temporarily abates) with many lives lost and many others shattered, and perpetrators are called to account, if not in their lifetime then often enough in the history books. Still, this does not prevent another cycle of violent trauma playing out.

Leys, it seems, sees a global populace that can clearly be divided between victim and perpetrator, and while to some degree we all do (as I have done in the preceding paragraph), and those distinctions do pointedly matter, taking an individualist-oriented moral high ground fails to address the recurrent traumatic cycles that have marked every epoch of human history. Such cycles now pose an even greater danger to an increasing number of people, as well as to nonhuman animals and the earth itself, due to advanced technological capabilities and global mobility. It is not, then, that I refuse to distinguish between those traumatically acting out destructively and those who are traumatically acted upon destructively. Rather, I propose that there is a desperate need for new understandings of the way trauma works cyclically and in assemblage in order to better recognize, intervene in, and prevent traumatic cycles.

My notion of cyclical haunting picks up on theories suggestive of the potential of trauma transmission. Allowing for an intergenerational transmission of trauma does not equate to claiming the same traumatic experience of the survivor forebear, nor does it mean license to claim verbatim knowledge or cognitive memory of the traumatic event(s). It does not even necessarily involve "remembering," as we commonly think of it, at all. Most people will never be aware of the trauma passed on to them, let alone specific events or details, but lack of consciousness of a traumatic legacy does not prevent its being carried from one generation to another. Even with little to no cognitive knowledge, it is possible for an individual to exhibit posttraumatic symptoms from which they can and do act, speak, and write.

When I speak of traumatic event(s), I do not mean to suggest that I see the traumatic encounter as a static or fixed occurrence. In an interview with Jordan Greenwald, Lauren Berlant offers a heuristic from *Cruel Optimism* (2011), in which she describes a more fluid, open-ended, affect-tinged view of event:

> An episode is a perturbation in the ordinary's ongoingness that raises to consciousness a situation that follows from something without bringing with it conventions or prophecies about what its ultimate shape as event will be. Episodes are defined first by causality, but their affective charge derives from confronting the enigma of their ultimate shape. Something has an impact: What will happen? I call this process the becoming-event of the situation. A situation usually gets its shape from the way that it resonates strongly with previous episodes. (Berlant and Greenwald 2012: 72)

I view the traumatic encounter, whether catastrophic or covert, as a becoming-event, an event that both reverberates with previous traumatic encounters and generates an affective charge destined to later, and again, resonate.

The lived, politically positioned, socially inscribed body is often absent from, or minimized in, these debates about psychic trauma. As Lisa Blackman makes clear, the body is "now no longer peripheral to humanities study" (2012: 4) and "sociology of the body" is now an "established subdiscipline of sociology" (3), but body studies and affect theory pose challenges to each other, despite the obvious and intimate relationship between the body and affect. Trauma transmissions are a contradictory operation in that they involve subjective and familial experiences of trauma in which shame, fear, anger, and other affects reinforce a sense of being bound to a body and subjectively and socially confined within it; they also exceed this boundedness in interrelational contagions. I align my conception of transgenerational trauma testimony with feminist thinkers who propose the practice of "thinking through the body" (Gallop 1988) and writing through the body, as well as those theorists who propose modes of intersubjective and transsubjective affective transmission.

This is to say that the chapters that follow focus on a seeming paradox: thinking (and writing) through affect, and specifically traumatic affect—which describes affect that is bound to, and by, trauma. My use of the term "traumatic affect" signals an attempt to address trauma in an affective framework and affect in a trauma theory framework. I bring this to bear on writing about transgenerational transmissions, exploring both the role of affect in trauma transmissions and the question of what it means for affect to lead the way in literary accounts of those transmissions. Highlighting an understanding of affect as "a state of relation . . . of forces or intensities" (Gregg and Seigworth 2010: 1), traumatic affect describes that movement of affect as stemming from traumatic experience.

The history of affect theory is multifaceted, with developments on different fronts and at different time periods. Traditionally, influenced by Plato, and later Descartes, Western thinkers have tended to view emotion as obstacles to higher functioning in social, political, and intellectual life, at best harmless or trivial indulgences and at worst hysterical and dangerous diversions from reason and common sense. The "affect theory" that has emerged in response to this historic devaluing is not just one theory; it is a complex, and often contradictory, jostling of theoretical approaches, some of which existed before the term "affect theory" gained currency. Baruch Spinoza, Enlightenment philosopher, was the first major Western thinker to challenge this essentially negative view of emotion and affect, and his work remains crucially relevant today, over three centuries later.

It is for this reason that I draw on his theory of affect and ethics throughout this book, and most notably in Chapter 2. But there are other important precursors to the contemporary, interdisciplinary "affective turn" in the humanities. Psychoanalysis theorized affect in relation to the libido and "life drive," and the feminist and queer theories that emerged throughout the 1970s, 1980s, and 1990s also proved influential. Holocaust studies made significant contributions, and it paved the way for the study of intergenerational trauma. The trajectory that led from trauma studies is thus seen as central to the rise of affect theory. Due to the diversity of thinking within the field, an introduction to affect theory in general, and specifically to the ways in which I work with it, will lay a foundation for more nuanced explorations in the following chapters.

The American psychologist Silvan Tomkins (1963) theorized a phenomenological approach to affect, and theorists such as Eve Kosofsky Sedgwick and Adam Frank (1995) returned to his work in order to critique the post-structural tendency toward abstraction and the hypersensitivity to perceived essentialism in the humanities in the twilight of the twentieth century. Recentering the affective reality of the body, Sedgwick and Frank highlighted the importance and productive potential of Tomkins's view of affect. Though there have been energetic challenges to this revitalization of his theory, namely from Ruth Leys, the reclamation of Tomkins provides a valuable starting point for understanding the subjective and interpersonal dynamics of transgenerational trauma and its testimony in literature.

Categorically detailing the specific ways in which traumatic affect is transmitted is beyond the scope of this project and the disciplines from which it emerges. There are numerous avenues of exploration, including scientific investigation and experimentation, and psychological clinical studies, and I am not equipped to theorize transmission on these fronts, suffice to say that universally agreed upon and scientifically verifiable knowledge is restricted at this point, and many questions remain as to the potential of affect in relation to transmission. I speak to some of the possibilities I view as most viable for our present capacity of knowledge, and as most convincing from an observational and experiential standpoint. Throughout the chapters that follow, readers will encounter various propositions about the ways in which traumatic affect might proceed, both in trauma transmissions, and in the writing of them. If it at times seems as if I utilize disparate theories and contradictory views, it is both because there are so many different conceptions of what affects are and do and because affects themselves are somewhat mutable, hence so too are their transmissive operations. What the various conceptions of affect share, though, is an emphasis on relation as constitutive of affect and thus its relevance to explorations of familial and cultural transmissions. Tomkins offers a useful vocabulary of affect that provides a foundation for understanding the ways in which affect might work within those contexts.

Tomkins describes *affect* as a distinct biological, innate response to stimulus. He relates this to biology and defines it as transcultural and universal. He uses the word *feeling* to denote the awareness of a given affect as it is experienced, and the ability to comprehend it as a subjective experience. He relates this to psychology and to individual interpretation of the story of affective experience. Tomkins casts *emotion* as affect and feeling filed away as memory, which he relates to biography and individual life experiences. This describes the way that affect, noted and recorded as memory (conscious or unconscious), leads to a sensitivity to the particular feelings associated with those experiences, resulting in a tendency toward certain emotions (feelings attached to memory) in response to certain stimuli. This simplified breakdown is not the last word (there are different accounts, many of which are insightful and have productive promise), but it does suggest variable possibilities of transmission and may help clarify the seemingly conflicting discussions of transmitted traumatic affect throughout this book.

Where I discuss affective autonomy and virtuality, I speak in terms of embodied affect as it escapes biological confines due to speed and intensity, and as it may transmit through the atmosphere and in those enigmatic yet undeniable engagements between the energetic and material realms. Teresa Brennan's work on the transmission of affect (2004) outlines numerous ways in which such movements of affect may proceed. Citing Marx and Foucault, who argued for a social constructivist view of subjectivity, she describes the transmission of affect as "a process that is social in origin but biological and physical in effect" (3). Brennan calls for a new metapsychology capable of gaining insight into the mysteries of affective transmission, and her propositions draw on both cultural theory and science to explore a range of possible modes that include sensory (she is particularly interested in olfactory transmission), hormonal, and in utero transmission. Though the process, in her view, is social in origin, it becomes individual and psychological to the extent that thoughts and beliefs are attached to the transmitted affect, thereby shaping subjectivity (and relationship). Crucially, she states that "feminine beings" (15)—not only women, but children, nonhuman animals, those racially ascribed into the realm of the feminine through discursive processes such as Orientalism (Said 1978), and those otherwise not exhibiting the standard signs of masculinity—bear a disproportionate degree of negative affect. I speak to this by way of an intersectionality framework in Chapter 5.

While Brennan's otherwise valuable exploration of transmission makes some unsubstantiated and less than entirely convincing claims regarding pheromones and the like, Sara Ahmed articulates a compelling approach to the transsubjective movement of affect in her materialist exploration of the cultural politics of emotion. Casting emotion and its circulation in terms of cultural practice, Ahmed shows how affects transmit through language and signs and between bodies, with varying degrees of "stickiness" (2004). Ahmed explores the question of what affect does. For her one of the most notable things it does is differentiate between people in ways that define their perceived value. As such, emotion works as prime political currency. For Ahmed, recovery from injustice (and I would add the trauma so often associated with it) involves exposure through testimony. And the work of exposure is "both political and emotional work" (200). This is central to my view of the poetics of transgenerational trauma. Drawing on Tomkins, Ahmed's account of shame focuses on the way that the shaming of Australia's Indigenous people has served a racist, imperialist, nation-building agenda. I address this history specifically in Chapters 4 and 5. Though Ahmed doesn't explicitly raise Tomkins's (1963) conception of "shame-binds," she does suggest the ways in which the consequences of the politics of shame translate into systematic injustice and shame-bound "minorities." This disparity is reflected in statistics showing that the suicide rate among Indigenous peoples is more than double that of non-Indigenous Australians (Mindframe 2016).

For Tomkins, shame-binds are processes in which various affects/emotions become bound to shame. When it comes to trauma, it stands to reason that shame would likely bind most commonly to fear, sadness, and anger, because these are the affects most associated with an experience of powerlessness. In terms of familial transmissions as they affect the youngest members, shame can attach to a great deal more. Traumatic shame-binds can wound the very fabric of developing subjectivity, and can in turn make traumatized children particularly vulnerable to further shame and shame-binds. For Tomkins, shame is, to borrow Ahmed's term, super "sticky" and its propensity for adhesion to other affects can repress the capacity for feeling in general. Joseph Adamson and Hilary Clark discuss shame-binds as "particularly crucial in understanding the significance of shame in psychodynamics" (1999: 15).

I would extend this to transmission, for it is those affective repressions and binds that are most likely to give rise to transmissive language and behavior, and that the poetics of transgenerational trauma can loosen.

Affect bound to trauma might be understood as what Tomkins calls a "script." Russell Meares (2000), writing within the context of clinical trauma studies, presents a compatible conception in his "traumatic memory system" (53), in which cognitive/affective/behavioral formations come into play, which he rather poetically refers to as "satellites of trauma" (112). The tendency of traumatic shame to bind in indirect ways was addressed by Gilles Deleuze (Negri 1990) when he described being struck by Primo Levi's repeated references to the Nazi camps producing a sense of shame at being human. It is not, Deleuze points out, that Levi suggests we are all responsible for Nazism, but that "we've all been tainted by it: even the survivors of the camps had to make compromises with it, if only to survive" (Negri 1990). Relating this to what Levi famously refers to as the gray area, Deleuze declares such shame "one of the most powerful incentives toward philosophy, and it's what makes all philosophy political." Freud made a similar point when he acknowledged poets and philosophers as having discovered the unconscious before him (Adamson and Clark 1999).

The writers that would testify to such operations mine both conscious and unconscious material (individual, familial, and social) as it relates to violations and movements of traumatic affect—through familial and cultural scripts. And the poetics of transgenerational trauma is political in that it reveals the shame-bound gray area of traumatic transmissions that taint us all, to greater or lesser degrees. I do not claim that such works are new, but rather that they have a new significance as expressions of what Julia Kristeva has termed "intimate revolt" (2002). A "new world order" that constitutes a "society of spectacle" means that "political revolt is being mired in compromise" (2), necessitating the (re)turn to the "sensory intimacy" of literature (3). Ann Cvetkovich also speaks to a contemporary reality in which "political depression" results from "the sense that customary forms of political response, including direct action and critical analysis, are no longer working either to change the world or to make us feel better" (2012: 1). But, she qualifies, if this sounds like a downer, there is yet positive possibility for dark "moods, and sensibilities become sites of publicity and community formation." Cvetkovich suggests the expression and circulation of public feelings "to generate the affective foundation of hope that is necessary for political action" (2).

I consider the works I survey to be examples of literature that encompass these potentials. They each emerge not only, or necessarily, out of a thematic of trauma but as renderings of trauma transmissions in structure and temporality, graphic panels, experimental grammar, and, of course, language itself. In her classic text, *The Words to Say It*, Marie Cardinal (1993) paid homage to the power of words:

> Words could be inoffensive vehicles, multicolored bumper cars colliding with one another in ordinary life, causing sparks to spray that did no harm. Words could be vibrating particles, constantly animating existence, or cells swallowing each other like phagocytes or gluttonous corpuscles leaguing together to devour microbes and repulse foreign invasions. Words could be wounds or the scars from old wounds, they could resemble a rotten tooth in a smile of pleasure. Words could also be giants, solid boulders going deep down into the earth, thanks to which one can get across the rapids. Words could become monsters, finally, the SS of the unconscious, driving back the thought of the living into the prisons of oblivion. (239)

Testifying to transgenerational trauma confronts the task of outwitting the Schutzstaffel (SS) of the unconscious who would drive back the thought of the living into the prisons of oblivion, or, in other words, denial. As Cardinal's writing suggests, this process is bodily and the power of words serves as a sort of salve.

This book addresses writing that embodies and translates traumatic familial events, despite the unreliability of traumatic memory, and I assert that this writing involves an ethical intricacy less black and white than the common association of a fixed "truth" in memoir and autobiography allows. This writing, despite its possible, or probable, factual unreliability, can nevertheless serve as an important site of testimony and witnessing. These texts do not seek to represent a single violent or original event or events in the past, or an individual or family history, so much as they express the unassimilated reverberations of traumatic affect by writing between and around trauma's paradoxical lack of registration and its belated hauntings. As such, this kind of writing cannot hope to tell the truth exactly; nor does it attempt to, if truth is taken to mean an objectively verifiable claim. It would be more apt to say that it does some work toward *undoing lies*. In *Three Steps on the Ladder of Writing* (1993), Hélène Cixous, writer, philosopher, and literary theorist, writes: "I circle 'the truth' with all kinds of signs, quotation marks, and brackets, to protect it from any form of fixation or conceptualization. . . . It is what writing *wants* [italics in original]. But 'the truth' is totally down below and a long way off" (1993: 6). Praising writers of texts that "say the worst," Cixous is quick to distinguish this saying of the worst from confession, stating: "I am not talking about religious people; these are poets. It's not about confessing oneself" (41).

My conception of the poetics of trauma distinguishes the kind of truth of which Cixous speaks from hard evidence and fact. When the kind of truth a writer is called on to bear witness to is not a straightforward disclosure, the writing might be thought to constitute the art of unlying. If absolute truth is an impossibility the next best thing is to move in the direction of it, to at least not knowingly lie, to attempt to undo lies in the act of writing. "Our lives are buildings made up of lies," elaborates Cixous. "We have to lie to live. But to write we must try to unlie" (36). This writerly unlying is not just the unlying of the construct of the self, but also of the familial foundation and the cultural turf on which that self has been built. Defining truth as "the thing you must not say," Cixous calls it the miracle of the child and the poet who walk toward home (in the direction of truth): "And for this home, this foreign home, about which we know nothing and which looks like a black thing moving, for this we give up all our family homes" (1993: 36).

When it comes to trauma, truth is not only the thing you must not say, but also *the thing you cannot say*. The thing you cannot say, as such, may best be expressed creatively, imaginatively, poetically, and affectively. Words, however malleable, can never completely convey the visceral surge of terror or profound shame, or the subjective splitting at the root of trauma, and yet, when set loose in linguistic or structural experimentation they get closer to doing so than when confined in orthodox mores and routine strategies. This writing practice makes possible communication of that which evades rational thought and conventional genre limitations. It also allows for testimony outside what Ernst van Alphen calls indexical memory. Arguing against the transmission of trauma between generations, van Alphen insists that memory is fundamentally indexical in terms of continuity between event and memory and that this is therefore inherently individual and cannot be transferred (van Alphen 2006: 485–6). But as Marianne Hirsch points out, this objection only holds if you view memory as a purely cognitive indexical operation. In this sense, van Alphen would be more compatible with Leys's approach than mine. Hirsch (2008) argues, as do I, for a view of memory that encompasses bodily and affective imprints. My understanding of the poetics of transgenerational trauma is in keeping with Hirsch's assertion that "postmemorial work" endeavors to "reactivate and re-embody more distant social/national and archival/cultural memorial structures by reinvesting them with resonant individual and familial forms of mediation and aesthetic expression" (111).

Since trauma creates a condition of unreliability in its telling, it is an act of empowerment for a writer to knowingly work with this unreliability, to bring imagination to bear on the psychic and bodily remnants and traces of trauma in order to produce a literature that offers itself to witnessing and unlying. The dreamlike quality of traumatic memory would seem to lend itself to poetic and novelistic treatments and to memoir/fiction fusions. I do not use the now dated term "faction" because I do not want to forge an assumed alliance between memoir and factual account in this writing (though of course it may contain some factual accounts). "Autofiction" is another term used in literary criticism to describe the practice of bringing the contradictory styles of fiction and autobiography together in one work. It is a preferable term for several of the works I examine since it leaves out the explicit claim to truth. As Shirley Jordon (2013) suggests, this "slippery hybrid" involves a "privileged connection" to trauma, but it falls short because some testimony to transgenerational trauma is not memoir. Natalie Edwards (2012) analyzes the controversial work of Christine Angot, declaring it "relational autobiography."

This is interesting because a subjective slant and the impossibility of objective fact is implicit in the relational, but ultimately none of these terms quite captures the nature of the texts I examine. To endorse an assumed alliance between memoir and factual account, when the memoir in question involves traumatic operations, would be to do violence to the nature of traumatic memory by attempting to force it to conform to a dualism that favors fact over affect. When it comes to the perplexing territory of transgenerational trauma, such conformity refuses the opportunity for a unique process of artistic production and testimony, one that enables vital expression of, and engagement with, traumatic affect for both writer and reader. A few words about the term "the poetics of transgenerational trauma"—poetics refers to both the study of formal techniques in poetry and literature generally and alternatively to the craft of writing poetry. My usage of "poetics" relates more to the latter as it extended to include the art of writing poetically and/or experimentally in testimonies of transgenerational trauma. Further, the surveyed texts not only testify to trauma transmissions, but also are themselves transmissive texts, and I speak to the dangers of writing and reading this testimony in Chapter 2.

The texts have been selected because each demonstrates distinct features of the poetics of transgenerational trauma, in content and form, because each of the texts arises out of a compelling context, and because each makes an important and spirited contribution to literature. All are contemporary works written by women. Being contemporary and authored by women are not essential qualifications of this testimony, as I detail in Chapter 1, but it is also no accident. If feminized beings are conditioned and positioned to carry negative and traumatic affect, it is hardly surprising that they will be at the forefront of testimony to such operations. The textual interpretations offered in the following chapters focus on eight texts: Alison Bechdel's *Fun Home: A Family Tragicomic* (2006), Hélène Cixous's *Hyperdream* (2009), Marguerite Duras's *The Lover* (1992), Pat Barker's *Regeneration Trilogy* (1999), and Alexis Wright's *Carpentaria* (2006) and *The Swan Book* (2013).

I count each of these as masterful works that proffer crucial contributions to our understanding of trauma and its transgenerational transmission as it has played out throughout history, its operations in literature and in culture, and its creative potential. It is not my intention to romantically aver that writers somehow transcend trauma by virtue of being able to work with it in the production of literature. That would be sheer folly given the number of artists and writers who have displayed conscious awareness and creative capacity around trauma only to ultimately succumb to its ill effects (i.e., probable suicides such as Primo Levi's, confirmed suicides such as Anne Sexton's, and the many who have met addicted, alcoholic, or otherwise reckless and untimely fates). Many who initially survive traumatic experience and go on to work with its presence productively, sometimes brilliantly, in various art forms or endeavors are later felled by it, overtly or covertly lured into its deathly embrace. Likewise, I am wary of claims that conflate writing with the therapeutic cure of trauma. But as I argue in the coming chapters, each of the selected works serves to facilitate a reckoning with trauma. There are certain questions at the heart of this book: How does a chronicle of transgenerational trauma reveal the processes of transmission and the cultural conditions and collective trauma associated with it, thereby becoming a social force of political import? And what might motivate a writer to undertake such a daunting project? Each of the works surveyed demonstrate different tactical approaches to the challenging brief in the first question, as the chapters that follow detail. Along the way, I make some suggestions as to the personal and political motivations and benefits of such works.

In the first chapter, I conduct a comparative reading of two novels touted as autobiographical: Elizabeth Smart's *By Grand Central Station I Sat Down and Wept* (1991) and Marguerite Duras's *The Lover* (1992), arguing that the latter is an example of the poetics of transgenerational trauma, while the former, despite many similarities, is not. *The Lover*, set in the dying days of French colonial Vietnam, and most celebrated for its erotic tale of the affair between a teenaged French girl and a rich Chinese man, is a postmodernist classic with translations in over forty languages. Duras is said to have been surprised by its success, and she went on to renounce it, declaring it "an airport novel," written while inebriated, which is quite possibly true since Duras, who wrote the book in her twilight years, having already published over forty works, was alcoholic (Mastroianni 2015). Debate continues as to the weight of its contribution to literature; I side with those who view it as an accomplished text. In my reading, its achievement is not diminished by the insobriety of the writer, or by Duras's own assessment. If for some it is the "disconnected musings of a seventy-year-old writer" (Mastroianni 2015), it is to my mind an example of the (aged) organic fracturedness of traumatic experience. Duras's backtracking on her initial description of the novel as autobiographical, her casting into doubt its factual reliability, might be read as traumatic symptom of both writer and text. Even its drunken production might be considered a part of its (symptomatic) traumatic testimony.

Situating the poetics of transgenerational trauma in relation to the significant literary and feminist notion of écriture féminine (Cixous 1981), a controversial conception that seems to be enjoying something of a revival, I argue that Smart's novel exhibits the qualities of écriture féminine, while *The Lover* both qualifies as écriture féminine, and crucially departs from it. This comparative reading shows how the traumatic and feminine are implicated in, and by, one another in patriarchal culture and in écriture féminine. In proposing the poetics of transgenerational trauma, I also draw on Julia Kristeva's notion of the "strange body" (1984) to complicate the question of gender, arguing that the writing of transgenerational trauma is not defined by a particular biologically determined or gendered writing body.

Next I consider the ethics of writing (through) a history of familial trauma and the possible dangers of this testimony. I contextualize Alison Bechdel's graphic memoir, *Fun Home: A Family Tragicomic* (2006), and Hélène Cixous's fictional memoir, *Hyperdream* (2009), in a broader discussion of genre (and genre resistance). *Fun Home*, a cult classic by the author of the popular and long-running comic strip *Dykes to Watch Out For*, is set in rural Pennsylvania. The book tells the story of Bechdel's childhood and early adulthood, wrangling with trauma relating to verbal and emotional abuse, homophobia, and the probable suicide of her homosexual father. *Fun Home*, inspired—as much recent graphic memoir has been—by Art Spiegelman's powerhouse transgenerational trauma testimony *Maus* (1996), joins the ranks of graphic works that have successfully tackled transgenerational trauma post the Second World War. Graphic memoir has perhaps been the most prolific and fruitful of literary genres in terms of trauma testimony, in large part because it facilitates ready and direct "access to non-verbal and highly affective embodiment and materiality of trauma, subjectivity, emotion and experience" (Chute 2012). As exacting and demanding as the process of creating graphic memoir must be, the poetics of transgenerational trauma seems an even more daunting challenge for those, such as Duras and Cixous, working with language only. In this case, the writer must find ways to birth the "embodiment and materiality" (Chute 2012) of trauma with words alone, hence the heightened use of poetry, metaphor, and linguistic and structural experimentation.

In *Hyperdream*, Cixous achieves this in poetic prose by bringing her sharp critical eye for the cultural underpinnings of personal experience and the personal underpinnings of political realities to bear on her keen poetic impulses. A novel/memoir hybrid, *Hyperdream* is about the tender ties between living and dying, a relationship between an ailing mother and her carer daughter, and the specter of a traumatized Europe. "I write at length, and without interruption," Cixous once said in a public talk about her writing process. "As if I were a runner, a marathon runner. . . . And when I don't write, I sleep, and when I sleep, I dream, which means I write" (New York State Writers Institute 2007). This relentless day/night, waking/sleeping writing process gives rise to an elliptical narration that demonstrates the power of poetic language in trauma testimony. Working with Spinoza's theory of affect, I argue that in depicting trauma and enacting writing as a social force, these texts, as diverse examples of the poetics of transgenerational trauma, constitute a specific mode of literary testimony involving a particular affect-ethic. There is, I show, a substantial difference between testimony in which personal history becomes a portal for the illumination of cultural conditions, and testimony in which this portal remains closed, or at least obscured.

Turning my reflection on familial trauma to focus on Indigenous understandings of family, I go on to examine the postcolonial and cross-cultural testimony of Australian author Alexis Wright. Her groundbreaking novel *Carpentaria* (2006) followed several notable publications (1998, 1997a,b) and put Wright, an Aboriginal land rights activist, academic, and educator, firmly on the map in Australian letters. The story is set in Australia's Top End, where the Aboriginal people of the region live in the long shadow of colonialism, only to have a multinational mining corporation move in on traditional sacred land. Hailed an instant classic by critics, *Carpentaria* took the better part of a decade to bring to completion. This is understandable given the scope of its ambition and the innovating complexity of its testimony to transgenerational dispossession. Bringing together Derrida's post-structural figuring of hauntology and Nicholas Abraham and Maria Torok's psychoanalytic concept of the "phantom" in my reading of *Carpentaria*, I argue for a deconstructive reading of the phantom, outlining a view of the affective operations of the poetics of transgenerational trauma as a record of historic trends of transmission. Specifically, I show how trauma can operate as social and political inheritance, and I examine the crucial role of cross-cultural literary testimony in bearing witness to the crimes of colonialism and Indigenous cultural heritage.

Continuing my engagement with hauntology, Chapter 4 brings together the strands of my argument in what I call "cyclical haunting," a concept that draws on Deleuze and Brian Massumi's work on the virtuality and the autonomy of affect to describe the way historic and social currents of traumatic affect feed into, and out of, subjective and familial experience. I consider these operations in light of Pat Barker's *Regeneration Trilogy* (1999), three books that observe the profound sufferings of the First World War and life for British people, home and abroad, during that period. The trilogy is notable for its inclusion of numerous, meticulously researched real-life characters, including the poets Siegfried Sassoon and Wilfred Owen, the writer Robert Graves, and the anthropologist/psychiatrist William Rivers (Rivers appears in all three books). These remarkable books were written by an Englishwoman not yet born when the "Great War" raged; an ex-teacher with a degree in history and economics from the London School of Economics, who likes to describe herself as "an ordinary mum from up north" (Riding 1995). Despite that seeming distance, it turns out that there was, as with the other texts I survey, significant personal investment and involvement in the project. Barker, who was raised by her grandparents, was conceived during a wartime fling. She had been told her father had died in the war, and her grandfather had also fought and sported a bayonet scar on his back, which the young Barker was sometimes allowed to touch while listening to him recount war stories (Riding 1995). Having learned of Rivers's work through her husband, a Professor of zoology, Barker began her lengthy research. Though that research provides the spine of the trilogy, and much of its compelling weightiness, it would seem that the heart of *Regeneration*'s antiwar politics is Barker's own lived experience of transgenerational trauma. The result is that these novels, blending nonfiction and fiction, reveal a dynamic between interpersonal realms and networks beyond them: movements, collectives, institutions, communities, creeds, religions, subcultures, nations, governments, terrorism, and globalism.

The hypothesis of cyclical haunting as applied to Barker's trilogy adds a further dimension to the understanding of transgenerational trauma testimony. I argue that despite (and because of) the crucial role of personal experience in the poetics of transgenerational trauma, such literature should be respected as political account rather than simple subjective revelation or fictional story.

Chapter 5 charts connections between gender, race, and the environment, demonstrating the ways in which the poetics of transgenerational trauma witnesses to intersected injustices and traumas. Returning to Alexis Wright's *Carpentaria* (2006), and extending focus to her follow-up novel *The Swan Book* (2013), this speculative chapter ponders cyclical haunting beyond the human. *The Swan Book*, Wright's third novel, is even more innovative and high-stakes than the celebrated *Carpentaria*. It tells the story of a young Aboriginal rape survivor, Oblivia, first adopted by an old woman immigrant and later kidnapped by an Aboriginal politician. *The Swan Book* projects the concerns of today—the severity of posttraumatic experience among Aboriginal Australians, the retraumatizing policies of present-day government, the threat of human-induced climate change—into a not-too-distant future in which global warming has already wiped out the Northern Hemisphere on page one. Employing the framework of intersectionality, I show how the novel exposes traumatic intersections of injustice in society in relation to gender, race, and age. *The Swan Book* is unique in its depiction of trauma transmissions that exceed human society. Nonhuman animals are threatened and becoming extinct at an unprecedented rate, and there are claims from the scientific community that the consequences of climate change are poised to increase to levels that endanger human life and community. Challenging entrenched humanist and speciesist preoccupations with trauma, I show that human trauma transmissions routinely impact the environment and other sentient beings. Employing material from the environmental sciences and critical animal studies, I argue that these considerations are urgent and necessarily feminist in orientation, and that the literature that exposes this constitutes a radical form of political action and activism.

Finally, in conclusion, I expand on the question of "how" and "why" in relation to the poetics of transgenerational trauma. Building on the tacit implication throughout the book that trauma is not static or an entirely negative experience, assuming it is satisfactorily survived (physically and sufficiently psychically), I link Abraham and Torok's understanding of introjection to the Deleuzian notion of becoming in acknowledgment of the creative facets and potentials of trauma.

As my readings of the surveyed works reveal, the writing of traumatic transmissions is an act of courage because the writer faces the ethical dilemmas and discomfort of negotiating a way through the gray area of which Deleuze (after Levi) speaks; this testimony also involves writing of, and through, traumatic affective binds. The writer who undertakes this task acts as a kind of lantern bearer. The very expression of affect can be bound by shame, and the degree to which it is permissible or disallowed varies between individuals, families, and cultures. Thus, art and literature become indispensable pathways for the recognition of trauma and affect as social forces. As Adamson and Clark state, "In art and literature, shame and repression are diminished, and the richness of emotional life, its stimulation and turbulence and nuance, is investigated in its complexity" (1999: 15). It is here, at the forefront of this claim, that I place my conception of the poetics of transgenerational trauma.

Why, it might be asked, does the claim to this writing being primarily social and political matter? It matters because it rocks the intellectual and institutional traditions that unwittingly enable the continuation of a social organization that breeds deathly and damaging cycles of trauma. My insistence that this testimony is political involves a challenge to the common perception that traumatic and traumatizing acts are isolated anomalies affecting unfortunate individuals, rather than the organic consequences of an entrenched patriarchal and ruthlessly capitalist social and political system. It is a system that dominates the entire planet, causing women, children, men, people who identify as nonbinary or genderqueer, and nonhuman animals to suffer unnecessarily. It is a system in which the vast majority of us are, in one way or another, implicated.

1

L'écriture Féminine and the Strange Body

Few of the founding texts that established the enormously productive field of Holocaust studies, or the works that came to the fore throughout the 1990s that took the examination of literary testimony as their project, gave sustained focus to the question of gender in relation to trauma. This is an understandable omission, especially for the pioneers of Holocaust studies, many themselves survivors, who were struggling to understand the diabolical psychic, social, and political operations that led to the Shoah, and its traumatic legacy. Since the 1990s, gender studies and trauma studies have proceeded side by side and the "scholarly fields of gender and trauma have been profiled, elaborated and intertwined in various theories and disciplines, to a various extent" (Festic 2012). The question of gender in relation to transgenerational trauma is a productive one, as scholars like Marianne Hirsch (2012) have confirmed and demonstrated, but even recent major publications in trauma theory, such as *The Future of Trauma Theory: Contemporary Literary and Cultural Criticism* (Buelens, Durrant, and Eagleston 2014), which takes a decidedly interdisciplinary approach to reevaluating trauma theory in the twenty-first century, fails to substantially address gender.

At the most obvious level a connection between gender and trauma can be made in terms of lived experience. For example, being or becoming a woman is associated with heightened traumatic encounter in the form of rape and violent crime, partner and family violence, historic (and still prevalent in degrees depending on location and context) educational disadvantage, and exclusion, constraint, and underrepresentation in public life. In theorizing a poetics of transgenerational trauma, my interest in gender lies more in the ways in which this poetics constitutes a feminist practice rather than in claims prescribing the biological sex of the practitioner. In this chapter I tease out the similarities, differences, and intriguing departures between what has been formulated as "feminine writing" and the writing of transgenerational trauma. In doing so, I evoke critical considerations around gender and writing in order to show that the poetics of transgenerational trauma is not a straightforwardly gendered writing; rather it is produced via strange-bodied traumatic memory and its affective circulations.

Reading trauma theory, one repeatedly comes across an interpretation that to speak or write trauma is to attempt to liberate the unconscious and express experience not representable in language. The claim is that trauma is not readily available to conventional discourse in language. This claim is based upon a general understanding of trauma responses as "the often delayed, uncontrolled repetitive appearance of hallucinations and other intrusive phenomena" (Caruth 1996: 11). Here, the subject is rendered speechless by delay, by a lack of psychic registration, and the seemingly incoherent reverberations of belatedness.

The post-structuralist feminists Hélène Cixous and Julia Kristeva highlight another area of the unsayable, or at least the not sayable in ordinary language. In Cixous's works (Cixous 1981a,b), this is depicted, more or less, as writing the body (that which remains outside of figurative and conventional language) and writing the experience of woman (marginalized in phallocentric culture). Cixous has famously asserted that "feminine" and "revolutionary" embodied writing challenges cultural and literary gender operations. Relating this practice to the affective and bodily depths Cixous does not primarily refer to the physical body or biology, but to the body as a "complex of social and biological processes" (Oliver 1993: 174).

Kristeva (1984) relates unrepresentability to what she calls the "semiotic chora" (the term "chora" is borrowed from Plato). Following on from, and complicating, Jacques Lacan (1977), she relates the semiotic to the maternal, which predates paternal (patriarchal) law and the subject's entry into the Symbolic Order. Lacan establishes the Symbolic Order as the realm of signification and language and of social reality. In Michel Foucault's nonpsychoanalytic political philosophy, such social operations are alternatively theorized as "discourse" (1980), which describes organizations of knowledge, language, bodies (individual, textual, institutional), materialities, activities, and power that are specific to particular moments in history and that change throughout history. The chora's prelinguistic "semiotic aspect of signification indicates what is 'below the surface' of the speaking being" (McAfee 2004: 18). It is bodily and linked to the energy of the drives. Its relationality is to the maternal, but it is not simply somatic; it is also linked to the liminal, the thetic, and language, however socialized and conditioned. For Kristeva then, the subject is involved in a signifying process that cannot be reduced to categories of simple representation. Though she resists the idea of sexed writing, even in metaphorical terms, it is this inference of the prelinguistic maternal that has been read as implying a feminine element in language, resulting in a differently nuanced comprehension of what Cixous explicitly denotes as *écriture féminine* (feminine writing). Despite these developments in the period preceding their writing, those at the forefront of literary trauma theory, such as Cathy Caruth and Shoshana Felman, do not appear to have engaged with the question of sexual difference or the gender relations of, and within, language, when formulating their textual theories of traumatic writing. Even the psychoanalytic theorist Maria Torok (Abraham and Torok 1994), who takes an interest in both the literary operations of trauma and sexual difference, seems nevertheless to keep the two concerns separate in her work.[1]

I realize that recourse to these works by Cixous and Kristeva may, at first glance, seem dated due to their association with the second wave of feminism, but I cast them into a very specific context: the revisiting of notions of feminine writing in relation to transgenerational trauma and its transmissions. Such an examination necessarily requires engagement with the influential texts on écriture féminine, since they inform my positioning of trauma, as a first move in this book, in relation to questions of gender and writing. Despite their differences in detail, both theorists share the view that the desire or need to speak, to write, or to testify, contradicts trauma's predisposition to elude language, though neither names trauma explicitly.

Caruth refers to trauma as "the story of a wound that cries out, that addresses us in the attempt to tell us of a reality or truth that is not otherwise available" (Caruth 1996: 4). Felman articulates the pull to express trauma as a yearning to "*seek* reality" (italics in original) by exploring the "injury inflicted by it" in an effort to "re-emerge from the paralysis of this state" and move on (Felman 1995: 33). In extolling writing that "consists in saying the worst," Cixous appeals to us to "go and see, and not only see but inscribe the abyss we are" (Cixous 1993: 42). In Kristeva's view the language of the Symbolic Order is repressive, while the poetic language of the semiotic "reactivates" repressed material (1980: 136). So it is that the desire for voice and reckoning calls forth experience that resists (conventional) language, drawing us into therapy and/or the arts, into writing and reading, and into spaces and relations in which affect can lead the way.

In this chapter, I focus on two autobiographical novels and classics of poetic prose, *By Grand Central Station I Sat Down and Wept*, by Elizabeth Smart (1991), which I hold to be a rendering of feminine writing as described by Cixous, and *The Lover*, by Marguerite Duras (1992). *The Lover* has been widely written about, and I acknowledge that in many ways it reads today as a decidedly twentieth-century text. I have selected it because I view it as a solid starting point for my examination of the poetics of transgenerational trauma, revealing, as I argue in this chapter, something of its gendered and imperialist operations, which I address with developing nuance in later chapters. It is my hope, then, that even those readers most familiar with *The Lover* and corresponding criticisms might remain open to a fresh reading from a posttrauma turn, postaffect turn, twenty-first-century vantage point.

My aim is to position my theorizing of the poetics of transgenerational trauma by situating it in relation to a significant literary and feminist theory to a) show how the traumatic and feminine are implicated in, and by, one another in certain writing practices, and b) assert that the production of the poetics of transgenerational trauma has less to do with biological sex and more to do with the resonance of traumatic affect in bodily inscriptions. The notion of écriture féminine, as championed by Cixous during the late 1970s and early 1980s, sought to challenge phallocentric and logocentric gender relations with a vision of a feminist and revolutionary writing. Contentious from the start, it gave rise to international disputes about what constituted the feminine and whether or not a gendered casting of language was useful or advantageous. As well as highlighting gendered aspects of language and writing, écriture féminine also demonstrated a celebratory conceptual approach to writings that sit outside the dominant literary modes and the norms of the commercial publishing industry. In my examination of two such texts, I illuminate both crossovers and diversions between écriture féminine and the poetics of transgenerational trauma, showing that écriture féminine might be thought of as a kind of traumatic writing, and that the poetics of transgenerational trauma is, at root, a form of feminine writing that focuses on the operations of the transmission of trauma, familial and cultural. My suggestion that écriture féminine constitutes traumatic writing does not equate to a claim that "woman" is inherently traumatic, but rather that within a patriarchal cultural formation, writing the feminine—the affective, the chora, the subliminal—speaks of, and out of, currents of traumatic affect more readily than other, more conventional, forms of writing. My assertion that the poetics of transgenerational trauma is a form of écriture féminine is made in relation to Cixous's notion of a socialized, metaphoric "system of cultural inscription readable as masculine or feminine" rather than in relation to her statements that locate écriture féminine in embodied terms. I argue that both écriture féminine and the poetics of transgenerational trauma seek to destabilize dichotomies in which qualities attributed to the masculine are privileged (such as logical and rational thought and language) by way of profoundly affective writing practices, but that they also diverge in crucial ways.

Revisiting feminine writing

When contemplation of the body in writing trauma inevitably led to questions around gendered social, theoretical, and literary operations, my undergraduate reading of Cixous's exuberant texts celebrating écriture féminine came to mind as a seemingly obvious portal for reflection. No sooner had the thought occurred than reticence set in: the breathtakingly bold concept of écriture féminine, as proposed by Cixous, has been, for all its lyrical glory and emancipatory promise, a sticking point. Cixous herself admitted it was more a framework for exploration and a rallying cry rather than a theory proper, stating: "It is impossible to define a feminine practice of writing, and this is an impossibility that will remain, for this practice can never be theorized, enclosed, coded—which doesn't mean that it doesn't exist" (Cixous 1981a: 253). While it is not possible to do justice to the debates around feminine writing within the breadth of this chapter, I would like to draw out at least a couple of the issues raised in those debates in order to clarify my embrace of the term, and to position my view of the poetics of transgenerational trauma in relation to it.

The idea of subversive writing proposed by the so-called "French Feminists" generated a great deal of discussion, and dissent, particularly from American scholars and more materialist-oriented feminists such as Anne Rosalind Jones (1981), an early commentator and critic. The question as to where Kristeva should be positioned in relation to écriture féminine and to any notion of women's writing per se has also been debated. Following Jones, a number of feminist writers, most notably Kelly Oliver (1993), teased out the similarities and differences between Cixous and Kristeva. Though Kristeva wrote about her concept of revolutionary, and in some sense feminized, writing around the same time as Cixous was publishing on écriture féminine, their propositions were constructed in distinct ways. This disparity is key to my understanding of the poetics of transgenerational trauma. For Cixous, écriture féminine redresses patriarchal social and literary operations through the practice of a bodily writing, while Kristeva theorizes a revolutionary practice of/in language that facilitates social and political revolution. In "Sorties" (1981b), Cixous critiques the binary oppositions that culture, philosophy, and literature are based upon, positing her "qualifiers" of masculine/feminine as a way of critiquing this binary imbalance and phallocentric, logocentric social and political order. Conversely, Kristeva's revolutionary writing takes place in what Oliver calls a dialectic oscillation between the Symbolic Order—the dominant discourse of making sense—and the disavowed semiotic, which speaks the unconscious and drives via the musicality of poetics and avant-garde writing, and which is most evident in tones, rhythms, and gaps (Oliver 1993: 95).

In Kristeva's view, the semiotic is more active in this oscillation in revolutionary writing than in traditional literatures, and she conceives of the semiotic as preverbal and linked to the maternal. It is this gendered aspect of Kristeva's semiotic that has seen it linked to Cixous's characterization of the feminine in literature and to Kristeva's being associated with Cixous's écriture féminine, despite the fact that Kristeva herself has emphatically rejected the claim to a "woman's writing," stating, "There is nothing in either past or recent publications by women that permits us to claim that a specifically female writing exists" (Kristeva 1987: 111). Interestingly, though Cixous has often been charged with essentialism for her conception of a feminine writing, and though she herself fanned the flames of such charges by waxing lyrical about women writing in the same breath with which she promotes the glories of écriture féminine, Cixous has been careful to distance her "feminine" from "socially determined" sex.

Some Cixous passages *do* muddy the waters, such as when she writes: "Woman must write herself: must write about women and bring women to writing, from which they have been driven away as violently as from their bodies " (Cixous 1981a: 245). Cixous also states that while men are "coaxed toward social success, toward sublimation," women "are body" and to her mind this calculates as "more body, hence more writing" (257). These read as direct equations of woman, body, and writing. On the other hand, she stresses the cross-gender potential of feminine writing. Unsurprisingly, many failed to grasp the complexity of the apparent contradictions of Cixous's vision, which at one level advocated the writing of women, while at another went to pains to stress the metaphoric and nonbiological foundation of écriture féminine. In "Sorties," Cixous argues that there is a socialized "immense system of cultural inscription readable as masculine or feminine," which can be either reinforced or disrupted via the production of signs and relationships of power and production (Cixous 1981a: 93). She stresses that she uses masculine and feminine as "qualifiers of sexual difference," as cultural signifiers as it were, and that the "difference is not, of course, distributed according to socially determined 'sexes'" (93).

This claim would appear to be verified by the fact that Cixous wrote her PhD thesis on James Joyce. She has also repeatedly hailed Jean Genet as an exemplary practitioner of écriture féminine, along with Latin American writer Clarice Lispector. In my conception of the strange body, I propose a casting of "feminine"/feminist writing that loosens lingering associations with the activisms of the "second wave" women's liberation movement and revives it in the twenty-first-century present. In the pages that follow, I outline the poetics of transgenerational trauma as a related, but distinct, challenge to the patriarchal bearing and heritage of society at the deepest strata through language and literature, one generated from a locus beyond the specificity of the given individual body or its biological sex. So long as culture is bound by binary oppositions in which the masculine is privileged, the term "écriture féminine" remains useful, if for no other reason than that conceptions of revolutionary and feminine operations and writings remind us of the gendered conditions in which we participate in culture, write, read, and theorize.

The strange body

Lauded a masterpiece by Angela Carter, and widely held to be a gem of poetic prose, *By Grand Central Station I Sat Down and Wept* chronicles Smart's passionate affair with the married British poet George Barker, with whom she bore four children. It was first published during their four-year affair in 1945. In her foreword to the 1991 publication of the book, Brigid Brophy defends it as a "novel" despite stating that it is little more than "the bare three lines of a love triangle, and even those have to be inferred from the narrator's rhapsodizing or lamentation over them" (Brophy 1991: 8). This comment is crucial because though the book is a fine example of écriture féminine as espoused by Cixous—poetically somatic, penetratingly affective, and stunningly unconventional at the time of its publication—its narrative is, by and large, confined to the conditions of the affair. *The Lover*, by Marguerite Duras, is a critically acclaimed experimental memoir, hailed as one of the greatest autobiographical novels of the twentieth century. It is ostensibly about Duras's teenaged affair with a wealthy Chinese man in the dying days of colonial Saigon. In *The Lover*, Duras too demonstrates the feminine in and of language—that which is bodily, affective, and in Kristeva's terms, semiotic, though here we need remember that Kristeva's "semiotic" does not refer to de Saussure's structuralist theory of semiotics. Her semiotic is the emotional underbelly of the Symbolic Order. But, as I will show in my comparative reading of these texts, Duras also illuminates transgenerational and intergenerational trauma and the traumatic shame-binds of patriarchy, imperialism, and racism. As Maxine Hong Kingston says in her introduction, "The couple with no names in *The Lover* also reach each other through history that moved populations singly and en masse to and fro across the earth and into its every corner" (Kingston 1992: vi). Above all, it is the traumatized relation with the other that Duras mines—erotically, familiarly, and culturally.

Brophy notes the "liturgical" (1991: 9) nature of Smart's work, its "plundering classical mythology" and "mastery of metaphor" (10), and she likens the book to the work of "the only other supreme prose-poet of our age, Jean Genet" (11), whose work, we may recall, Cixous holds as exemplary of écriture féminine. Brophy declares the text's "insistent rhythm" to be the "rhythm of a throb," stating that "even when its rhythm expresses the throb of pleasure, the pleasure is so ardent that it lays waste the personality which experiences it" (Brophy 1991: 9). Pounding with poetic immediacy in the first person, present tense, Smart's text explodes in the manner Cixous espouses in "The Laugh of the Medusa" when she says, "A feminine text cannot fail to be more than subversive. It is volcanic; as it is written it brings about an upheaval of the old property crust" (Cixous 1981a: 258). Smart's prohibited and fecund desire does "shatter" the hallowed institution of marriage, and in her giddy rapture, she imagines she can "break up the truth" of the Second World War and of the meeting places of powerful men with her expectant adulation:

> With it I can repopulate all the world. I can bring forth new worlds in underground shelters while the bombs are dropping above; I can do it in lifeboats as the ship goes down; I can do it in prisons without the guard's permission; and O, when I do it quietly in the lobby while the conference is going on, a lot of statesmen will emerge twirling their moustaches, and see the birth-blood, and know that they have been foiled. Love is as strong as death. (Smart 1991: 66)

War, traditional marriage, the law, and other "masculine investments" are present in passing in Smart's novel, but only as fantasised and surmountable obstacles to the narrator's central mission of loving and desiring.

The Lover is primarily set in 1929, between the world wars, but the stench of war pervades the young girl's French heritage, and the never-ending tensions of the colony are palpable throughout. War, the patriarchy, and the masculine investment in violence are personified in the figure of the narrator's disturbed and disturbing brother, a bully, thief, gambler, and layabout manipulator. As she explains to her lover following yet another meal in which her family has steadfastly ignored him in a flagrant display of racist and colonial snobbery: "My elder brother's cold, insulting violence is there whatever happens to us, whatever comes our way. His first impulse is always to kill, to wipe out, to hold sway over life, to scorn, to hunt, to make suffer" (Duras 1992: 54). Later, when the narrator is older and living in France during the liberation of Paris, the elder brother shows up, having previously duped her out of her share of her mother's estate. He's on the run (the narrator suspects he is an anti-Semitic informer), and he promptly steals her rations and savings (77).

The affair in *The Lover* is also prohibitive. In fact, it is illegal (Duras was fifteen and under the age of consent when the affair commenced). Like Smart's affair, Duras's was subject to derision, punishment, and the law, but in *The Lover* there is no countering with romantic and exalted claims to love's overcoming realities such as war, colonialism, or racism. The desire the narrator shares with her Chinese lover is intoxicating in its way, but somehow always measured in relation to the culture in which it is conducted and tempered by its shaming gaze, which manifests as a kind of self-consciousness. This is evident in passages such as, "He gives me my shower, washes me, rinses me, he adores that, he puts my make-up on and dresses me, he adores me. I'm the darling of his life" (63) and descriptions of the Chinese lover washing her:

> under the shower, slowly, as she used to wash herself at home at her mother's, with cool water from a jar he keeps specially for her, and then he'll carry her, still wet, to the bed, he'll switch on the fan and kiss her more and more all over. (Duras 1992: 91)

Scenes like this depict the self-consciousness of a girl who takes refuge in sexual pleasure and comfort, and in doing so holds her inherited shame and grief at arm's length until an older incarnation manages to write it. In introducing my theory of a poetics of transgenerational trauma I preserve something of écriture féminine's most nonessentialist guise for the purposes of exploring the body and affectivity in the writing of trauma, while insisting that this poetics is rather the writing of a "strange body" (Kristeva 1987: 111). This strange body is capable of testifying to complexes of social operations and realities well beyond not only a given subject, but also a given generation.

Kristeva views radical writing as writing in which gender is displaced and replaced by an enigmatic strange body. This strange-bodyness is not gender absence or oblivion, but a space in which gender is shifted out of its moorings and confines. Positing revolutionary composition within the timeless, lawless realm of the unconscious, Kristeva holds that writing "ignores sex or gender and displaces its difference in the discreet workings of language and signification (which are necessarily ideological and historical). Knots of desire are created as a result" (Kristeva 1987: 111). Oliver (1993) points out that in "The Laugh of the Medusa" Cixous also suggests a similar idea when she envisions a writing that surpasses the metaphoric confines of the masculine and the feminine to become writing that is "not masculine or feminine but in between. It is bisexual. The between seems to exist within each of us, the presence of difference within" (Oliver 1993: 175). This puzzling reference to bisexuality in relation to feminine writing has to do with the description of Medusa put forth by Cixous—a feminine head with phallic tendrils for hair—an image taken to represent bodily, affective, feminine writing that appears in dynamic relation to the masculine principles it subverts. Clearly then, this refers not to bisexuality as a sexual orientation, but to an experience in which both potentials of gender are operative, something more akin to Kristeva's vision of the semiotic as written through the Symbolic.

For Kristeva, who sees writing as a reaction to the radical split of the speaking subject, this shift is described by way of the conceptual metaphor of birth rather than the conceptual metaphor of sex. "The eternally premature baby," she writes, turns to language as an act of desperation, "prematurely separated from the world of the mother and the world of things, remedies the situation by using an invincible weapon: linguistic symbolization" (Kristeva 1987: 111). The subjective operation that takes place in such a development is one in which a network is constructed where drives, signifiers, meanings, and, I would add, affects, "join together and split asunder in a dynamic and enigmatic process. As a result, a strange body comes into being, one that is neither man nor woman, young nor old" (111). In this conception, revolutionary writing privileges the disavowed semiotic, which speaks the unconscious. This resonates with understandings of trauma as involving a process of subjective splitting proposed by significant trauma theorists like Freud (1922), Jean Laplanche (1999), and Cathy Caruth (1995, 1996).

The roots of Duras's love affair lie deep in the traumatic soil of her family and the meeting of cultures, and even at her young age, our heroine, a budding writer, understands the limits of its power in surmounting them. This is a telling difference between the texts. Smart sympathetically portrays the harm she does to Barker's wife, as well as her own suffering, which becomes most acute when the affair finally falters. And the world of others does cross her path: there are gossips, well-meaning then abandoning friends, and a section in which she goes to live with her disapproving mother and disappointed father. But it is always Smart's psychosexual world of desire that is center stage of the novel. The affair in *The Lover*, on the other hand, is only one strand of a richer, more intricate, and layered fabric. Despite its title and reviews suggesting otherwise, *The Lover* is dominated by Duras's family—her "mad" (30), ferocious, and widowed mother, malicious older brother, and beloved and doomed younger brother—and their familial transmissions. Even her weak, adult lover is dominated by familial transmissions: he devours his young lover but finally forsakes her, thanks to his dependence on the money and approval of his father.

As significant as the characters of the narrator's brothers and lover are, it is women that *The Lover* is most meaningfully preoccupied with—chiefly the mother, but also a school friend, Hélène Lagonelle, whose beauty our nameless narrator admires and covets. There are intimate memories of, and musings on, the lives of women she knew in wartime Paris: an American named Marie-Claude Carpenter, and another named Betty Fernandez. Perhaps most poignant is her description of the "beggar women of the towns, the rice fields, the tracks bordering Siam, the banks of the Mekong" (Duras 1992: 86). Here Duras portrays the tragic lives of the native women of the colony as lived out in poverty—bearing children not wanted, who cannot be fed, and who die—women walking, walking, and ending up in Calcutta (97). "My memory of men is never lit up and illuminated like my memory of women," says the narrator (66). In a very real sense, the gendered trauma of women in the conditions of colonial patriarchy is more the story than the narrator's scandalous adolescent affair. Through her relationship with her deranged mother and these various women, Duras's protagonist reveals the toxic circulations of traumatic affect at the heart of the fading French empire. The shame-bound traumatic transmissions of colonial culture become her mother's shame-bound traumatic transmissions, which in turn become the narrator's—a spiraling circle of transmission.

Smart also exposes affective operations, but these appear as more intimately contained than those in *The Lover*. The affects most present in *By Grand Central Station* are joy, fear, guilt, and sadness; and these affects circulate within the love triangle of which the narrator is a part. This is evident in passages like the following, in which the narrator mourns the anguish of her lover's wife:

> On her mangledness I am spreading my amorous sheets, but who will have any pride in the wedding red, seeping up between the thighs of love which rise like a colossus, but whose issue is only the cold semen of grief? Not God, but bats and a spider who is weaving my guilt, keep the rendezvous with me, and shame copulates with every September housefly. My room echoes with the screams she never uttered, and under my floor the vines of remorse get ready to push up through the damp. (Smart 1991: 31–32)

Smart writes this woundedness of the other, but she never strays far from her obsessive insistence on the romantic and narcissistically transcendent paradigm within which she frames her story. By contrast, Duras seeks not only to write the woundedness of her narrator's life and those who immediately surround her, but also to write the woundedness of history. So it is that Smart's novel more closely aligns itself with the contentious blurring between écriture féminine and its perceived affiliation with "women's writing." Of the two texts, *The Lover* demonstrates most perceptibly the writing of the strange body of which Kristeva speaks. Duras's nameless, ageless narrator travels through time, one moment as a mature woman speaking of her past, and in the next as a young girl in her present, and yet again as an omnipresent eye tracking old friends in Paris or beggar women en route to Calcutta. The poetics of transgenerational trauma is generated less through a preoccupation around gendered experience (although it may depict a great deal of it) and more through strange-bodied traumatic memory and its affective circulations.

Smart's richness of imagery, ripeness of phrasing, and poetic skill cannot be denied. *By Grand Central Station* exhibits a poetic excess and sustained grandeur of prose that teeters at times on the brink of purpleness without crumpling into it. Duras's is a less flamboyant, but more densely affective testament to love and loss. Her narrator encompasses a subjectivity which, in addressing the magnitude of transgenerational trauma transmissions, is "split asunder in a dynamic and enigmatic process" reflecting the strange body of the transgenerationally traumatized subject. Such a body writes not only out of the strangeness of this radical split of the speaking subject, but also out of the fractured, shame-bound, fearful, and grief-stricken legacy of chronic and multigenerational trauma. Perhaps the only literary body stranger is that of the psychotic writer. Smart writes out of a desiring, self-absorbed femininity, while Duras, much older than Smart at the time of writing, morphs lucidly into a strange-bodyness oceanic enough to bear transgenerational multitudes.

At this juncture I want to make some qualifications about my co-opting of Kristeva's strange body. Namely, I distance myself from her preoccupation with the maternal preverbal as the site of subjective splitting to establish the traumatic nonverbal (in the language of the Symbolic Order) and traumatic subjective splitting as the conditions of the strange-bodied writing I propose. As Judith Butler says in her critique of Kristeva's postulating a semiotic writing as a "specifically feminine locus of subversion of the paternal law within language" (1988: 104), there are issues with Kristeva's formulation. For Butler, these include Kristeva's casting the semiotic as minor to the Symbolic major, the questionable construct of maternal body as prediscursive (that is, pre-Symbolic Order), the limits Kristeva places on the potential of the semiotic as a libidinal source of subversion (105), and the suggestion, as Butler reads it, that in Kristeva's theory of the semiotic "homosexuality cannot be a culturally sustainable activity" (110). Ultimately, contends Butler, "Kristeva offers us a strategy of subversion that can never become a sustained political practice" (106). The problem with Kristeva's original thinking on the semiotic and poetic language is the positioning of the maternal as organically and inevitably prior to cultural formation and the social.

Butler reconfigures the semiotic, using Foucault's (1980) theory of sexuality as constituted within discourse, with a series of deft moves that seek not to disprove Kristeva's general view of culture and the Symbolic renouncing of the feminine (in language and in body), but to question

> any theory that asserts that signification is predicated upon the denial or repression of a female principle ought to consider whether that femaleness is really external to the cultural norms by which it is repressed. In other words, on my reading, the repression of the feminine does not require that the agency of repression and the object of repression be ontologically distinct. (117)

In this way, Butler frees the semiotic from its restraints as aspects of being and language dependent on a prediscursive "maternal libidinal" (117). Instead, she views the maternal and its feminine libidinal economy as constructed by historically specific discourse, in other words as discursive effects. As Foucault also broadly established, where there is power there is resistance. Writing the semiotic, then, can be seen as libidinous resistance to this positioning of the maternal and feminine within the discourse of patriarchy. So it is that having based certain ideas on Kristeva's understanding of the semiotic, I ultimately pass over Kristeva's maternal and draw on Butler's recasting in my usage of Kristeva's strange body as the radically split subject that produces the poetics of transgenerational trauma.

This brings me to another salient point regarding the distinction between écriture féminine as enacted *By Grand Central Station* and the strange-bodied transmissive testimony of *The Lover*: the notable discursive change that has taken place since Cixous and Kristeva first introduced their conceptions of feminine writing. Bearing out Foucault's calculations regarding the construction of sex and sexuality via discourse, during these first decades of the twenty-first-century seismic shifts have been underway in relation to increasing identifications with, and understanding and acceptance of, nonbinary and multiple nontraditional positions regarding gender and sexuality. These include gender fluidity, transgendered transitioning, intersexuality, and asexuality. This development obliges us to think beyond strict and traditional gender categorizations in consideration of writing and testimony, even if we are thinking through them metaphorically. For example, when prominent "TERF" (Trans-exclusionary Radical Feminist)

Germaine Greer denigrates transgendered people and communities, she misunderstands a crucial point that I champion. It *is* possible to be born biologically female, to be a feminist, to work with feminist theory, and to be concerned, as feminists have broadly and traditionally been, with the lived experience of women born into the female sex and their writing, while at the same time to be open to identifications and lived experiences that are nontraditional, nonbinary, or not biological from birth. The strange body, then, does not require or reinforce either/or in-the-world trajectories or experiences; it does away with gender as a blunt instrument and admits its precarious complexity in traumatic testimony. To hold such a tension is not to maintain that these amount to the same lived experiences, but as the emergence of non-Western feminisms has taught us, no one feminism can efficiently, reliably, and routinely encompass the entirety of female experience in all its diversities and cultural differences.

The strange body of the poetics of transgenerational trauma challenges not only dichotomous gender roles maintained by the patriarchy, but also hackneyed popular perceptions of "women's writing," with its attendant lowly "genre" status and marketing tropes like "chick lit." We need only, as a momentary exercise, entertain how ludicrous the prospect of marketing "men's writing" seems to be reminded of just how problematic this term "women's writing" is. Yet it is also important to remember that its appearance was contextual: it emerged at a time when Western women were forcing their way into areas, such as politics and publishing, from which they had been historically barred. Though the term came into currency in recognition of women's entry into the public world of writing and literature in rising numbers, it has since become an albatross that all too often positions writing by women at a classed remove from the center of public debate and culture. My adoption of Kristeva's strange body contests both the remaining tendencies toward biological essentialism and the persistent propensity for trauma testimony by women to be commonly seen and marketed as personal accounts and therefore not political. Women now make up a substantial portion of the publishing industry—they are writers, readers, and publishing professionals—and one would hope the days of women writers and their books being roundly patronized are long past. But there is still a tendency for stories written by women that center on subjective and familial experience to be assumed less socially and politically significant than works by male writers, even if they bear witness to vast social operations. As this book is dedicated to proving, the strange-bodied poetics of transgenerational trauma demands to be taken seriously. At the same time, it is not neutral when it comes to gender. Rather, as I will show, this kind of testimony is fundamentally feminist in nature.

I want now to return to the matter of trauma and woundedness as a somewhat shared characteristic of both écriture féminine and the poetics of transgenerational trauma to show that the distinction lies in the way in which the latter testifies more decidedly to multigenerational transmissions. Cixous, whose father died when she was ten years old, often addresses trauma explicitly in her writings. Some ten to twenty years after her work on écriture féminine in the 1970s, Cixous talked about shame and the trials of writing through wounds and the body in a series of writings (1991, 1993, 1998). Unsurprisingly, discussions of the wound and the scar also feature prominently in trauma theory. Caruth, for example, links the wound to repetition and to the voice, by way of Freud's analysis of *Gerusalemme Liberata* (1820) by Tasso. It is in relation to this story that Freud coins the term "traumatic neurosis," which Caruth (1996) says, "emerges as the unwitting re-enactment of an event that one cannot simply leave behind" (2).

Reading Cixous (1998) and listing various definitions of the word "stigma," with its connotations of branding, infamy, disgrace, and Christian iconography, Kathryn Robson settles on an understanding of stigma as marks "impressed upon the skin, imprint the individual's past on the body, so that the stigmatized body becomes a site where history and identity are inscribed" (2004: 76). Wounds might be open, fresh, possibly weeping, presumably vulnerable to infection, while scars are *imprinted* wounds, *inscriptions*. The kind of injury embodied in *By Grand Central Station* and *The Lover* can, I argue, be contrasted in terms of the wound and stigmata. Both books employ experimental strategies that enable the writing of traumatic gaps that resist factual account and the orthodox benchmark of so-called objective recount. Both assert, and celebrate, the illogical splendor of sexual and writerly desire over socially prescriptive customs. Both equally challenge the "old property crust" of conservative literature through innovation and the blending of the genres of memoir and fiction. As such, both works are examples of feminine and revolutionary writing, but *The Lover* goes further in illuminating cultural and collective operations of trauma through the writing of familial trauma. *By Grand Central Station* represents woundedness, while *The Lover* represents stigmata as a "site where history and identity are inscribed" by the very processes of the transgenerational transmission of trauma.

Brophy (1991) makes an emphatic pronouncement on *By Grand Central Station*: "The entire book is a wound" (9)—and it surely is a throbbing wound of thwarted, satiated, and damaging desire. Smart occasionally hints at the traumatic operations that surround, and perhaps inform, this woundedness in lines like, "I am shot with wounds which have eyes that see a world all sorrow, always to be, panoramic and unhealable, and mouths that hang unspeakable in the sky of blood" (Smart 1991: 23), but the traumatic connections between the personal and the cultural, the individual and collective, are not realized and quarried as they are in *The Lover*. It is not the affair, nor the narrator's holy/hell incantation of it that energizes Duras's text, as is the case with *By Grand Central Station*, but rather the dark, echoey, lonely latency of intergenerational trauma. Her narrator writes:

> The story of my life doesn't exist. Does not exist. There's never any center to it. No path, no line. There are great spaces where you pretend there used to be someone, but it's not true, there was no one. (Duras 1992: 8)

In other words, Duras writes not just a subjective wound, or a triangular dynamic of woundedness, as Smart does, but a transcultural traumatic constellation of wounds and scars in which the narrator finds herself morphing, unsupported, into womanhood.

Robson conceives traumatic narrative as emerging from the wound (2004: 28), but Cixous is right when she says that writing can never *be* the wound itself, and neither can writing alone be its healing. Writing inscribes a scar that marks the site of the wound. The scarred transgenerational poetics of *The Lover*, with its impossibility of absolute healing across history, also inscribes the sweeping effects of French imperialism. This undead history reverberates around, and within, both the sexual and creative awakening of the young girl and the melancholic recollections of her older incarnation. Just as Butler cautions against "the illusion of a true body beyond the [paternal] law," I resist presenting the strange body in the poetics of transgenerational trauma in hyperbolic terms, as capable of somehow transcending the traumatic legacy of patriarchal imperialism. Instead, I position this strange-bodied writing as a stigmatatized site through which an "open future of cultural possibilities" (Butler 1988: 117) might take shape.

Finally, I consider the treatment of time as another significant point of difference between écriture féminine and the poetics of transgenerational trauma as manifest in *By Grand Central Station* and *The Lover*. The latter enacts what Caruth calls the "delayed appearance" and "belated address" of trauma (Caruth 1996: 4), alternating between first and third person, present and past tense, creating subjective shifts of intimacy and distance, in which time precedes in a nonlinear manner capable of crossing continents, seas, decades, and narrator selves. Despite its poetic obscurities in relation to time and its refusal of literal disclosure, time is fundamentally conventional in *By Grand Central Station*, which proceeds by way of chronological first person, present-tense narrative, beginning with the beginning of the affair, charting its course, and ending with the end of the affair. Here I extend Kristeva's conception of the strange body as gender shifted out of its moorings to include the way that in traumatic experience time is shifted out of its moorings.

In Caruth's view, the problem of traumatic memory is its inability to fully witness the traumatic event. The immediacy of the traumatic experience involves "a gap that carries the force of the event" and this process compromises and/or alters cognitive function, resulting in a loss of knowledge of the experience and conscious memory. The shock and force of trauma, in other words, appears in the very "collapse of its understanding" (Caruth 1996: 7). Since the traumatic experience is by nature not integrated at the time of its occurrence, it cannot become a normal cognitive memory that takes its place in a chronological narrative or "completed story of the past" (153). Caruth also raises the perplexing matter of the resistance of some "survivors" to accept a therapeutic "cure," citing a common ambivalence to outing what of the traumatic story and experience they feel they possess lest such steps "imply the giving-up of an important reality, or the dilution of a special truth into the reassuring terms of therapy" (vii). The poetics of transgenerational trauma, then, in its textual embodiment, offers something of a strange-bodied working-through of trauma, but one that, rather risking being lost when spoken and witnessed, memorializes trauma, immortalizes it, and testifies to it, by creating a continually available loci of witnessing and empathy.

By Grand Central Station features a solid, if lyrical, and self-possessed narration. The narrator suffers, is fragile, exhilarated, and diminished by turns, yet she remains subjectively coherent with an orderly sense of time and place throughout. Smart's prose is far from simple reporting on the progression of a substantial affair that encounters various complications. Much of the novel's power and poetry comes from the many passages in which nothing of significance happens on the external plane. It is in mining the inner world of the narrator that the prose takes flight, with its numerous allusions to mythological and metaphorical references. In this sense there is continual play between inside and outside time, and the inside time does have a kind of timelessness about it, an archetypal quality, as if it speaks not just for this one woman in love with a man less available and possessable than she would have it, but for the unbridled libidinousness and frustrated desires of all womankind. It is a narrative that engages with this archetypal collective unconscious, to couple both Cixous's and Kristeva's foci on the importance of the unconscious in feminine writing with Carl Jung's well-known notion of the collective unconscious (Jung 1981).

By contrast, *The Lover* testifies to a more complex unconscious operation. In the poetics of transgenerational trauma, the family of origin, as the foremost site of transmission, is explicitly or implicitly present in the narrative in such a way as to situate it as the locus of traumatic affect transmissions. In *The Lover*, the family is introduced on page five and thereafter they remain a formidable force. In *By Grand Central Station*, there is no mention of the narrator's family until well into the novel and her parents exist only as peripheral figures, as outsiders to the drama of the affair. The narrative of *The Lover* breaks every rule in the book in terms of conventional literary practice: in the first paragraph the first-person narrator is introduced as old, though referenced as young. In the next, the narrator begins to reminisce about her adolescent self. This interweaving of present-day awareness and perspective and retrospective recollections of youth continues until the narrator assumes first-person present tense, announcing herself as aged fifteen and a half, about to board the ferry on which she is fated to meet her Chinese lover. In one passage, the precocious young narrator states:

> I already know a thing or two. I know it's not clothes that make women beautiful or otherwise, nor beauty care, nor expensive creams, nor the distinction or costliness of their finery. I know the problem lies elsewhere. I don't know where. I only know it isn't where women think. (Duras 1992: 18)

The narrator continues, recounting her observations of women in the streets of Saigon and "upcountry" who "save themselves up for Europe" in what amounts to a pithy critique of gendered colonial life. "They wait, these women. They dress just for the sake of dressing. They look at themselves," she says, concluding with, "Some kill themselves" (18–19). In the next sentence the narrator has shifted back to a mature, reflective self who declares, "This self-betrayal of women always struck me as a mistake, an error" (19). This shifting, strange-bodied narrator, speaking from alternating past and present tenses, encapsulates the belatedness and after-wounding—the tendency to repeat or revisit—of traumatic experience. And so it is that time circulates between a never solid past, present, and future, and subjectivity slips in and out of ages, looking backward in one sentence and forward in the next. Many creative writing teachers in a modern-day undergraduate writing program would disapprove of a student taking such liberties with narration, but Duras, writing as a mature-aged and masterful author, shows that just as trauma defies logic, so too does much of the writing that testifies to it.

The inference of herstory

The first nod toward a poetic of transgenerational trauma in *By Grand Central Station* comes on the last page. Smart (1991) writes of her son:

> Look at the idiot boy you begot with that night. He is all the world that is left. He is America, and better than love. He is civilization's heir, O you mob, whose actions brought him into being. He is happier than you, sweetheart. But will he do to fill in these coming thousand years? (Smart 1991: 112)

The novel Brophy calls "one of the most shelled, skinned, nerve-exposed books ever written" (1991: 13) winds down with this gesture toward the generations that came before, come after, and exist alongside the blistering affair that had until then gripped the text. Duras, less surprisingly, given her movements through time and across generations and continents, also closes with a reference to the next generation with a melancholic passage about her Chinese lover's arranged marriage to a rich Chinese girl: "Through a lie he must have found himself inside the other woman, through a lie providing what their families, Heaven, and the northern ancestors expected of him, to wit, an heir to their name" (Duras 1992: 116).

In another striking resemblance, both texts end with lines that recall the lover and proclaim the continuity of affective relationship, but this parallel belies a notable difference, a difference that can perhaps be summed up in Caruth's conception of history, which she says, like trauma itself, can only be grasped in the "inaccessibility of its occurrence" (1996: 18). The most critical move of the poetics of transgenerational trauma is its illumination of this operation of traumatic transgenerational history. Caruth elaborates that it is the "constitutive function of latency" in history that ensures the "indissoluble, political bond to other histories" (18). Perhaps the next, and most radical, move of the poetics of transgenerational trauma is here, in its potential for uncovering the ways in which certain historical and cultural events implicate others through experimental or mega narratives in which those implications manifest in familial and cultural dynamics and legacies.

As my reading of *By Grand Central Station* and *The Lover* demonstrates, the poetics of transgenerational trauma is aligned with the subversive impetus of (a strange-bodied) feminine and revolutionary writing, but écriture féminine and revolutionary writing is not always aligned with the project of the poetics of transgenerational trauma, with its undertaking of testifying to traumatic familial and historical transmissions. Écriture féminine retains its relevance in the present era, not as a static and provable theory (which it was not fashioned to be in the first place) eternally bound to "women's writing," but as a contemplative model that facilitates consideration of the metaphoric workings and collapsing of the traditional binary of gender in traumatic writing and literature. In other words, in deferring to Kristeva's strange body

I am following on from Cixous's acknowledgment that a gendered writing can't be formally theorized, and folding into strange-bodyness the idea that the various metaphoric possibilities—of writing as feminine, as bisexual, as unsexed, and as traumatized—might somehow coexist.

The strange-bodyness I put forth stands for an admission that the gender operations (or not) of literary production, including my conception of a poetics of transgenerational trauma, can never be fully knowable or theorized. It stands too for the assertion that even in the face of this impossibility, trauma, affect, and the body demand voice and require witness. When this demand is met in literary testimony as it is in *The Lover*, it is nothing less than witnessing to the transgenerational effects of French imperialism, particularly as they are visited upon women. In other words, Duras writes not just her story, but "herstory."

2

The Ethics of Writing (through) a History of Familial Trauma

Memoir and associated genres, such as memoir fusions and fictional memoir, autofiction, faction, and works of fiction based on real-life characters and events, pointedly call up the question of ethics in ways that fiction and poetry generally don't. When a writer writes (through) a history of familial trauma, the question of ethics becomes even more pressing. Lives can be damaged, relationships destroyed, and what has been published can never be made entirely private again. And there are dangers inherent to undertaking trauma testimony, especially when that trauma has been witnessed and experienced firsthand in the context of overwhelming, intentional, and senseless suffering. There is a price to pay for remaining tender to trauma, for not hardening against it, and this tenderness is essential to its literary witnessing and testimony. There are consequences to gaining entry to its story, to the sensitivity required for entry. "That sensitivity," says Mona Simpson, writing about Primo Levi, "like its antidotes, has side effects" (2007).

Trauma, however directly inaccessible, denied, transmitted, acted out, or written out of the unconscious (in which the past remains present), is not abstract and disembodied but bound to, and by, affect in certain affective configurations of grief. Melancholy, sadness, anger-rage, anxiety-fear-terror, embarrassment-shame-humiliation, and numbness emerge as markers of transgenerationally transmitted trauma. The power of this affective movement and manifestation has to do with its potential for ethical encounter, which is constitutive of the poetics of transgenerational trauma. This potential is the means by which writing is carried beyond a simple account of trauma limited to personal identification and the peculiar pleasure of sharing hard luck stories. In this chapter I argue that affective-ethical encounter is capable of producing an increase of subjective and social power through a textual reckoning with trauma within and beyond the family.

The poetics of transgenerational trauma appears most commonly in genre as fiction, poetry, memoir, or some kind of hybrid. It may also be observed in critical memoir, fictocriticism, and autoethnography, though I do not, strictly speaking, examine those forms in this book. Characterized by an uncanny ability to reveal the operations of trauma in ways that exceed it as thematic content, this writing often defies strict genre category, or at least pushes genre envelopes. It is writing in which traumatic familial experience—for my purposes defined as the traumatic events or experiences of one generation passed down to another, or traumatic events or experiences within the bounds of the family, or, more commonly, a combination of the two—appears as crucially connected to, and reflective of, social reality. This chapter speaks to the dangers of this kind of testimony and the ethics of writing familial trauma via Spinoza's affect theory.

While many forms of traumatic testimony and writing explore cultural conditions by virtue of their intrinsic link to historical and collective events, testimony with a primary or significant focus on familial trauma is all too often considered merely personal. On the contrary, in the poetics of transgenerational trauma the preoccupation with the familial past is not a self-indulgent, individualist, backward gazing, but a grappling with the nexus of social and individual trauma, as it remains operative in the present. I consider these and other points in light of Alison Bechdel's graphic memoir, *Fun Home: A Family Tragicomic* (2006) and Hélène Cixous's fictional memoir, *Hyperdream* (2009). Neither involves the blatant dangers associated with firsthand witnessing to catastrophic collective trauma that Levi enacted in *If This Is a Man* (1959) and his many other post-Holocaust writings. But both books take other kinds of risks that come with certain hazards—risks that many people, including some writers, take pains to avoid and risks that one who would engage with the poetics of transgenerational trauma must take.

The danger of writing and reading the poetics of transgenerational trauma

Fun Home and *Hyperdream* reject formulaic and sensationalistic treatments of trauma in order to write what Cixous calls—citing Genet—the "nether realms." It is this access to affective nether realms that increases the perception and understanding so crucial to softening trauma's hold. Cixous (1993) describes this writing in her own practice as that which comes from "deep in my body, further down, behind thought" (204). This is not fanciful waxing lyrical about writing. Cixous is aligned with an ethical position taken up by the French poet and Holocaust survivor Charlotte Delbo, and the philosopher Gilles Deleuze. Jill Bennett (2005) elaborates on both in addressing traumatic memory as operative outside conscious, cognitive processes, which she credits for the affinity between trauma and the avant-garde that results in the "politicization of 'trauma art'" (14). A self-proclaimed aficionado of Spinoza, Deleuze bases his differentiation of ethical art from moral art on Spinoza's affect-ethic theory, in which ethical action is determined by the needs of a given being: whatever leads to expansiveness and well-being is ethical; whatever diminishes well-being is unethical. This is contrasted with the imposition of externally defined and predetermined moralistic frameworks based on notions such as "good" and "evil," "right" and "wrong."

For Deleuze, and Spinoza before him, ethics involves a capacity for transformation (unlike morality, which is more static and concerned with maintaining an externally constructed code of behavior). It achieves this capacity by refusing a given outside to thinking in which such moral codes are located. In this way, ethical art refuses to shore up already established assumptions or to tell cautionary tales. The experiments of *Fun Home* and *Hyperdream* are in keeping with Deleuze's vision of ethical art. Bechdel references *Fun Home*'s self-aware process of fearless familial examination (Chute and Bechdel 2006: 1013), pointing out that other than her coming out nothing really happens in the book apart from her father dying. The content, she insists, is essentially her engaging in "extremely involuted introspection" around that one event (1008). When Cixous says that she "writes at length without interruption, as if I were a marathon runner" (2011), she alludes to the internal trance and meditative space so palpable in her creative work. *Fun Home* and *Hyperdream* take the rejection of the idea of a given outside to thinking as their starting point, and thereafter their corporeal reasoning (which is not a rationalistic thinking, but a bodily, affective one) leads the way. The result is that the poetics of transgenerational trauma rejects framing trauma through a moralistic edifice, and its narratives do not seek resolution to, or the redemption of, trauma. Likewise, characters are not cast as clear-cut victims and perpetrators, but as actors in a social drama that exceeds them.

"Morality," says Bennett, "operates within the bounds of a given set of conventions, within which social and political problems must be solved" (2005: 15). By contrast, the experimental and/or multilayered drive of the poetics of transgenerational trauma involves, in part, a desire to depart from the established framework within which social and political problems are traditionally viewed and addressed. This literature illuminates not only social political problems, but also the established framework within which they exist. Ethical art is characterized by the primacy of sustained sensation over an intention to communicate ready-made meaning (18), which of course does not preclude this art also communicating meaning. In trauma writing, what this means is that the meanings made come from within the inside thinking (that which has refused the "given outside to thinking") and the hackneyed meaning-making common in more conventional trauma narratives is sidestepped.

Delbo contrasts common/ordinary memory, as the realm where events make sense, with sense/deep memory, as the terrain in which the psychic imprint of trauma lives on. This can be summed up in her statement that trauma is "always in the present, although not continuously felt" (Bennet 2005: 25). In their diverse ways, both *Fun Home* and *Hyperdream* privilege the sustaining of sensation over conventional communication and meaning-making, even if the arising of sensation in textual space, however radically inscribed, is never completely divorced from orthodox meaning (or in Kristevan terms, even if the semiotic necessarily appears in the language of the Symbolic). These texts have a heightened capacity for visceral and affectively charged composition, and as I show in the following section, it is precisely this capacity that enables their ethical disposition. I will return to this point about ethical integrity in the conclusion, but for now I want mainly to establish the poetics of transgenerational trauma as an ethical rather than a didactic enterprise.

In proposing this, I am attempting to describe how and why poetic and experimental trauma writing gets beyond the representational and into the "deep memory" of familial and cultural history. I am also making the claim that it is possible to have sense memories about the trauma of another and so to write (out) of a multigenerational traumatic lineage. Although I argue for the political value of such a practice, I am also obliged to consider its possible dangers. If the poetics of transgenerational trauma involves a heightened capacity to be affected, what is required not only of the writer, but also of the reader? And does this writing demand or create a requisite readerly disposition? If, as I maintain, the poetics of transgenerational trauma is an affectively charged textual embodiment of trauma transmissions, it follows that both its writers and readers are rendered vulnerable to being overwhelmed by traumatic affect, possibly to personal detriment.

Anna Gibbs (2006) points out that though all writing operates affectively to some degree, fiction and creative nonfiction involve a visceral operation that goes so far as to "challenge the fixity of our own bodily limits." It is this paradoxical discovery of the other/self via the loss of the self in ethical art that makes it so intoxicating. Gibbs says that to read such writing "is to lend one's body to the words of another, to be—albeit temporarily—possessed by alien affects and to put ourselves at risk of being transformed by them" (160). I would add that the affects by which we are possessed as readers are not always as alien as we may presume. Though a reader might not have been subjected to the specific traumas of the text, they may nevertheless relate to the affect generated by it through their own history of trauma. To read such writing is to lend one's body to the words of another in order to understand the traumatic experience of another individual, culture, and time, and/or to lend one's body to the words of another in order to reclaim and access that which is repressed within one's body.

I momentarily return to Levi as an example. His account, in *If This Is a Man* (1959), of the unspeakably tragic last moments of a nameless, disabled child whom prisoners called Hurbinek *feels* unbearable to read, even as a childless person not yet born when the horrors of Auschwitz doomed Hurbinek. One experiences heart-wrenching pain, impotent rage, and overwhelming sadness.

This is affect and love at work, the ethical witnessing to the profound suffering of another, but it is also empathy, an empathy based not in equivalence of experience or suffering or trauma, but in the depths of one's own inherent vulnerability. Reading Levi's honoring of Hurbinek connects me to my own experiences of infant abandonment, however different and more routine and privileged than the criminal context that orchestrated Hurbinek's abandonment, illness, and premature death. It is from this place that I recognize Hurbinek's aloneness. My own experiential understanding of even fleeting feelings of abandonment for the small child who is utterly dependent on others for survival meets my affectively imagining Hurbinek's experience, even though I still cannot relate in terms of identifying with Hurbinek's heinous circumstances and abysmal condition. If, in addition to that, I was a reader who had a child, or who had lost a child, witnessing Hurbinek's death through Levi's words becomes at once less safe. If I was a reader who had survived Auschwitz, and who had lost a child there, reading this account may not just *feel* unbearable; it may actually *be* unbearable and attempting to read it may threaten grave psychical menace.

Beyond literary performativity, then, lies the more complex matter of interactivity, which Gibbs views as entailing webs of "feedback loops" (2006: 162) between writer and writing, writer and imagined reader, writer and actual reader, and so on and so forth. When Shoshana Felman asks how the self is acted upon by writing and reading traumatic testimony and to what end, she comes to a bold conclusion: "A 'life-testimony' is not simply a testimony to a private life, but a point of conflation between text and life, a textual testimony which can *penetrate us like an actual life*" [italics in original] (1995: 14). Gibbs addresses the dangers of trauma testimony via the of post-Holocaust literary writings of Levi, Paul Celan, and Jean Améry, stating that numerous such writers died in untimely and suspicious circumstances, in accidents that were probable suicides. This raises the issue of safety outside established sets of conventions, within which social and political problems are approached. Clearly, there is no solving genocide, no convention within which it can be made to make sense or be justified, and seemingly no end to its traumatic shock waves. Likewise, the capacity for transformation in ethical art, and by extension, the poetics of transgenerational trauma, cannot guarantee that the transformation it proffers will be necessarily cheery, felt as positive, or lead to a desired outcome.

The writer willingly enters into a world of trauma because, perhaps, of the recognition that since they must in any event inhabit it, they may as well make art with it. Writers also write trauma because, as Gibbs maintains, in many cases the need to be heard, to testify, is stronger than the pull to avoid traumatic experience (2006: 165). The need to be heard outside of conventions of morality demands unflinching witnesses. Such antiescapist texts are suitable only for readers willing to follow the writer into the traumatic story and squirm in a relational, interactive dynamic that inspires identification, empathy, or defense or refusal, shame, compassion, or some combination or roller coaster ride thereof. Identification involves readers connecting to traumatic experiences or lineages through either affective encounter or the content of the traumatic narrative. Empathy is the visceral and felt imagining of the experience of another. Defense might operate as a preoccupation with judgment, appraisal, or cynicism, and refusal is signaled by rejection of the text either initially or during the course of reading.

But if the writer and reader willingly enter the world of trauma, there are those sometimes less willing who get co-opted into the journey. In conversation with Hillary Chute, Bechdel described the tensions in her relationship with her mother during the creation of *Fun Home*, and her mother's displeasure and incredulousness at the prospect of the project. She spoke, too, of her own misgivings in the face of this relationship, confessing that she didn't even tell her mother about the book until she had already worked on it for a year:

> I wanted to get a purchase on the material before I had to grapple with her feelings about it. I felt like I could very easily be dissuaded from the whole project. Her initial reaction, I think, was to laugh. She just thought it was absurd. She didn't ask me not to do it, which I was really grateful for. At some point, though, she told me she was going to have to cut me off from any further information about my father. She felt betrayed—quite justifiably so—that I was using things she'd told me in confidence about my father. So she wasn't going to tell me anything else. But then a year or so later, she gave me a box of letters that Dad had written her before they were married. My mom's a bit of a mixed-message kind of person—but maybe she gave me

> the letters because she thought they'd act as a counterweight to other things she'd shared with me. At any rate, the letters were a rich treasure trove, very helpful in fleshing out my father's character. (Chute 2006: 1006–07)

Bechdel's recollections illustrate the kind of ethical bind the writer of familial trauma often experiences: on the one hand ethically bound (in Deleuzian terms) to testify and on the other ethically concerned with the impact such testimony might have on those implicated, or otherwise involved in, their experiences of trauma.

Distinguishing Holocaust writing from other traumatic narratives, Gibbs states that such writing "carries the responsibility of writing on behalf of others, of representing, and in some sense speaking for, voices which have been silenced. How can one ever do this adequately?" (2006: 167). The poetics of transgenerational trauma is closer to Holocaust writing than other kinds of trauma writing in that both involve significant traumatic experience and history beyond the individual. In testimony of culturally transmitted trauma, there can be no easy answers, no quick fixes (or any fixes), and no feel-good, transcendent moral to the story. In such writing, some traumatization of the reader is unavoidable: it is the price of trauma being given voice, the conditions of its being heard. In an era of "trigger warnings," the assertion Gibbs makes that the secondary trauma induced in readers is "essential because it speaks to the ultimate communicability of traumatic experience as traumatic experience, and without this, healing either at the individual or social level cannot take place" (2006: 169) goes against the grain. When it comes to the poetics of transgenerational trauma, any potential for healing at the "social level" is only possible in multiplicities of subjective healing, and therefore, such healing can only be accomplished in humble measure by networks of individuals writing and reading texts. Though such writing brings with it a danger of the transmission, or retriggering, of trauma and so-called negative affects like shame, fear, and grief, this danger is, nevertheless, an indispensable element of the practice. The distressing aspect of writing and reading trauma might be viewed as something of an occupational hazard. Since transgenerational transmissions of trauma elude logical and reliable recall, such engagement is necessarily motivated and informed by traumatic affect, and as always this will not be contained within a given body, but rather spreads between bodies: animal and physical, textual, and institutional.

The idea of affect leading the way is affirmed by Cixous repeatedly in all her creative and theoretical works. It is also a conviction held by Deleuze and Delbo for whom "deep thought entails circumventing conventional thought and moving into darker regions" (Bennet 2005). Motivated by complex energies and connections, affect is the current in which thought proceeds in such a way as to be "integral to the composition of an artwork" (37). This prospect of thought proceeding from affective encounter is critical to my view of the ways in which transgenerational traumatic writers like Bechdel and Cixous generate their textual testimonies. Though my choice of two pointedly different and singular texts to illustrate the affect-ethical operations of the poetics of transgenerational trauma may initially confound, this disparity is optimal for drawing out the range and variables of the practice. The dissimilarity also highlights the points that this poetics is defined less by a specific genre or thematic content and more by a certain kind of experimental and affective process.

Spinoza's affect-ethic and the social

Fun Home tells the tale of Bechdel's childhood and early adulthood in an all-American family in which all is not as it seems. Bechdel charts her relationship with her obsessive, closeted father, Bruce—namely his outing and mysterious death a short time after she came out as a lesbian while in college—with witty, frank, humorous commentary and poignantly and precisely drawn illustrations. A bestseller, *Fun Home* is a relatively recent example of graphic memoir trauma testimony (this genre has made an impressive contribution since it was pioneered in the wake of the Second World War). *Hyperdream*, by contrast, is a meditative elegy about age and fragility, time, the bonds and tensions between mother and daughter, and the chasm left by the death of a dear friend, interweaving the traumatic familial history of the narrator with the traumatic history of Europe via the exchange of a bed that may or may not have belonged to the philosopher, critic, and writer Walter Benjamin before his suicide while on the run from the Nazis. Despite their different moods, milieus, and aesthetics both books exemplify the "corporeal reason"

(Hardt 2007: x) associated with the seventeenth-century affect theory of the Dutch Jewish philosopher Baruch Spinoza, widely thought of as the "source, either directly or indirectly, of most of the contemporary work" (ix) on affect emerging in multi- and interdisciplinary contexts today.

In basic terms, Spinoza (1996) defines affect as a causal relation between body and mind that has both productive and destructive potentials, stating that his understanding of affect relates to the "affections of the body by which the body's power of acting is either increased or diminished, aided or restrained" (70). Affect necessarily involves cognition because it is the capacity of the mind to perceive affect that motivates response and action. Spinoza's ethics are an elegant elaboration on this view of affect. In his theory of ethics the power (alternatively described as the *beingness*) of a being is either increased or diminished by any given action. That which increases the well-being/power of a being is ethical. That which diminishes it is unethical. The role of affect in the generation of this ethical capacity is key for Spinoza:

> Whatever so disposes the human body that it can be affected in a great many ways, or renders it capable of affecting external bodies in a great many ways, is useful to man; the more it renders the body capable of being affected in a great many ways, or of affecting other bodies, the more useful it is; on the other hand, what renders the body less capable of these things is harmful. (137)

For Spinoza, then, affect and ethics are so bound up with one another that it may be more accurate to speak in terms of his affect-ethic than his affect theory. It is in this way that the writing and reading of (and through) individual and collective trauma might be viewed as an ethical exchange. The poetics of transgenerational trauma, with its heightened capacity for affect, is a literary production that renders the body capable of being affected in a great many ways, and its being affected in a great many ways has the power of affecting other bodies. Looking past the seemingly obvious fact that all literature points to cultural processes and conditions to some degree, the trauma writing of *Fun Home* and *Hyperdream* involves a particularly complex ethic that surpasses the individual account in its acknowledgment of the sensory and social potency of trauma and its transmission. It does this by addressing cultural processes and conditions through narratives that mine subjective and relational spheres.

In *Fun Home* this can be seen in the way the movements of these spheres play out in the social swirl. At one point (2006: 102–05) Bechdel's father takes her and her siblings to New York City with a family associate called Roy, who, she later realizes, seems to have been her father's lover. Hanging around the Village only weeks after the Stonewall riots, an eight-year-old Bechdel absorbs more of the world and its sly homoerotic, homophobic, and homo-advocacy nuance than she can possibly process. In *Hyperdream* a recurring family story revolves around an item known as "Benjamin's Bed," which seems to stand as a memorial of the many losses—subjective, familial, and continental—sustained as a result of anti-Semitism. The narrator writes: "They were forever fleecing me, says my mother, one time Germany, one time my father's brother, one time Algeria. She gives a cackle of laughter that remembers, remembers—remembers" (Cixous 2009: 55). Then follows the story of the bed, a story in which the mother, amid a group of refugees, hears of a man, Mr. Benjamin, who is fleeing his apartment and selling his bed. It is a tale the narrator has heard before, but she submits to yet another rendition of it because as her mother reminds her "without that bed you wouldn't be here" (56). The story, the bed, the anti-Semitic history of Europe gets mixed up, enmeshed with the comings and goings of the mother's wartime life and the changes within the family.

In Spinozan terms, these books constitute an ethical practice in the sense that they privilege the somatic, affective, and expansive agency of writing that increases the power of beingness and the power to perceive and understand familial traumatic history and its origins in cultural traumatic history (which cannot readily be understood logically). Conversely, a conventional, affect-poor logic would enable little more than a prosaic recount of the already known and knowable of traumatic experience (which is, in relation to familial and social transmissions, necessarily severely limited in terms of direct access), too flat to court perception and understanding. In claiming that this writing exceeds a personal account (within which both memoir and familial testimony are traditionally framed) to illuminate the social, I am suggesting that such writing sheds light on currents of traumatic affect that are both manifold and refused (in which conscious knowledge is met with rejection) or denied (in which the operations of traumatic affect are not conscious or are minimized), and that it is via these refused or denied affective exchanges that trauma is transmitted. The social, then, in relation to the poetics of transgenerational trauma, is the circulation of traumatic affect within and beyond the family, and the sharing within communities and collectives of cultural traumatic legacies.

Bechdel's graphic memoir black comedy

Fun Home: A Family Tragicomic (Bechdel 2006) is a gloriously multidimensional depiction of the artist and author's childhood and adolescence in a dysfunctional Pennsylvanian family during the 1960s and 1970s. *Fun Home*'s nonlinear and recursive narrative epitomizes the nature of traumatic memory and the way in which it returns to haunt survivors. This is particularly evident in the repetition of frames recounting the possibly suicidal death of her obsessive and closeted homosexual father, which, in turn stand in for other unspeakable and refused losses and identifications that trouble the family. These panels are interwoven with Bechdel's own coming out story, as well as anecdotes and allusions, literary references, theoretical underpinnings, and daydreaming musings. An insightful expression of trauma in structure, language, and drawing, *Fun Home* is, as Julie Watson (2008) observes, "densely intertextual" (51) and "punctuated by the rhythmic movement of self-questioning and self-commentary" (27). Bechdel's captions are humorous, poignant, clever, and reflective articulations of frames based on photographs, maps, letters, social records, and Bechdel's memory and diary, knitted into thematic strands interlacing subjective, familial, and social upheaval into a rich textual fabric. One of its most striking achievements is the way this intertextuality manages to testify to the very process of familial transmissions of traumatic affect.

Judith Herman (1997) coined the term "Complex Post-Traumatic Stress Disorder" (CPTSD) to distinguish between the posttraumatic state resulting from the experience of chronic trauma and the effects of a more straightforward and short-lived experience of trauma known as Posttraumatic Stress Disorder (PTSD) (American Psychiatric Association 2000). Herman argues that chronic trauma, such as that experienced by a child at the mercy of a regularly abusive or neglectful parent, a spouse whose spirit is broken by long-term domestic violence, or a prisoner of war, is markedly different, more complex, and significantly harder to diagnose and treat than the PTSD stemming from a one-off event, such as an accident or attack. Though both kinds of trauma and posttraumatic states may be indicated in transgenerational transmissions, this conception of a chronic, particularly complex posttraumatic state is especially compelling in writing that features familial transmissions. The nexus of trauma and affect theories facilitates exploration of both the ways in which transmission takes place transgenerationally and the ways this process can be written. While the issue of transmission is given due consideration in affect theory, it is less prominent in trauma theory, so I want to reiterate my understanding of the term "traumatic affect." In order to avoid an abstracted transgenerational trauma theory whose relation to the body (individual, familial, and social) and affect is underplayed, my casting of transmission focuses on traumatic affect as affect that is bound to, and by, trauma. Echoing Jean Laplanche (1999: 109), I engage with affect as the bodily (and relational) representative of trauma. In this way I forge a critical connection between trauma and affect and trauma theory and affect theory.

A psychological and comprehensive examination of the process of transgenerational trauma is beyond the scope and literary focus of this work. My more contained intention in this chapter is to expound on my view that the affects at the heart of transgenerational trauma—shame (including rage, which I see as stemming from a combination of anger, shame, and fear), fear (including anxiety), and grief (including sadness and melancholy)—are also the affects principal to the writing of it. Affective language is crucial in both the transmission of traumatic affect and the poetics that portrays it. As Denise Riley says (2005), there is a "gulf between the ostensible content of what's said, and the affect which seeps from the very form of the words" (2). This not only suggests one of the ways trauma is transmitted familiarly and across generations but also its capacity to create and shape, fracture and rupture, subjectivity, and its potential for transmissions beyond the family. Constellations of traumatic affect are an implicit presence in the works I engage with, and those constellations represent modes of overt transmission between adults and children, such as physical assault, neglect, incest, and the experience or witnessing of violence and verbal abuse, as well as more subtle strains of transmission in which, for example, a reasonable statement might be made in a covertly shaming tone and manner. Ruth Leys makes a valid point about psychic trauma becoming, over time, a "debased currency" (2000: 2). Where once it was related to only indisputably horrific and traumatic experiences such as the Holocaust and other violent crimes, it is now routinely applied to passing upsets and employed in claims of victimhood that may have questionable motives. Even so, it is important to note that there is a difference between debasing and misusing the concept and word "trauma" and covert trauma. There are commonly less extreme and more subtle realms of experience, which nevertheless, despite relatively benign appearances, do qualify as psychically traumatic in that they are experiences marked by a lack of registration in the first instance, due to speed of occurrence or shock and belated symptomology. *Fun Home* masterfully testifies to these more understated traumas and nuanced transmissions.

During a conference presentation on the rise of graphic testimony, Hillary Chute (2012) hailed the capacity of graphic memoir to deal with "subjectivity in the space of image and caption" by virtue of "visual intimacy." Noting Art Speigelman's reference to the genre as "bodies on the page," Chute pointed out that such texts have a singular ability to "reconstitute lost bodies" and to carry affect across language in a current of visual immediacy, affirming Speigelman's claim that graphic memoir is a way of "materializing history." *Fun Home* features a vigorous, moving, and surprisingly funny narrative that flows fluidly backward, forward, and sideways in time. Bechdel undermines any tendency toward self-pity or grandiosity with painstakingly sophisticated layers of irony in which the text and drawings bounce and spark off one another playfully. The result is so nuanced, finely balanced, and well integrated on the page that it becomes impossible to see the drawings and language as separate entities, as either written text with drawings or drawings with written text. Asked in an interview why she felt the narrative needed to be so intricate, Bechdel replied:

> I went over and over it, constantly tweaking the connections between what had happened already and what was still coming. . . . Everything in the book is so carefully linked to everything else, that removing one word would be like pulling on a thread that unravels the whole sweater. (Chute 2006: 1007)

This intricacy exemplifies the dense complexity of Bechdel's relationship with her family, and especially her father. With multimediatized memory as its pulse, *Fun Home* speaks of this difficult relationship, of the way she and her father mirror each other yet are consistently at odds, and the losses and refusals that both bind and isolate them in their cross-gendered and melancholic identifications. They are similar and different, alienated and close, bound in an ambiguous and love/hate relation that carries melancholia down the line, from one generation to the next. A sense of vulnerability in struggling with this ambiguous relationship even after the death of her father infuses every element of Bechdel's text, including her noteworthy partial use of color. Her father loves color; she loves black and white. In a gesture that both accepts and rejects the father her text is black and white but for several evocative and somewhat mournful shades of green-gray.

The doublings and layerings of paradoxes, inversions, and sharp observations are expressive of the dynamics of shame, grief, love, and intelligence within her family, and these doublings and layers depict how trauma transmission influences the shaping of subjectivity. Bechdel weaves her story of transmission into, around, and out of the historical legacies of the oppression and persecution of artists, women, and homosexuals. As Watson (2008) says, Bechdel pulls off a remarkable feat by filtering her familial story—an essentially middle-class American childhood, with a few twists and proverbial skeletons in the cupboard—in such a way as to graph "the personal as a site of struggle for liberation that has analogs in human rights battles being waged around the world, particularly for homosexuals and women" (53). In this way, *Fun Home* emerges as a powerhouse of political critique firmly grounded in the personal. Bechdel's frozen affect and stymied grief around her father's untimely death and life of deceit are reflective of a society in which affect and grief are routinely suppressed.

For example, in one narrative loop about the death of her father Bechdel describes the severity of her denial, writing: "For years after my father's death, when the subject of parents came up in conversation I would relate the information in a flat, matter-of-fact tone," above a frame in which she sits in a café reporting her father's death with a heartless: "My dad's dead, he jumped in front of a truck." At the bottom of the frame the following text appears,

"Eager to detect in my listener the flinch of grief that eluded me." In the next frame she sits stone-faced opposite her companion, who responds with a predictably horrified "God, I'm sorry" (45). This is a stark example of the way traumatic affect, and its interplay with imagination, drives the words (and pictures) in the poetics of transgenerational trauma.

This scene also hints at the way constellations of affect, as the bodily representatives of trauma, are transmitted transgenerationally through processes psychoanalytic theorists Nicholas Abraham and Maria Torok refer to as incorporation, encryption, and entombment. For Abraham and Torok, incorporation describes an experience of loss of a love object that has not been properly mourned and in which the other is incorporated and internalized in such a way as to encrypt (Abraham and Torok 1994: 131) the subject along with the lost other. The loss need not be absolute, as in death, to be experienced as traumatic, and may relate to relational losses of other kinds. Incorporation denotes various kinds of internalization in which an "unbearable reality" is removed from consciousness and confined to an "inaccessible region of the psyche" (Rand 1994: 102). Abraham and Torok describe incorporation as the refusal to reclaim and/or integrate the part of ourselves that was "placed in what we lost; incorporation is the refusal to acknowledge the full import of the loss, a loss that, if recognized as such, would effectively transform us" (Abraham and Torok 1994: 127). Of course, in the case of a child this is not so much refusal as *developmental incapacity*, in the sense that a child cannot comprehend the implications of such investments and losses, even though they may acutely experience their impact. Even once an adult, a subject can struggle to comprehend the implications and the need for this reclamation when what was incorporated includes the traumatic affect and losses of an adult on whom the child depended (for both psychical survival and emotional sustenance)—precisely because it was traumatic.

In this way traumatic familial loss forms crypts that result in what Torok refers to as "the illness of mourning" (110), which is a pathological grieving process that mourns not the loss of the love object per se, but the "secret" inherent in the loss. This is not a secret in the normal sense (though in the case of Bechdel's father's sexual orientation this common understanding of the word secret was also operative). The secret for Abraham and Torok is the site of a trauma experienced as shameful, and its attendant subjective splitting. Abraham and Torok speak of the entwining of shame and grief this secreted tomb involves when they state, "Every time an incorporation is uncovered, it can be attributed to the undisclosable grief that befalls an ego already partitioned on account of a previous objectal experience tainted with shame" (Abraham and Torok 1994: 131). The crypt is formed within the subjective splitting that occurs with the transmission of the secret and critically it is only constructed when the transmitted shameful secret is "the love object's doing" and when the "object also functions for the subject as an ego ideal. It is therefore the *object's* secret that needs to be kept, *his* shame covered up" [italics in original] (131). Bechdel's splitting off from her own grief can be viewed as a sign that she had entombed her father's secreted (in both senses of the word) sexuality. Given the evolutionary dependence of children on their caregivers and their age-related ego identifications and propensity toward idealization of family members, particularly parents and elders, it is not difficult to see how the family environment can so readily become a hotbed of entombed transmissions.

This scene in the café where Bechdel seeks in the other what she refuses in herself demonstrates the unflinching candor so critical to the success of *Fun Home*. The penetrating scrupulousness with which Bechdel constantly exposes and interrogates herself is evident in frames that show her checking her misplaced pride. In one drawing she sits contemplatively on a jetty at sunset smoking a cigarette and pondering whether she might be constructing her father's repressed homosexuality as inappropriately heroic. Above the frame she writes, "There's a certain emotional expedience to claiming him as a tragic victim of homophobia, but that's a problematic line of thought." Below right in the frame she adds, "For one thing, it makes it harder for me to blame him" (2006: 196). This point about authorial integrity is key, though, because it is the ethical foundation that justifies the production of a work that may not have had the blessing of another whom the testimony involves, or that risks affecting others negatively. Even though Bechdel felt herself to be on shaky ground before her mother's disapproval, and expresses doubts as to whether she would have proceeded if her mother had outright asked her not to, her steadfast focus on herself and engagement with her own working-through process throughout the text ensures that Spinoza's affect-ethic supports her project. Creating *Fun Home* clearly involved her own expansion of beingness and potentially those of readers, and as such its production can be considered an ethical enterprise.

Dizzying flourishes of theoretical and literary references also inform a compulsive analysis that speeds alongside insightful ruminations and reconnections with dissociated emotion. For example, one page featuring panels depicting the family gardening begins with a comment on Proust:

> After the lilac passage, Proust describes Swann's garden in a feat of both literary and horticultural virtuosity that climaxes in the narrator's rapturous communion with the pink blossoms of the hawthorn hedge. (93)

A frame in which Bechdel's father is shown admiring a potted lilac precedes this. The caption reads, "If my father had a favorite flower, it was the lilac." Various other references to lilacs and Proust follow, along with a reminder that her father had been reading Proust the year before he died (92). The family gardening scene, intercut with narration about the narrator of Proust's story spying a little girl in a garden, ends with a final caption declaring, "If there was ever a bigger pansy than my father, it was Marcel Proust" (93). These two pages alone, rich with overlapping, traumatic meaning-making demonstrate the way Bechdel melds literary, theoretical, and lived experience to both amusing and somber effect.

Fun Home is a fearlessly honest performance that rebuffs a simplistic good/bad moral paradigm that would cast Bechdel herself as victim and her parents as villains. Rather, the narrator and her family are presented as intimates in a struggle between personal integrity and cultural tensions and prohibitions, the past and the present. For example, in one section Bechdel describes the courtship of her parents and the oppressions and delusions on both sides that led to the ill-advised marriage taking place and being sustained. In the beginning their mutual love of the arts and literature, and in particular F. Scott Fitzgerald, bound them. As Bechdel says, "If my father was a Fitzgerald character, my mother stepped right out of Henry James—a vigorous American idealist ensnared by degenerate continental forces" (66). Elsewhere she states, "I employ these allusions to James and Fitzgerald not only as descriptive devices, but because my parents are most real to me in fictional terms" (67). Bechdel goes on to describe a cold relationship, recalling only two displays of affection between her parents in her entire life with them: a chaste kiss goodbye and a hand placed on a back while watching TV, both of which "astonished and discomforted" the young Bechdel (68). Later she shows scenes of antagonism and muted misery that emanated from the unfortunate union to engulf the entire family. This refusal to cast her parents as the fall guys and her empathetic desire to understand the murky makings of their relationship is notable in a society in which the denial, repression, and acting out—in the sense of unconscious compulsions—of traumatic affect are the accepted, enabled norm on one hand and demonized (when observable as obviously bothersome or criminal acting out) on the other.

Against this tendency toward denial, there has emerged a kind of writing that almost exalts in trauma—a popular/ist mainstream genre that has enjoyed widespread publication and readership throughout the past couple of decades. The term "misery literature," reportedly coined by *The Bookseller* magazine, has been used to describe narratives of hard-core and extreme child abuse. The *Guardian* identified "mis-lit" as the latest craze in a 2007 online article titled "So Bad It's Good" (Addley 2007). Noting Frank McCourt's 1996 bestselling memoir, *Angela's Ashes*, and Jung Chang's hit, *Wild Swans* (1991), as seminal forerunners, Addley (2007) cited Dave Pelzer's memoir, *A Child Called It* (2001), which "details the story of his outrageously cruel childhood at the hands of his alcoholic mother, who beat, starved, stabbed and burned him," as the herald text for a plethora of hellish tales, including Stuart Howarth's incest memoir, *Please, Daddy, No: A Boy Betrayed* (2006) and *Damaged* (2007) by Cathy Glass, the harrowing tale of a foster carer and her attempt to give a severely abused girl a safe and loving home. Addley complained that the "charts are groaning with real-life accounts of neglect, violence and sexual abuse" before proclaiming incredulously that the UK bookshop Waterstones had introduced a dedicated "Painful Lives" shelf. *Fun Home* is an entirely different kind of writing against denial. Bechdel's testimony is a courageous text that both refutes the refusal of trauma *and* the pop bent of "inspiration literature," to refer to a less derogatory genre tag, with its tendency to revel in trauma and feature individualistic glorifications of survival. I set the poetics of transgenerational trauma apart from the moralistic, dualistic, and theological perspectives characteristic of such works. In the works I explore what is evident is less disclosure and more a resonant and alive revelation of trauma in the play of poetics and experimentation, fertile in the perceptive promise that Spinoza maintains as so crucial in his affect-ethic.

Cathy Caruth cites Dori Laub as suggesting that massive psychic trauma "precludes its registration; it is 'a record that has yet to be made'" (1995: 6). The question of how and why a writer might go about making a literary record of a record that has yet to be made is an interesting one, and it is helpful in teasing out the differences between the poetics of transgenerational trauma and those more conservative testimonies previously mentioned. Spinoza's central claim is that "the more the body is rendered capable of these things [being affected in many ways and being capable of affecting others], the more the mind is rendered capable of perceiving" (Spinoza 1996: 137). This means that affect leads to perception, which leads to understanding, or what he more commonly refers to as reason (though this is a bodily process of reasoning that does not privilege logic and rationality over affect—hence corporeal reason). Spinoza goes so far as to say, "Self-esteem can arise from reason [understanding], and only that self-esteem which does arise from reason is the greatest there can be" (143). In Spinoza's view, then, the most valuable form of self-esteem, perhaps the only true form, comes about through a reflective "power of understanding" (143). It is this that makes the literature I read significant: its facility for enacting and aiding this process. The poetics of transgenerational trauma, with its enhanced capacity for inducing affect that leads to perception, therefore enacts some measure of transformation of, and through, trauma.

Conventional trauma testimony elicits affect in its readers too, of course, but it is a more foreclosed experience of affect. This kind of writing wears its trauma upon its sleeve, so to speak, purporting to "know" and wholly represent its individualist traumatic content, so there is less capacity for the reader to enter into the testimony in such a way as to generate a dynamically interactive perceptive response. Here the reader is situated as outside the known and uniquely experienced trauma story; in other words the reader is positioned as a voyeur. The poetics of transgenerational trauma knows that it cannot fully know or represent the trauma of which it speaks, and this unknowing is met by experimental attempts to get ever closer to realities and truths not otherwise available. The Spinozan writer writes to raise self-esteem—not in some superficial and clichéd sense of the word, but in the grand Spinozan sense in which an increase of self-esteem is an increase of beingness. Caruth makes the point that "in trauma . . . the outside has gone inside without any mediation" (1996: 59). She goes on to say that Freud's ultimate contention is that "it is traumatic repetition, rather than the meaningful distortions of neurosis, that defines the shape of individual lives" (59). In the last pages of *Fun Home*, Bechdel signals the deathly nature of traumatic repetition in considering her father's love of Joyce's *Ulysses*, asking in one panel: "But how could he admire Joyce's lengthy libidinal 'yes' so fervently and end up saying 'no' to his own life?" (2006: 228). In its paradoxical creative aptitude for giving voice to this deathly transgenerational "wound that cries out" (Caruth 1996: 4), Bechdel's *Fun Home* serves as an affirmation and reclamation of life, in the wake of her father's forsaking of it.

Cixous and the poet-thinker's "book of mourning"

On the inside jacket of *Hyperdream*, Hélène Cixous's 2009 "novel," the text is referred to as a "book of mourning." And on the back cover, her good friend, philosopher Jacques Derrida, who is also a spectral figure in the book, makes the claim that for a writer to be "great" they must be a "poet-thinker"—"very much a poet and a very thinking poet." These are apt descriptions for a poetics of transgenerational trauma that does not incorporate visual representation and that testifies to even subtler transmissive operations than *Fun Home: A Family Tragicomic* (Bechdel 2006). In this book, Cixous achieves amplified affect, immediacy, and intimacy with traumatic transmissions through language alone and through strategies such as rhythmic repetition and eccentric phrasing and grammar charged with a steaming emotive heat, and a narration that is more about interior and relational experiences than it is plot or story-centered. The rhythmic repetition and eccentric phrasing and grammar that appear throughout this work is particularly evident in passages such as:

> For forty years we thought of death of life of death of death of life after that of death then of life, after death of death after death of life of the going away then of the coming back, we get away from it, the further away we get the closer we are we run to every window for forty years the same storm, each time we get away from it we think of death, we are giving life to death, I would say we're putting death to death my friend would say, let's not talk about it he would say, we're giving life to death, each time we talk about it let's not talk about it anymore my friend would say, we don't talk about it anymore. (Cixous 2009: 89)

This passage pulses with trauma in language that sputters and trips over itself, confused in its reference points and its attempt to wrangle with the death in life and the life in death. Cixous's lyrical honesty is most evident in scenes of relational proximity, in which she is confronted with her mother's aging body or her history with her mother:

> –Get up, I say.
>
> –We're going to do the cream cheese, says my mother.
>
> I say: unction, she says: cream cheese.
>
> A creased, crumpled, crinkly, tucked, puckered and gathered time, everything twofold, "when I was a girl" says my mother, her body shrunken supple flexible fold turn bend under the floppy shift of crinkly, twisted, kinky skin. Perfect little buttocks, all the old age is in the corkscrew legs.
>
> I am afraid of the legs. (2009: 55)

At other times it is anger, frustration, and impatience rather than fear and a sense of vulnerability and mortality that is expressed.

Elsewhere in the book the narrator describes the way the mother, clearly suffering from dementia, laughs without knowing what makes her laugh and forgets that she has told stories before, blaming the daughter for mistakenly believing she has already heard her stories:

> My utter exasperation yesterday, for the twentieth time in two months, teeth on edge, it's the third in the space of two days I've heard this one, sumptuous tales, modest chefs-d'oeuvre and rich in lessons, it set my teeth on edge. (58)

This seemingly negative affect, however, works in tension with a luminous love that shines through when she later adds, "At the same time I want to stray, I want to hear every last one of my mother's words, she whom I love more than myself" (59). Cixous's preference for the exploration of internal and relational worlds over plot and external event yields beautifully affective sentences, such as, "Before-the-death-of-Mummy, a time with no beginning where one finds oneself troubled, gaze cut off. The body-veil lets the Other show through [no full stop]" (55). Reading Cixous's novel one is struck by a palpable sense that she draws her words up from the bodily depths, from dreams and dark recesses of memory and affect. It is a writing practice she discusses at length in her theoretical work.

In *The Laugh of the Medusa*, perhaps her most famous text, in which she agitates for écriture féminine, Cixous says, "Poetry involves gaining strength through the unconscious. . . . The unconscious, that other limitless country, is the place where the repressed manage to survive" (1981a: 250). The unconscious is also thought to be the place where the delayed, uncontrollable, repetitive symptomology of trauma comes from, the unlocatable place where trauma survives in its strange limbo of registration. Later in *Medusa*, Cixous describes writing as working in "the in-between, inspecting the process of the same and of the other without which nothing can live, undoing the work of death" (1981a: 254). By "undoing the work of death" she means that this practice is "not fixed in sequences of struggle and expulsion or some other form of death but infinitely dynamized by an incessant process of exchange from one subject to another" (254). It is thus the unsurpassed capacity of poetry to undo the silence and death of trauma and bring it to light and life so that it might be used to inspect the "process of the same and of the other" in a way that is "dynamized by an incessant process of exchange from one subject to another."

It is in her use of poetic and experimental prose in creative writing that Cixous most illustrates what she praises theoretically as the affective aptitude of the revolutionary text, though as those writings show, Cixous can't help being poetic even in the supposedly rigidly accustomed confines of academia:

> Text: my body—shot through with streams of song . . . what touches you, the equivoice that affects you, fills your breast with an urge to come to language and launches your force; the rhythm that laughs you; the intimate recipient who makes all metaphors possible and desirable. (1981a: 252)

This is Cixous's notion of "writing the body,"[1] a useful concept in terms of *Hyperdream*, her novel/memoir about a woman/Cixous nursing her aged mother, while in lingering grief over the death of a dear friend (Derrida) several years earlier.

At first glance *Hyperdream* does not seem as obvious a rendering of the poetics of transgenerational trauma as *Fun Home*. Cixous's writing is darker and characterized by angst, but there are no overt traumatic familial events in the novel. The familial trauma is nebulous and in the undertones. It is, in the relationship between mother and daughter, more reflective of "structural" trauma, which Laplanche (1999) theorized as a universal operation through which subjectivity is formed in infancy, than "historic" trauma, which denotes trauma accumulated through familial and cultural nurturing (or lack of it) and via historical and collective events. The narrator tends her mother and feels distress, but there is little spectacle in the story and no stereotypically dramatic scenes. It might even be read as a poignant meditation on the passing of the seasons of life. Yet *Hyperdream* is a transgenerational traumatic text, even if it expresses a radically different realm of experience to the violent trauma of "mis-lit" or the florid dysfunctions of *Fun Home*. Demonstrating that familial trauma does not always involve horrific tales of childhood exploitation or rampant parental instability, *Hyperdream* enacts what Laplanche (1999) refers to as *afterwardness* (my italics). This is an idea and term elaborated from Freud, whose perception of trauma evolved over the course of his career and across much of this thought. Freud's abandonment of his early seduction theory, which stated that hysterical patients continued to suffer from the effects of sexual assaults that occurred in childhood, and his turn to fantasy, is roundly viewed by many as a betrayal of survivors of child abuse, but his notion of *Nachträglichkeit*, translated from German as deferred action, or afterwardness, has stood the test of time and proves highly productive in conceptualizations of phylogenetic heritage and its writings.

In *Nachträglichkeit*, it is not simply that a trauma or traumas that took place in the past return in the present. The word describes the way an impossible event—a trauma that, due to its shock or speed, was never established as an occurrence in consciousness—is registered, with disproportionate affective discharge, by a subsequent, and often seemingly trivial, or at least not necessarily traumatic, experience. For Laplanche, this second movement of trauma is what defines an experience as traumatic; what is not known (the first instance of trauma) is represented by a reverberation that appears belatedly. Afterwardness describes the way this reverberation takes place in association with a secondary event. Laplanche views the transmission of trauma from mother to child in infancy as central to the development of subjectivity, and he uses the term "implantation" to describe the unavoidable message inscribed from the other, stating that this message involves a (traumatic) intrusion of the "reality of the other" (Caruth 2001). It is this he refers to as structural, in that it is inevitable and formative. Cixous skillfully illuminates the operations of afterwardness in passages such as this one:

> I can see myself weeping later on soon for everything that this morning gets on my nerves, this very day I am jealous of today I am filled in advance with regret for the scene I'd like this instant to exit from, in advance I regret each of the distressing feelings that troubles me in this scene in which I feel trapped and in which I will later and in vain want to be trapped again as in a dream. (2009: viii)

Here Cixous seems to be summoning up all the unspeakable angst of her structural relation to her mother, a relation not only haunted by her mother's imminent death, but by her first years of life. Jennifer Cooke unwittingly references structural trauma when she says that Cixous is concerned with "communicating the mysterious unknowability which can rest at the heart of our closest relationships" (2011: 4).

Historic trauma is also apparent in *Hyperdream*, albeit in a more amorphous way than in *Fun Home*. This is evident in the narrator's musings on, and encounters with, her mother and in the tense relationship with her brother that hovers in the background. Big picture historic trauma is most apparent in a long, curious chapter titled "Benjamin's Bed" in which a war-torn Europe infuses the tale of a family treasure. Though little of the tale is explicitly told in the text, there is a sense of the terror and hardship of twentieth-century life in Europe bearing down on the family, even many years after the world wars. In a sly way, *Hyperdream* merges structural and historical trauma. The protagonist is structurally heir to the impact of historic traumas on her mother, as well as struggling to negotiate her own historic trauma. The writing is so present and close that the breathing of the women is almost audible as the daughter painstakingly anoints the ailing mother's body. In this scene in which the condition of dependency so fundamental in familial transgenerational trauma is reversed in the traumatized daughter's care of the dying mother, the fragility and frustrations of aging and loving are embodied on the page so palpably it is as if the reader is watching and listening through a cracked door. As Cooke observes, Cixous's writing "brings out the singularities and enigmas of relationships; emotions are described with poetic intensity and a very visceral lyricism" (2011: 4). I would add that Cixous's writing also brings out shared traumas.

Cixous's use of grammar is also notable, and it is critical to her visceral lyricism. In *Hyperdream*, grammar is given to meaningful lapses—paragraphs ending with hanging commas and words abandoned to space mid-sentence, that are perhaps illustrative of traumatic gaps within subjectivity and language. Such use of grammar operates as an internal affective logic (as opposed to a logic born of the traditional rules of grammar). Reiterations of traumatic affect and recurrences of love and pain tumble forth in sections like the following: "'*I go on living*' I told myself, thought marvelously bitter, bitterly marveling, '*I went on living, therefore losing.*' I was thinking, '*it's without end*'" (Cixous 2009: 60). Bennett could be talking about *Hyperdream* directly when she says, "The poetics of sense memory involve not so much *speaking of* but *speaking out of* a particular memory or experience—in other words, speaking from the body *sustaining sensation*" [italics in original] (2005: 38).

Just as *Hyperdream* communicates the mysterious unknowability of structural trauma, so too it demonstrates the disconcerting tenacity of second wounding, or as I prefer to call it, after-wounding. Cixous lost her father to tuberculosis at the age of ten, and as Kathryn Robson points out "Cixous's texts repeatedly return to the father's death without satisfactorily assimilating or containing it: the story of loss can never be completed in Cixous's writing" (82). Indeed, though the narrative is focused on Cixous's mother, *Hyperdream* opens with a reference to the loss of her father:

> Thursday was the first day of the month of death of my dead my father the dead, my number one dead my first death the fiftieth first day, how fresh this death this dead I was thinking, this death that does not get any older. (Cixous 2009: 4)

If second wounding is indicated by a depiction of trauma as not so much locatable in an individual's past as in its nonassimilation and return, it manifests as the way in which the not known of trauma becomes known—the event or posttraumatic symptom in the present that calls up the distressing affect of a wounding from the past that has not been consciously registered or processed. I prefer to use "after-wounding" in place of second wounding because as Herman figured in her positing of CPTSD, so often childhood trauma tends to produce a chronic form of posttraumatic experience, in which the psychic injuries of the past can be triggered often, relatively easily, and by a greater variance of stimuli. The idiom of after-wounding refers both to the notion of second wounding and to the concept of afterwardness, so critical to Laplanche's theory of trauma. It encompasses overt traumatic experience, such as the death of Cixous's father when she was ten, as well as harder-to-identify subjective splittings, such as the vague structural and daily psychic schisms and woundings shared between the narrator and her mother.

In *Hyperdream*, Cixous does not focus on her father explicitly again after the opening lines, but the repeated refrain of Derrida's demise indicates an intensity of after-wounding that summons the traumatic absence of her father. The melancholic motif of the loss of Derrida thus evokes Cixous's lifelong grief over the untimely death of her father. In the poetics of transgenerational trauma, it is not only a discreet second wounding that exposes a distinct original one. Trauma might be exposed less in a discreet second wounding than in a multiplicity of woundings, manifest as a mess of hypersensitivities, seemingly nonsensical reactions, projections, re-creations, disturbances, or hallucinatory interpretations of events, which may, in certain circumstances, involve a baffling and overwhelming flooding of affect. This is reflective of the diverse ways in which structural and historical trauma is transmitted within the multigenerational legacy of a family, to a greater or lesser degree, producing specific effects/affects, symptoms, and trajectories within the life of a subject and family. The texts I survey explore the ways constellations of traumatic affect (and much else besides) are operative in internal and relational symbiotic dynamics. Such symbiosis doesn't just mean these affects exist in the mutability and mutuality of transmission and binding. This process also involves a web of shame-bindings that extends well beyond the core constellation of traumatic affect, and well beyond the family of origin, as Bechdel's testimony so deftly shows, and as *Hyperdream* also reveals in subtle symbolism, such as the mother's umbrella, which seems to function as an important marker of gender, class, and character.

Yet, if the force of trauma and transgenerational trauma is formidable there is a power greater and mightier in love. The affirmation of this is at the heart of both *Fun Home* and *Hyperdream*, and this is reflective of a conceptual position I take. For Abraham and Torok, love is the art of introjection (1994)—a term and process I speak to more fully in Chapter 3. Kristeva has a similar understanding of love, associating it with psychic space (Kristeva 2002). For Brennan, its hallmarks are discernment and living attention (Brennan 2004). By whatever name or framing, the promise and sway of love is always working—in more or less measure—against, within, and upon the adhesiveness of trauma and its constellations of affect. If love inspires and facilitates the work of introjection and its arterial flow in grieving, or what Laplanche calls unweaving (1999), its actions and expressions are as complex, immeasurable, and uncategorizable as those of transgenerational trauma. *Hyperdream* reveals the slippery thawing grief process that takes place when love and literary action go to work on familial transmissions. This matter of grief as a crucial component of the poetics of transgenerational trauma warrants further explication.

In basic terms, mourning was for Freud a normative and healthy response to loss that runs its course and resolves, thereby freeing the libido from the lost love object (not necessarily a person) to cathect anew. Melancholia was presented as pathological, a stuckness in which the detachment and decathecting of libido is not accomplished in a timely manner. Though Freud later revisited his thinking, acknowledging that the distinction between the two was not as neat as he originally proposed, this early model remains useful, if only in passing. In "Mourning and Melancholia" (1917), Freud identified the common ground between mourning and melancholia as the loss of love object, one in which the specific attachment between the ego and the love object causes significant disruption in the face of loss. In other words, both processes involve identification—the blurring of boundaries that makes the love object a narcissistic experience that equates loss of other with loss of self. Another shared trait is the ambiguous love of the object, a love/hate relation, but the psychic effects of this ambiguity differ between the two processes.

Freud states: "Melancholia is in some way related to an object-loss which is withdrawn from consciousness, in contradistinction to mourning, in which there is nothing about the loss that is unconscious" (Freud 1917: 244). Many have addressed, and variously utilized, Freud's conceptions of mourning and/or melancholia, and it is not my intention to follow suit here, suffice to say that I use the term "grief" in this book to describe that tumultuous space between mourning and melancholia in which there is flux and movement between the two. This is a space most pertinent to the poetics of transgenerational trauma, in that crypted transmissions necessarily result in melancholia, but the work of love and the affect-ethic of literary trauma testimony enact mourning. This grief space is one in which the reader can share; it relates not only to individual experiences or particular familial configurations of trauma, but to social operations with wider effects. In my discussion of transgenerational testimony it is in the indeterminate vortex between healthy mourning and pathological melancholy that the challenge of introjection meets its possibility in language.

Abraham and Torok speak of the breast-filled mouth, the empty mouth, and of the replacing of the breast with language as a form of introjection when they say, "Learning to fill the emptiness of the mouth with words is the initial model of introjection," and "Since language acts and makes up for absence by representing, by giving figurative shape to presence, it can only be comprehended or shared in a 'community of empty mouths'" (Abraham and Torok 1994: 128). In the meeting of language and love, an emancipating energy is unleashed that loosens the hold of shame-bound transmissions.

Cixous's affective, experimental ruminations and free associations are means by which she speaks the inexplicable and enigmatic territory between structural and historical trauma. And in its depiction of after-wounding, *Hyperdream* offers a portrayal of the inevitable collapse of structural and historical trauma into one another.

Spinozans

Deleuze declares toward the end of "Ethology: Spinoza and Us" (1992), "Writers, poets, musicians, filmmakers—painters too, even chance readers—may find that they are Spinozists; indeed, such a thing is more likely for them than for professional philosophers" (630). The writer of trauma transmissions engenders a textual encounter that increases the power of understanding around trauma as a collective operation. *Fun Home* addresses not only Bechdel's task of confronting repressed traumatic grief, but also the consequences of her parents' failure to do so, and the intricate interplay between individual and familial repressions and socially produced norms and homophobic shame-bound prohibitions. Through its dreamlike poetics *Hyperdream* demonstrates the resonance of a collapse between the kind of structural trauma of which Laplanche speaks and the kind of historic trauma addressed by theorists like Caruth and Felman.

The poetics of transgenerational trauma is summoned from affective depths and brought to the light of perception and understanding in the space occupied by writer and reader. Its power of understanding emerges from the truths fashioned not just by conscious memory and historic detail, but also in and by the operations of the text: the blurring of defined genres and the process in which the unconscious imprint and temporality of trauma is manifest textually, affectively, and strategically. Such a methodology can be viewed as feminist in that it seeks to acknowledge and illustrate the somatic agency of writing and the gendered relations and conditions overlooked in more orthodox literature and its readings. It is trauma writing that highlights the difference between prosaic story and poetic and bodily expression, between representation and enactment, between voyeurism and victimhood and performances of perception, understanding, and empowerment in the Spinozan sense.

Spinoza's vision of ethical and political action center around the idea that affects resulting from external causes, which may be experienced as positive or negative (in the case of trauma they are usually painful or problematic), are superseded by encounters informed by internal causes, which are necessarily positive and joyful. This does not equate to isolation because in Spinoza's thinking subjective autonomy and the expansion of beingness leads to increased receptivity and engagement with the world of others (hence the ethical potential of affective reckoning). When it comes to external causes that are traumatic in nature, it can be difficult if not impossible to replace the affects produced by that experience, which are likely to manifest as "passions" (for Spinoza the passions are negative and diminishing; they are affects run riot, detached from understanding), with another, nontraumatic internal experience, one which can facilitate understanding. The process of engaging with art and literature, either as producer or reader/audience, is one way in which an internal experience can be generated in the face of external injury. In this way, the poetics of transgenerational trauma constitutes ethical action with political potential.

Books like *Fun Home* and *Hyperdream* cast into doubt perceptions of social ontology as "out there" by explicating dynamic relations between the micro and macro and networks of trauma both within the family and beyond. The poetics of transgenerational trauma involves an affective and productive exchange that offers both writer and reader the opportunity of transmuting trauma. In the face of this, the functional descriptor of "survivor" falls short, both because it is a word generally reserved for those who have passed through traumatic extremes (and as such it does not usually represent those who have experienced more covert or less severe trauma), and because in contending with this potent practice we do far more than simply survive.

3

Hauntology and the Spooked Text

The history of colonialism is long and bloody, dating way back to ancient colonialisms of the Vikings, Alexander the Great, and the Roman Empire, which dominated between 27 BC and 476 AD. This chapter is most directly concerned with patriarchal imperialism as manifested in the boom of British colonialism that rode the wave of eighteenth-century modernity and the Industrial Revolution. From the late sixteenth century to the second half of the twentieth century, Britain was such a formidable global power that during its ascent it enacted an unprecedented brand of colonialism: it claimed the world's largest island, a landmass about the same size as the continental United States, and set up a penal colony there, some 9,459 miles away from London, the beating heart of the British Empire. The "First Fleet" of eleven ships sailed into Botany Bay on January 18, 1788, carrying 751 convicts and their children, two of my own ancestors among them, who had, in the process of surviving the three-month voyage, met aboard the "Scarborough." After relocating to Port Jackson, an area known as "cadi" to the local Cadigal people, Captain Arthur Phillip raised the British flag, and the convicts disembarked, along with 252 marines and their families. So it was "Australia" came into being.

Before the establishment of the penal colony, some 750,000 Aboriginal and Torres Strait Islander people populated Australia, as their forebears had done for many, many millenniums. Today, as a result of the consequences of colonization, they number only around 669,900, around 3 percent of the entire Australian population. Australia became an independent nation, a constitutional monarchy to be precise, in 1901. This means that although the Commonwealth of Australia is governed by Parliament in adherence to the Australian constitution, the reigning British monarch is still technically the Australian reigning monarch and head of state. The term "postcolonialism" is most often understood as a field of study in which the legacies of imperialism and colonialism are analyzed in literature or other cultural productions. The "postcolonial era" also describes a period following formal colonialism in which its effects are still being felt and/or enacted. This chapter uses the term primarily in terms of the latter, but also in reference to the way in which the operations of colonialism and modernity are reconfigured in neocolonialisms, and in relation to cross-cultural literature that testifies to these realities, most especially from the point of view of Indigenous lived experience.

Alexis Wright's second novel *Carpentaria* (2006) is a fierce epic that both honors Indigenous sovereignty and culture and attests to the ravages wrought by colonization. Set in the fictional coastal town of Desperance, on the Gulf of Carpentaria in northwest Queensland, the novel centers on the infighting between local Aboriginal communities, and the greater challenge that befalls the region when a multinational mining corporation sets up on sacred land. But even more than this "plot," the novel is about masculinity as played out in the characters of, and relationships between, Norm Phantom, an old Aboriginal mystic and local leader; his son, Will; and their family friend, Mozzie Fishman. This chapter reads *Carpentaria* and other select texts in light of Jacques Derrida's post-structural conception of hauntology (1994) and the psychoanalytic theory of Hungarian-French analysts Nicholas Abraham and Maria Torok (1994) in order to examine the ways in which writing and literature can testify to the traumas of colonialism and genocide even centuries after their initial impact. I do not read for "hidden" traumas. I am concerned with a more ambitious venture. In Chapter 1, I claimed that the poetics of transgenerational trauma had the capacity to reveal operations of traumatic and transgenerational history, to illustrate what Caruth means when she says, "The traumatic nature of history means that events are only historical to the extent that they implicate others" (1996: 18). In Chapter 2, I explored the affect-ethics of the "Spinozan" writer and the dangers of the poetics of transgenerational trauma. In this chapter, I elaborate on these assertions by drawing on theories of hauntology to explore certain characteristics unique to postcolonial testimony, including non-Western perceptions of family, time, and reality. The enquiry is not so much whether or not a given text contains "specters": the question is the degree to which the specter is present, the ways in which it is conjured, and whether or not it is consciously acknowledged and articulated.

Wright is from Waanji country in the highlands of the Gulf, which can be found on a map of Australia between far north Queensland to the east and the top end of the Northern Territory to the west, south of Indonesia and Papua New Guinea across the Arafura Sea. Though Wright has close personal ties with the region and community she portrays, she identifies *Carpentaria* as fiction. A formidable presence in Australian public life, Wright is a distinguished research fellow at Western Sydney University, an award-winning and critically acclaimed author, and a researcher and educator with extensive experience working in government departments and Aboriginal agencies. As such she is at the forefront of Australian literature and Indigenous advocacy. Wright's commentary on her own creative process shows that in working on *Carpentaria*, she was keenly aware of the need to invent a way of writing that could embody both the negative effects of colonialism and her proud Aboriginal heritage. The resulting text is experimental, allegorical, sometimes humorous, and often startlingly lyrical. Its language is a combination of Anglo regional working-class and Indigenous English—a raw vernacular that snaps into poetry or vulgarity in a narrative that swings from prosaic plot development to grand happenings. It features an impossible-to-categorize blend of voices and influences and is driven by an almighty imagination, one capable of evoking the "Dreamtime" and depicting dysfunctional community in the same passage.

Otherwise known as "the Dreaming," Dreamtime is an ancient Aboriginal animist spiritual tradition that tells the creation stories of the sacred era in which ancestral totemic beings made the world and everything in it. Dreamtime is not just a set of beliefs about the origin of life in Australia; it is also a form of law and cultural learning in which the ways of specific Aboriginal nations are maintained and passed on from generation to generation. Reviewers (Syson 2007; Guest 2008) have used words like "dreamscape" and "magic" to describe Wright's fiction. Seeking some kind of genre marker for this unclassifiable work, I myself used the term "magic realist" to describe some the book's twists and turns in an essay for the Copyright Agency's Reading Australia Program (2015). There have been pertinent criticisms of this tendency of white intellectuals to cast the Dreamtime as mere fable, and to describe Aboriginal experience and writing in exotic terms (Wolfe 1991; Ravenscroft 2010). Jeanine Leane, a Wiradjuri scholar, points out that this recenters whiteness. Positioning Aboriginal stories of place and spirituality as outside (Western) reality, "the discourse surrounding [Aboriginal knowledge] slips into familiar vocabulary and generic codes: magic, superstition, myth and the supernatural—western readings that label the knowledge of 'others' unexplainable" (2015: 156). The term Leane uses for Wright's fiction is "Aboriginal realism" (155).

Since 1770, when Captain James Cook claimed the east coast of the continent now known as Australia, the First Peoples of this land have experienced incalculable trauma and devastation. They have suffered epidemics of imported disease, rape, and dispossession. They have been decimated by massacres and displacement into missions. Families have been torn apart and many Indigenous people and communities remain disadvantaged by questionable present-day policies and internationally denounced government failures. In short, the "settlement," otherwise known as the invasion, of Australia has cast its original human inhabitants into a perpetual state of loss and mourning. Yet, the novel is not only about trauma and loss—it is also a celebration of Aboriginal history and culture prior to the invasion; of Aboriginal resilience and heroism in the generations since; of Aboriginal refusal to be defined by Western notions of time; and of Aboriginal language and story in all its guises, traditional and contemporary. Though Wright resists framing Indigenous people as simplistically passive and victimized, *Carpentaria* is, at its core, a text of and about mourning and the questionability of modern notions of time. The novel testifies to the heritage of trauma via cross-cultural witnessing, but more than that it reveals the way a transgenerational traumatic text can serve as an important account of trends of transmission across extended stretches of time in the absence of the usual marker of evidence: official written record.

"Traumatic writing" or "post-traumatic writing" describes writing that represents usually catastrophic or apocalyptic traumatic experience, such as the Holocaust (LaCapra 1999, 2001). In literary theory, traumatic writing has been positioned as an attempt to liberate the unconscious and speak the unspeakable and the literally unthinkable (Caruth 1991, 1996; Felman and Laub 1992). Some have hailed the singular capacity of poetry to say the proverbial unsayable, but the claim is perhaps better made that poetry (as well as other arts such as visual art and music) expresses the *otherwise* unsayable. The great German poet Rilke affirmed the intimacy between the poetic word and affective silence when he wrote, "Words gently end at the edge/of the Unsayable" in "Sonnets to Orpheus" (Rilke 2002). If words can't exactly speak what most resists being spoken in words, poetic words can, Rilke avows, get right up close. I once attended a master class[1] with eminent American poet Michael Palmer in which he spoke of the likeness between poetry and dance in their ability to express the otherwise inexpressible through rhythm, meter, and gesture (made physically or viscerally in language). Palmer spoke too of the poetic reach to say the unsayable and poetry's attempt to articulate the potential, and prior-to-language, of experience. If we think of that potential and prior-to-language unsayableness as the existential unsayable, I asked him, what of the poetics of the traumatic "unsayable," which is not potential nor prior to, but in a sense both timeless and ever present? In answer, Palmer mentioned psychotic poetry (which I imagine means poetry having schizophrenic qualities) and its incantatory "outside the psyche" quality, before admitting that he hadn't given the matter of the traumatic unsayable much thought.

I take up that question in discussing the work this kind of writing does and the means by which it might be accomplished, showing how writing charts movements between the past and the present within a current of heightened affect capable of generating a textual embodiment of trauma spanning generations. In doing so, I refer again to Caruth's definition of psychic trauma as not simply indicating repression or the failure to process an event of the past: trauma *is* the past operative in the present. When Caruth challenges the idea of trauma as a "single violent" or "original event" in an individual past (1996: 4), she hints at that which is at the heart of both Derrida's and Abraham and Torok's hauntologies, sharing, as they do, the quality of traumas not locatable in a single violent or original event in an individual's past. These frameworks also share an evocation of the unassimilated nature of trauma, the way it is not known in the first instance, and its tendency to make its presence known belatedly (4). For this reason these theories prove useful in identifying the ways in which the past in the present operates culturally and textually. Affirming Caruth, Jill Bennett adds: "Traumatic memory is, in this regard, resolutely an issue of the present" (2005: 40). Bennett's point that trauma is resolutely an issue of the present is also crucial to my conception of the poetics of transgenerational trauma as spooked text, though as will become clear, Derrida's hauntology questions even the notion of a static "present."

The poetics of transgenerational trauma is a particularly haunted textuality that actively engages with the specter, either in its amorphous ghostly form or its more pointedly named or indicated phantom/s. In order to write this kind of text a writer must defy the conventions that would deny such séance. This is why haunted textuality is more likely encountered in creative writing than in formulaic, journalistic, or academic writing. Derrida speaks straight to the point when he says, "A traditional scholar does not believe in ghosts—nor in all that could be called the virtual space of spectrality" (Derrida 1994: 11). Part of the efficacy of the poetics of transgenerational trauma as a super-spooked practice of writing is that though it is unable to fully articulate trauma in language, it nevertheless speaks of, out of, and to, that which hovers between presence and absence, unnamable, and unknowable in the usual sense. Such literature is able to do this by way of a kind of channeling. Before taking up my exploration of what such channeling might involve, I briefly speak to non-Western conceptions of family and the Australian postcolonial context.

(Post)colonial story and cross-cultural witnessing

On the surface, Wright's novels appear to depart from my previously stated view of the family as central in the poetics of transgenerational trauma. But I maintain they crucially broaden understanding of the familial and ways in which transgenerational trauma operates in culture and in text, particularly in non-Western and cross-cultural testimony. The nuclear family unit does not figure as such in Australian Aboriginal culture. Traditionally both immediate and extended family as well as the community at large raise children. Generally speaking, Aboriginal people speak in terms of their "mob" or "country" (meaning the specific area of land that is their heritage and its Dreaming) over "family" in the sense that people of Anglo origin usually intend. This is not to say that immediate family is of no consequence, or that there are no family units in Wright's work. But it is important to expand my conception of the family to include non-Western customs and societies in which family is traditionally extended to the degree that it can be considered communal.

Considered stylistically radical and commercially risky, *Carpentaria* was published by Giramondo, a small, independent publisher, after every major publisher in Australia had rejected it. The timing of its publication was eerily significant. Not long after *Carpentaria* hit the shelves the *Ampe Akelyernemane Meke Mekarle: "Little Children Are Sacred" Report* (Wild and Anderson 2007) was released, documenting endemic child sexual assault in remote Indigenous communities (domestic violence and alcoholism have also been identified as serious problems in Indigenous communities, as they are in mainstream society). This proved a catalyst for action: the conservative coalition federal government introduced the Northern Territory National Emergency Response, a program of welfare, law enforcement, land tenure changes, and policing, commonly known as "the invention." As *The New York Times* (Perlez 2007) reported, the very same day the novel was announced as the winner of the prestigious Miles Franklin Literary Award, Prime Minister John Howard imposed a "ban on alcohol and pornography in the Northern Territory as part of an effort to combat child abuse, which a government report found to be widespread in Aboriginal communities." The *New York Times* also noted that while promoting *Carpentaria*, Wright was prevailed upon to respond to Howard's move as an Indigenous advocate. This is unsurprising given that Wright is both an established activist and the author of the nonfiction title, *Grog War* (1997), about endemic alcoholism in an Indigenous community and the corruption that thwarted attempts to address it. Wright reportedly expressed wariness with the strategies of the government, suggesting preelection posturing rather than genuine concern for the well-being of Indigenous people might have fuelled the drastic and speedy policy development. Wright's literary work has not only challenged the national silencing of Aboriginal people (evident in their underrepresentation in Parliament—there are notably far fewer Indigenous people in government in Australia than there are Māori representatives in New Zealand, which passed legislation to ensure their participation); it has also introduced an entirely new voice, a new way of speaking, of representing the postcolonial context.

When I first configured my reading of *Carpentaria* in relation to theories of hauntology, I was unaware of Grace Cho's 2008 book *Haunting the Korean Diaspora: Shame, Secrecy, and the Forgotten War*, in which she engages with Abraham and Torok in a second-generation, experimental, and autoethnographic exploration of transgenerational haunting relating to war. There are crossovers between her exploration of hauntology and mine, and I might just as rightly present the invasion of Australia as a forgotten colonialization, given the way mainstream Australia proceeds, by and large, as if it never took place, the many persecutions of Indigenous peoples assigned to a blend of tacit collective denial and secrecy. The likes of Howard, his eventual successor Tony Abbott, and Pauline Hanson, the once rising independent star whose policies are expressions of thinly veiled malcontented bigotry, have famously refused to accept either governmental shame or blame for the devastation brought upon Aboriginal Australians. In fact, Hanson first came to power in Queensland in 1998 as leader of the One Nation Party on that very platform, alongside her ardent campaigning against the "Asian invasion."

Hanson was reelected into Parliament following the 2016 federal election, this time with her sights set on immigrants from the Middle East (previously she targeted Asian immigrants). The majority of politicians, across party lines, are content to let Indigenous communities struggling with the crushing aftermath of centuries of trauma carry the shame and blame for the problems within those communities. The dispossession of Aboriginal Australians has been so extreme as to have—but for their tenacious connections to country and each other—cast Aboriginal Australians into a diaspora in the very land their ancestors have inhabited for eons. Cho describes her experience of the postwar Korean diaspora in the United States as having grown up in the absence of a "public discourse" (2008: 11), but makes clear that despite this silence subsequent generations are haunted by the "traumatic effects of what we are not allowed to know" (12). Wright taps into both the silence and the haunting surrounding the original colonization, and the continuing neocolonization, of Australia.

Gabriele Schwab, who studies stories for their potential to "carry" transgenerational trauma in light of Abraham and Torok's work (2006: 98), observes that "writing from within the core of trauma is a constant struggle between the colonizing power of words and the revolt of what is being rejected, silenced" (95). The challenge of writing from within the core of overwhelming collective and multigenerational experiences of trauma is part of the quest Wright set for herself in creating *Carpentaria*. The novel resists "being framed by the history of dispossession and marginalization that so often defines Aboriginal people as silent and passive victims" (Molloy 2013: 1) in a variety of ways, including its bold performance demonstrating the power of storytelling, the agency of witnessing and testimony, and the affective capacity of posttraumatic poetics.

Chapter two opens with the following passage:

> One evening in the driest grasses in the world, a child who was no stranger to her people, asked if anyone could find hope. The people of parable and prophecy pondered what was hopeless and finally declared that they no longer knew what hope was. The clocks, tick-a-ty tock, looked as though they might run out of time. Luckily, the ghosts in the memories of the old folk were listening, and said anyone can find hope in the stories: the big stories and the little ones in between. So . . . (2006: 12)

Here writing is a tribute to loss as well as an affirmation of life. Drawing on customs, folklore, and oral traditions practiced over time immemorial, Wright takes storytelling from its place in the center of her culture and plants it at the starting point of her cross-cultural testimony with the beautiful line: "The ghosts in the memories of the old folk were listening" and the reassurance that hope can be found in the "stories." Aboriginal and Torres Strait Islander cultures are estimated to be the oldest living cultural history in the world, dating back to at least 50,000–65,000 years (Australian Government 2013). The destruction of Aboriginal languages is one of the many long-term consequences of colonialism. Of the estimated 250 languages spoken before my forebears and their fellow prisoners stepped ashore only fifty remain in use today (Lo 2013). What does it mean for a writer to witness to the devastating effects of colonization in the language of the colonizers? It seems Wright began *Carpentaria* with an intention to inscribe the pleasures and creativity of Indigenous language into Australian letters, and one can only imagine how overwhelming an undertaking it must have been for Wright to sit down to the first blank page. In "On Writing *Carpentaria*" (2007a), Wright discusses the epic and oral nature of Indigenous stories:

> I tried to come to some understanding of two principal questions: firstly, how to understand the idea of Indigenous people living with the stories of all the times of this country, and secondly, how to write from this perspective. (2)

Wright also speaks of wrangling with guilt for taking pause to write a "novel capable of embracing all times" (3) because of her sense of personal calling regarding the "urgent work to do in our communities, or more battles to fight over the high levels of ignorance fostered by this government in particular about Aboriginal rights in this country" (2–3). Wright was aware of a degree of privilege in even having the option to write a novel and she was alert to the enormous responsibility of performing an act of public mourning, testimony, and witnessing, and the impetus of such writing. Her reference to *Carpentaria* as a "novel capable of embracing all times" hints at its hauntological qualities.

Wright conceived of *Carpentaria* as a work that could not be constrained "in a capsule that was either time or incident specific." It would not conform to English as we know it. Her aim was to question such boundaries and codings and to explore how the ancient beliefs, stories, and spiritual and cultural practices of her people "sit in the modern world" (3). She was not interested in writing history per se, and on this point her thinking is aligned with Derrida's hauntology when she says that she could "find no reason to write history, in the sense of drawing on historical incident, when all times are important and unresolved" (11). Wright's treatment of time and memory is layered and complex. The reader of *Carpentaria* is obliged to release the expectation of being firmly situated in time as subtle slippages across narration confound orthodox assumptions about time, place, and experience. The book stands as a relation of presents that cast into doubt rigid notions of past and present as fixed temporal locations.

The temporal structure of the novel has obvious traumatic characteristics. It features a nonlinear and nonsensical circulation of mixed-up history that captures and conveys how the traumatized, colonized mind struggles with "bad realities" and "unacceptable history" (Wright 2007a: 5). Drawing on Stephen Muecke in her reflection on the process of writing, Wright speaks of the "layering of ancient forms and imaginative inventions that oscillates between the ancient and the modern" (4). She also evokes W. G. Sebald's analysis of Jean Améry's writing in noting that when the "thread of chronological time is broken, background and foreground merge," concluding that "terror dislocates time." This results in a postcolonial experience in which traumatic affect circulates "mingling centuries, and continuing through the whorls of time" (5). The poetics of transgenerational trauma is possible because in the unconscious, the space from which traumatic affect transmits (even if it sometimes passes through awareness in some shape or form), there is no sense of time in terms of the way we think of time in the conscious world. The question of time and transmissive possibility is even more complicated in posttraumatic literary testimony involving cross-cultural witnessing. Wright's postcolonial poetics of transgenerational trauma embody traumatic temporality in the ways outlined in Chapters 1 and 2, but also span much longer stretches of time, including old people knowledge from long distant ancestors, and knowledge from the land itself. In the opening pages, she writes:

> It takes a particular kind of knowledge to go with the river, whatever its mood. It is about there being no difference between you and the movement of water as it seasonally shifts its tracks according to its own mood. A river that spurns human endeavour in one dramatic gesture, jilting a lover who has never really been known, as it did to the frontier town built on its banks in the hectic heyday of colonial vigour. A town intended to serve as a port for the shipping trade for the hinterland of Northern Australia. (2007b: 2–3)

As Leane says in her insightful reading of *Carpentaria*, "The construct of 'history' defines time as a space that can be measured. Time flows in a certain linear direction where people 'make' history" (2015: 151). It is in this sense that *Carpentaria* is engaged with hauntology rather than concerned with history per se. Derrida refers to *Spectres of Marx* as "a politico-logic of trauma and a topology of mourning" (1994: 97). Though he builds his notion of hauntology around the figure of Marx and associated larger-than-life historical and political hauntings, it is explicit that he views the nature of the specter, and hauntology itself, as an essentially traumatic phenomenon. It is living with loss and with its timeless reverberations. If, as Derrida wrote in the early 1990s, it remains somewhat true that a traditional scholar does not believe in ghosts or in the virtual space of spectrality, and his challenge to orthodox perceptions of time is difficult to accept, we would do well to remember that many physicists are also questioning the reliability of what we call the past, present, and future (Greene 2005).

Derrida's specter versus the psychoanalytic phantom

Colin Davis's essay (2005), contrasting Derrida's notion of the specter and Abraham and Torok's concept of the phantom, affords a basic framework for thinking about the capacity of writing to embody the trauma of past generations and to illuminate the nature of traumatic memory. As Davis outlines, Derrida's hauntology is not a hackneyed belief in the supernatural, but a supplantation of its "near-homonym ontology" that replaces the "the priority of being and presence" with the figure of the specter, or ghost, as that which is "neither present nor absent, neither dead nor alive" (Davis 2005: 373). Hauntology has nothing to do with the genre of ghost stories and does not require belief in the paranormal. For Derrida, the specter constitutes the intrusion of a timeless other (person, work, or point in history) into our world, and this is an intrusion that cannot be accounted for in existing discourse or intellectual comprehension. This is where experimental writing has a distinctive agency.

Abraham and Torok's phantom, described as the site of transgenerational transmission and communication, marks the way in which the undisclosed traumas of one generation influence and disturb the life of another (Davis 2005: 376). Abraham and Torok themselves position the phantom as an intergenerational operation, an alternative to the individualist construction of Freudian thought. They claim its conception involves a "radical reorientation" of post-Freudian psychopathological theory in shifting the psychoanalytic focus beyond individual analysis. It does this by postulating that some individuals "unwittingly inherit the secret psychic substance of the ancestors" and that this is a condition in which that individual will become symptomatic as a result not of their own life experiences "but from someone else's psychic conflicts, traumas, or secrets" (Abraham and Torok 1994: 166). While

Marianne Hirsch (2012) and others at the forefront of memory and genocide studies have mined this territory, advancing understanding of second- and third-generation testimony, Abraham and Torok's psychoanalytic nuance and theoretically poetic elegance enable consideration of a more multifaceted multigenerational transmission.

The phantom is bound up with Abraham and Torok's concept of the secret, which is not just, or even, a secret in the usual sense, but an entombed event or experience bound to an internal silence, which results in a subjective split that is inherently shameful and diminishing. The phantom, then, is the manner in which the secret(s) of a previous generation embed in and haunt subsequent generations, with or without their awareness of the traumatic event or events. Abraham and Torok posit the phantom as the spectral presence of a departed ancestor operative in the living ego of a descendant. The phantom is a kind of possession in which the resident forebear seeks to keep traumatic and shameful secrets from discovery and exposure. Abraham and Torok's concept of the secret reveals the difference between shame in its healthy relation to interest and what I call traumatic shame (the term "toxic shame" was popularized by the self-help titles in the 1980s and the 1990s, but to my mind "traumatic shame" is a more accurate casting). Trauma is often associated with secrecy, in the standard definition of the word, but the transmission of trauma does not depend on this common meaning of secrecy. Abraham and Torok's notion of secrecy is inherent in transgenerational trauma, whether or not the trauma transmitted is a secret in the usual sense. For Abraham and Torok, the secret is an entombed traumatic event or experience bound to an internal silence that results in a subjective split that is in itself shameful and diminishing. The secret is a deathly experience with deathly consequences, and introjection is the only possible remedy (Abraham and Torok 1994: 157–58).

The psychoanalytic aim is to uncover the secret/s. Derrida is uninterested in the forensic investigation and goal of restoration that is inherent to the psychoanalytic project. Instead, he insists there is an ethical dimension to our relationship with the specter. This means that rather than seeking to integrate it or force it into language Derrida would urge us to encounter its otherness, its alien and incomprehensible nature, and to be committed to preserving it.

For Derrida, the ghostly secret is not a jigsaw puzzle requiring a fanatical effort to find missing pieces, but a mystery whose enigmatic nature does not preclude engagement. In this sense, Wright's fiction is a kind of antipuzzle in contemporary literature. It is work that insists upon, and courts, the presence of the ghost, refusing to cross-examine it, understanding that indeed the ghost cannot be respectfully communed with in such an environment, dedicated to the ethical mission of preserving and communicating it. There are "fairy-like" figures of folklore in *Carpentaria* that resonate with Derrida's idea of ultimately allowing unknowability:

> The *yinbirras*, they said, were related to all of the tribes. These Yanngunyi were people who lived beside other real people, and even though you could hear them going about their business, shouting at each other to listen, they would not let anyone see them because they did not want to be found, or made civilised. (Wright 2007b: 227)

Wright's novels are the creative equivalent of Derrida's hauntology in that both resist an interpretive project, a demand for an explanatory calculation or simple disclosure. By its very nature the specter defies intellectual access. Psychoanalysis also understands the limits of intellectual access, but it nevertheless seeks to circumvent those limits via a variety of strategies, including dream interpretation, free association, and, sometimes, hypnosis. In the early days of psychoanalysis, pioneers such as Pierre Janet, Josef Breuer, Sigmund Freud, and Sándor Ferenczi used diagnostic terms like "hysteria" and "shell shock" in relation to trauma and affect. During the 1960s and 1970s, Abraham and Torok took a pointed interest in transgenerational trauma, complicating traditional psychoanalytic theory by fusing philosophy, psychology, linguistics, and literary theory into a unique theory. At the forefront of the bourgeoning new "science," Freud before them had hypothesized trauma and affect in terms of individual identity, universally structured unconscious conflicts, neurosis, and fantasy. His most groundbreaking and enduring work on trauma was inspired by the endemic of severely traumatized men returning from the devastation of the First World War. Despite working within this framework, Abraham and Torok went to pains to distinguish between the traditional psychoanalytic approach to trauma and their own. In particular they aired concerns about the predetermined constructions that gained primacy in public consciousness and clinical practice, namely Freud's theory of the Oedipus complex.

Abraham and Torok reportedly influenced Derrida, who was instrumental in bringing about their publication (Davis 2005: 373). Paradoxically, despite his effort to help their writings reach a wider audience, it is thought to be partly because of the success of Derrida's hauntology that Abraham and Torok drifted into semiobscurity. Davis writes that adherents of deconstruction tend to give Abraham and Torok's hauntology "a distinctly Derridean inflection" (376). I too disavow an investigative project regarding Abraham and Torok's phantom, but I also reaffirm the value of the phantom as conceived by Abraham and Torok and its usefulness in thinking about the operations of traumatic affect in narrative.

Abraham and Torok use only one idiom, "the phantom," for their concept, while Derrida employs multiple words, "spectre," "ghost," and occasionally "phantom," interchangeably. The Derridean notion of the "ghost" will be applied to textual hauntings more diffuse, diluted, or hybrid than phantomological haunting, and the term "spectre" will be employed as a reference to either, both, or to haunting in general. I want to retain something of the specificity of the concept of the "phantom" while questioning the assumption that a return to the order of knowledge is necessary, or even achievable. In the following pages I tease out these related yet distinct spookings within *Carpentaria*, focusing on what the two theories agree on—the critical involvement of grief in spectrality.

Ghostliness

A text can be highly ghosted—without necessarily dealing overtly with traumatic content or history—by embodying the ghosts of distant generational traumas or cultural traumas so collectively well tolerated as to have become accepted norm. This kind of ghosting may be so fundamental to writing as to be its very foundation. Julian Wolfreys (2002) insists that ghostliness is not just an aspect of textuality, but rather fundamental to the act of representation and all storytelling. In his words, "The spectral is at the heart of any narrative of the modern" and "all forms of narrative are spectral to some extent" (1–3).

If transgenerational transmission of trauma is a social operation and force—that is, one that is both informed by the culture and history within which it takes place and one that in turn informs culture—Wolfreys's assertions are not as extreme as they may initially seem. But even if we accept his postulation that ghostliness pervades representation and story, exceeding genre and other specifics of textual production, it does not follow that all texts are equally spooked, or that the presence of ghosts is as profoundly encountered or politically enacted across all texts. When it comes to writing, it is the measure by which an experience, reality, or cultural condition resists communication in language that determines its propensity to ghostliness; hence ghostliness operates as an apparition of trauma.

Evident in elements such as mood, tone, and ambiance, ghostliness is channeled by a writer affectively as that which does not quite make it into text but which the text nevertheless conjures up. Toni Morrison's novel, *Beloved* (1987), is not only spooked with Sethe's murdered daughter, but also with the entire American slave trade, the history and impact of which is simply too colossal, communal, and prolonged to be written only as a phantomlike secret. A writer like Kathy Acker (1994a,b,c) may have been channeling ghostly traumas around patriarchy, misogyny, and sexuality too socially entrenched, eroticized, and romanticized to be revealed in any more exact and rational ways in her violent and confronting books. Haruki Murakami's (2000, 2006) surreal and atmospheric novels are ghosted with the specter of Japan's relationship to the West, the shared history of war and cultural produce. Texts such as these are more overtly haunted by Derrida's unsettling of established notions of time and reality than by Abraham and Torok's explicitly coded traumas.

It follows that a text can be both ghosted and phantomic. The ghostliness of *Carpentaria* has to do with the specters of Anglo invasion and colonialism, but also with the Dreaming itself, with its open-ended quality of forever time, as demonstrated by this passage:

> If you are someone who visits old cemeteries, wait awhile if you visit the water people. The old Gulf country men and women who took our besieged memories to the grave might just climb out of the mud and tell you the real story of what happened here. (2006: 11)

What might the nature of the besieged memories and the real story be? Whatever the answer, it is clear that they exist outside of the dictates of what we call time and outside of the realms we view as the strictly living and the strictly dead. The ghosting of the legacy of massacres and missions is manifest in copious references such as that made to "Uncle Micky's collection of bullet cartridges" (10) that were "used in the massacres of the local tribes" and which he picked up in a "fever which drove him on" (11). Likewise the mention made of "those whose fractured spirit cried of rape, murder and the pillage of their traditional lands" (27) and the "up-to-no-good Mission-bred kids" who "accidently hanged Cry-baby Sally" under the rivergum (2). The ghosting of the text lies in the silence of the old Gulf country men and women whose graves lie in the mud, in the traumatic muteness of those who dodged or were penetrated by the bullets and in the untold stories of the up-to-no-good Mission kids. It pulses in between the words and lines of this writing of what Katrina Schlunke refers to as a "dumb place . . . excessive to memorial," a place that "couldn't be accounted for," whose "story is untellable" (2004: 75). It is ghosted too with age-old conflicts among the Indigenous "poor old Pricklebush people" (Wright 2006: 23), brought to an ugly head by the stresses of racism, poverty, and, later, disagreements over the mine. Even conflicts predating colonialism by eons are called up. "People who had been getting on well," writes Wright, "living side by side for decades, started to recall tribal battles from the ancient past" (26).

Derrida insists that it is ethically necessary to speak of, to, and with the ghost, going so far as to state that there can be no justice without acceptance of some responsibility toward both the dead and the yet-to-be-born that were or will be affected by "wars, political or other kinds of violence, nationalist, racist, colonialist, sexist, or other kinds of exterminations, victims of the oppressions of capitalist imperialism or any of the forms of totalitarianism" (Derrida 1994: xix). It is apt to remember that for Derrida the specter is not a matter of the past spooking the present, or the dead spooking the living as such. His conception of hauntology refers to that which cannot be located in time as we know it and that which acts as a kind of continuum of presents less solid than we like to imagine. He speaks of a "spectral moment" as "a moment that no longer belongs to time, if one understands by the word the linking of modalized presents (past present, actual present: 'now', future present)" (xx).

Derrida maintains that the ghost should not be made to speak sensibly and precisely but should instead be engaged with as an uncertainty. The ghost in the poetics of transgenerational trauma might be thought of as the affective traces of traumas so far past or so unspeakably pervasive as to escape reference to a given time or an identifiable phantom. In the phantomic aspect of the poetics of transgenerational trauma, however, Derrida's post-structural hauntology and Abraham and Torok's psychoanalytic hauntology feed off each other in suspenseful density, because as well as translating what is translatable of the phantom, the transgenerational trauma writer also necessarily channels the ghostly specter of what remains unknowable, unspeakable, and atmospheric. Such channeled affect may be less influential in a text than the translated phantom in terms of narrative drive, plot, and character development, and rather spooks the text amorphously in an energetic manner. In this way, the poetics of transgenerational trauma affectively witnesses to intergenerational ghost stories.

The phantom

The phantom spooks by marking the site of a particular psychic splitting, or network of splittings, and the attendant shame and subsequent weakening of the living subject host to it. Abraham states: "All the departed may return but some are destined to haunt: the dead who were shamed during their lifetime or those who took unspeakable secrets to the grave" (Abraham 1994: 171). He views the phantom as a kind of signifier for "the gap produced in us by the concealment of some part of a love object's life" so that in phantomic spookings "what haunts are not the dead, but the gaps left within us by the secrets of others" (171). As Davis sets out, the central disparity between Derridean and psychoanalytic spectrality is found in this concept of the secret, which amounts to a traumatic gap. For Abraham and Torok the secrets of the lying phantom are unspeakable because of their roots in shame and prohibition. It is not that the secret cannot be spoken, but that it resists exposing its shameful core. Abraham and Torok hold that secrets "can and should be put into words so that the phantom and its noxious effects on the living can be exorcized," while for Derrida, "the ghost and its secrets are unspeakable in a quite different sense" (Davis 2005: 378). Derrida is not concerned with individual symptomology and its analysis, but with a tremendous historic, collective, multigenerational, and affective legacy. For him the secret does not resist being spoken because it is taboo but "because it cannot not (yet) be articulated in the languages available to us" (Davis 2005: 378), or at least, I would add, not in ways we would traditionally or routinely recognize as articulation.

My reading of the phantomized text integrates aspects of both these variations of the secret and eschews others. In keeping with Abraham and Torok's model, I treat the phantom as an evasive and inherited site of shame and prohibition within subjectivity, one that indeed has "noxious effects on the living." I also concur that the phantom can, and must, to some degree, and in certain respects, be "put into words" in such a way as to disempower and shrink its hold. But that, as I will later explain, is where I part ways with Abraham and Torok. For Abraham and Torok the phantom is a liar that purposefully misleads and eludes its hostage, but to my mind, though the phantom does involve deceit and denial, it is not just that the phantom lies and (mis)leads its unsuspecting host away from itself. The site of the phantom marks the formation of an entrenched traumatic lie in the sense that trauma shapes and changes subjectivity, especially that of children in relation to the familial other. This is evident in the figure of the flawed yet heroic protagonist of *Carpentaria*, named, remarkably and coincidently, Normal Phantom (Wright has a penchant for punny and metaphoric names) and his family.

Midway through the novel Norm, "an old tribal man" (Wright 2006: 4) who has lived all his days in the dense Pricklebush scrub on the edge of the northwest Queensland township of Desperance has been left by his piece-of-work wife, Angel Day, to cope with a household of troubled adult children. His estranged activist son, Will, is a loose cannon on the run, while a "ventriloquist" (211) cockatoo called Pirate provides company and solace. This reference to ventriloquism is uncanny given Abraham and Torok's use of the word to describe the way in which the phantom is cryptically and usually incomprehensibly vocal in the speech and writing of its harboring descendant, though it seems likely Wright intended it in the usual sense, as a description of the bird's faculty for mimicry. Despite the impact of phantoms upon his life, family, and community, Norm is something of a mystic and a respected elder. The shame and mourning that accompany the phantom might be regarded as the affective tombstones of a traumatic lie. In Norm's case the lie has been imposed by the dominance and assumed superiority of the colonizers, by the power of racism and imperialism to diminish culture and self-esteem in successive blows against generation after generation of his Indigenous forebears.

The poetics of transgenerational trauma makes possible a bearing witness to familial and cultural traumatic lies that are specific and explicit in nature though not necessarily verifiable in disclosure. It is less the factual telling of secreted stories and more akin to a translation of them. As Walter Benjamin shows in his essay "The Task of the Translator" (1969: 69–82), translation is not the straightforward transcribing from one source and language to another, but rather an art form in itself, an interpretive and creative act. If we consider traumatic experience as the source and the language of trauma as foreign—that is, outside of our language and unreadable in our own—then the work of the poetics of transgenerational trauma involves re-creating and recasting its material into a narrative in the given language of writing. Transgenerational traumatic writing mines familial life and traumatic experience, and the affects associated with them; snippets of history suggest the story that a writer of transgenerational trauma translates. So it is that by writing (through) familial or communal trauma affectively, drawing on various sources—stories, rumor, official records, documents, remembered conversation, gossip, diaries, letters, photos and memory (including fragmented, distorted, and unreliable memory), mythology and/or lived experience—a writer channels the unassimilated trauma of familial ancestors and collective history. Anything that constitutes the unassimilated nature of trauma, the very ways in which it has not been known and yet registers its attendance in individual and family life, may become the phantomic source material of the secret the writer of transgenerational trauma translates. This is not to say that what actually happens in a family, a traumatic event, or cultural history is of no consequence in its specificity, or that uncovering, speaking, writing, and reading those factual details is unimportant. That too has its vital role to play and its distinctive operations. It is a way of rethinking the truth of traumatic experience and of considering how, in the poetics of trauma, it may be testified without reliance on fact, enabling testimony, witnessing, and introjection around traumas and histories that for one reason or another cannot be reliably substantiated.

First- and second-generation traumatic writing, such as Alison Bechdel's *Fun Home: A Family Tragicomic* (2006), and the poetry of Lily Brett tend to be phantom-rich, and as such they are examples of what I am referring to as a mode of translation. Bechdel translates not only the phantom of her father's sexual and emotional repression, but also the historical and traumatic legacy around the oppression and persecution of homosexuals. Brett's collection *The Auschwitz Poems* (1986) is utterly infused with the energy, memory, and profound trauma of her survivor mother. Its deceptively simple poetics, appearing in lower case and unpunctuated, with titles like "Everything looked normal" and "I wear your face," packs relentless punches to the power base of the phantom. Her later collection *After the War: Poems* (1990) charts the posttraumatic experience with a focus on second-generation acting out and working through. Wright's works cannot so readily be described as "second generation" testimony for she translates traumatic experience from all the times before her, witnessing to many generations down the line.

In *Carpentaria*, both the knowledge and trauma of ancestors is not a matter of the past. They are operative in the present of the living. In Chapter 8, Norm, who has "secret conversations" with the "heavenly spirits at night" about the ways of the ocean and clandestine fishing locations (Wright 2006: 230), embarks on an epic voyage with a mission to bury Elias, his seafaring comrade, at sea. Here, delirious visions intensify the past-present style of narration so that the past is not only manifest in the present; it is even more real than it was in its initial occurrence. Norm is described as

> staring straight through reality to watch her [his wife, Angel Day] for the first time that long ago day when Elias had seen her. Looking so closely into her face, he was astounded at its clarity. He was shocked to see a secret intimacy residing within her. He had never before seen this face from her childhood transcending through the travesties of their life together. (243)

Another important point is that traditionally the Aboriginal worldview is much less individualistic than the worldview of Western society. So it is that in this novel transgenerational trauma is less of a personal or intimate account in which familial and cultural transmission is illuminated and more of a collective experience in which ancestral knowledge and trauma are interwoven in mythology and stories. For example, Wright writes:

> Everyone in Pricklebush knew of the poisonous countries out at sea, places where it was too dangerous for a man to go, where the spirits dwelt, like the Gundugundu men who were even more dangerous than Kadajala, the white-man devil, and those of the unhappy warring spirit warriors of the old wars. (276)

A seemingly simple passage such as this conveys an intricate interconnectedness of traumas and myth: Pricklebush is a slum in which Indigenous people struggle to live in relation to, and on the outskirts of, the white town of Desperance. This passing reference itself is heavy with history, as is the reference to "Kadajala, the white-man devil"—the colonizers and their descendants—and the "warring spirit warriors of the old wars," which have to do with Aboriginal conflicts in the time before the invasion. How then, does a writer like Wright pull off this kind of testimony in which all times matter from as far back as we have record of humanity of the planet?

During an interview (*The 7.30 Report* 2007), Wright spoke of a particularly painful event in her family history in which her great-grandmother was taken as a child, along with another little girl, by a notorious pastoralist whose workers are on record as having massacred Indigenous people. She said she was not sure if her great-grandmother's own family were among those killed. Kerry O'Brien went on to raise a comment Wright had made in an essay some years before the publication of *Carpentaria*, in which she wrote that she had "inherited all the words left unsaid in a family to save the peace" and that these were "words that have buried a thousand crimes and a thousand hurts." Asked what she had meant by that she replied:

> It's very hurtful for our family sometimes to talk about that history. And I think it gets passed down to the next generation through the following generations of not wanting to bring up hurtful things, hurtful things that happen to us even now.

How might a person inherit all the words left unsaid in a family that is part of a collective history of colonization and then go on to write out of that?

Transmitted affectively as well as by other means, the writer of transgenerational trauma writes with affect leading thought in combination, where relevant, with research, and in doing so testifies without certain knowledge of secrets and traumatic history, or with only patchy or distorted knowledge. It becomes possible then, to adhere to the specificity of Abraham and Torok's hypothesis of the phantom without approaching it as knowable data or a problem to be solved, but rather, as source material for an exploration and translation independent of concrete personal or familial revelations (but which may nevertheless also contain them). *Carpentaria*, as a text that demonstrates the dynamic play between the two conceptions of haunting, manages to convey layers of truth about Australia's history and a vision of contemporary Australia previously not articulated in Australian literature.

Introjection and the paradox of a "posttraumatic" poetics

Derrida eloquently expresses his view of mourning as "in fact and by right interminable, without possible normality, without reliable limit" (1994: 97). *Carpentaria*, Wright's "long song" (2007a: 7), is a creative act of the mourning so central in hauntology. "So," writes Wright, in the penultimate chapter of *Carpentaria*, "melancholy started to grow in the island's rich fertile atmosphere and competed for life just like any other seed planted on the island" (2007b: 378). Derrida views mourning as the trail of trauma, going so far as to suggest mourning is not only one kind of work and something that informs work, but also ultimately the *only work* and the very condition of production. He calls this "spectral spiritualization" (1994: 97). The inference is that traumatic compulsivity is an inherent aspect of labor, involving both repetition and a lack of an original, fixed motive for the action of work. Here Wolfreys's assertions about the ubiquitous ghostly nature of textual production come to mind. If repetition is characteristic of trauma, and mourning is an open-ended process with no categorical, identifiable beginning, no neat parameters, *and* the condition of production, the postcolonial poetics of transgenerational trauma can be seen as a particularly spectrally spiritualized occupation and manifestation. Circling back to Abraham and Torok, who wait patiently, now themselves spectral, I want to focus on mourning and "introjection" in relation to the poetics of transgenerational trauma. In his references to work, Derrida is describing the same process that Abraham and Torok understand as "introjection," although for Derrida the intention is encounter, while for Abraham and Torok it has analytic application. The term "introjection" itself has a long and problematic history, meaning many things to many theorists, so I take this opportunity to define my understanding and usage.

In claiming that the poetics of transgenerational trauma surpasses the mere telling of a traumatic tale to facilitate the work of introjection, I use the term in the Abraham and Torok sense. For them, introjection is the driving force of psychic life bound to and by love. It is not limited to the work of therapy, though therapeutic abreaction, binding, working through, and mourning can be crucial elements of it. They differentiate their view of introjection as a multifaceted, life-affirming, and enriching process from the various castings of the word in psychoanalytic orthodoxy, which conflate it with other processes, such as "incorporation" (Abraham and Torok 1994: 127). For example, Freud's use of the word "introjection" is akin to notions of internalization, which posits introjection as a reverse of projection, a process by which the ego adopts aspects of another as its own. Abraham and Torok contend that this better describes incorporation, which "denotes a fantasy" (Abraham and Torok 1994: 125).

The correlation Abraham and Torok make between introjection and love is particularly compelling; they view introjection as the work of love, as its living process. As psychoanalytic theorists, Abraham and Torok adopt the Freudian understanding that ties love to the life force, and thus it is the unifying drive at work in opposition to the anxious, traumatic, disconnecting impulses of the death drive (Freud 2011). Writing much later, Teresa Brennan (2004) goes to pains to distinguish love from affects that "work against bodily well being through stress-related illness." She describes affects of distress as the work of "disconnecting or deathly impulses." Linking love to the life drive suggests that love and the "deathly" affects "work in different directions, one for unification, the other against it" (36). While I embrace an understanding of love and the life forces as unifying, I am wary of any assumption of unenjoyable affects necessarily being antilife or deathly. Rather than casting all painful affect as related to the death drive and as "against" unification, I consider them residues of trauma, and as such necessarily resistant. It does not follow though that these need be viewed as necessarily outside or antilove. The potential of grief, in the process of witnessing and testimony, can be a unifying process if undertaken in a spirit of introjection and love.

Torok distinguishes their redefinition by announcing introjection as defined not by compensation but by expansion and enrichment (to return momentarily to Spinoza this is in keeping with his understanding of power, and with its ethical promise, as an increase in beingness). It is not a matter of introjecting an object, but of "introjecting the sum total of the drives, and their vicissitudes as occasioned and mediated by the object" (Torok 1994: 113). Abraham and Torok's introjection is a positive, intricate, life-affirming endeavor by which trauma, and indeed all experience, is endured, adapted to, worked through, and transformed through a process of openness, awareness, and expression (Abraham and Torok 1994). More broadly, for Abraham, Torok, and Rand, introjection ultimately "designates the driving force of psychic life in its entirety" (Rand 1994: 8). I adapt the term in keeping with their view of introjection as a lifelong process of attainment and integration, the "active expansion of our potential to accommodate our own emerging desires and feelings as well as the events and influences of the external world" (9).

Bringing traumatic affect to consciousness is a central concern of the poetics of transgenerational trauma. It is at this point that the critical difference between Derrida's hauntology and Abraham and Torok's phantom emerges, for though Abraham and Torok also confirm the mournful nature of hauntology, they do pursue, unlike Derrida, for whom spectral mourning is open-ended and essentially elusive, an endpoint, an outcome, a direct engagement, which might be said to constitute closure. Describing Abraham and Torok's view of haunting as the process by which "unfelt mourning, unassimilated trauma, the unwitting psychical inheritance of someone else's secrets—drive a wedge between us and our society," Nicholas Rand poses the question: "How can people be helped to initiate a process of introjection that has failed to occur spontaneously?" (Rand 1994: 22). I embrace this asserted need for introjection while declining an objective that presumes it possible to entirely introject transgenerational trauma. Further, I claim the writing and reading of the poetics of transgenerational trauma as ways (among others) in which people can be helped to initiate a process of introjection.

Let me return to Derrida briefly before proceeding on the matter of introjection. On point one of his three-part description of the specter as "thing" Derrida says, "First of all mourning. We will be speaking of nothing else" (1994: 9). We will be speaking of nothing else in everything we speak about. Work, the work of mourning, and the work of writing, "consists always in attempting to ontologize remains, to make them present, in the first place by *identifying* the bodily remains and by *localizing* the dead" [italics in original] (9). On point two he writes, rather poetically, that we cannot speak of "generations of skulls or spirits except on the condition of language—and the voice, in any case of that which marks the name or takes its place" (9). The condition of language is essential, but, if we are to speak of generations of skulls or spirits our idea of language may need to be expanded to include language (as a system of signs and symbols) outside of language proper, such as affect and the imagery of Indigenous mythology. Wright performs precisely what is called for here, stretching language in ways and in directions that convey the generations of skulls. On point three, Derrida insists, "Finally, the thing *works*, whether it transforms or transforms itself, poses or decomposes itself: the spirit, the 'spirit of the spirit' is *work*" [italics in original] (9).

This issue of work is crucial: the work of living, of art, of love, of writing, of reading, of introjection. Schwab (2006) notes Duras's comments in the preamble to her memoir *The War* (1986), to the effect that the text was in her view superior to literature. Schwab asks, "What is this piece if it is not literature and why does literature appear as shameful in comparison with it?" (2006: 115). I hazard to guess that Duras is communicating something complex about the nature of the poetics of trauma versus attempts to merely represent (traumatic) events in conventional literature. Duras appears to be aware that *The War* does something the average novel can't; that it possesses a palpable, powerful, and enriching integrity of testimony that surpasses that of standard storytelling or historical record. But if I go so far as to maintain that writing and reading can help initiate a process of introjection, I do so with qualification. I do not hold that the poetics of transgenerational trauma, or any other kind of writing, is therapeutic per se. In other words, it is unlikely to result in the kind of outcomes clinical psychoanalytic or psychology practices usually aim for. The introjection it involves is not a mandate to be obeyed, a search-and-destroy mission, or textual therapy, and yet it can bring about significant shifts in perception that may indeed be life changing in ways big or small. In relation to the poetics of transgenerational trauma, I distance myself from any psychoanalytic demands for hard-and-fast phantomic secret spilling and employ introjection in terms of the gentler, Derridean-style description of "psychic opening and expansion" put forth by Rand. It is here, in this understanding of introjection as it relates to spectrality, that I assert the significance of traumatic affect and its testimony.

Trauma presents an enormous challenge to the work of introjection since it resists being known, spoken, and written. When it comes to transgenerational trauma, a subject is called upon to address not only personal experiences of trauma but also traumas from preceding generations. This makes introjection even more elusive, and perhaps the most that can be achieved is a kind of introjection of understanding, a process in which the traumata of forebears and its familial legacies are acknowledged and, in some way, accepted. In such cases, transmitted affect appears as the incarnation of trauma, including transgenerational trauma, and it is this traumatic affect that offers enhanced promise for introjection through an intimate exchange, communicated and mediated by the process of writing and reading. However—and this is key to my argument—a vital aspect of the unique introjectory capacity of the poetics of transgenerational trauma is its paradoxical refusal of the credence that trauma can ever be entirely reckoned with, or tidily or lineally worked through. How could it be when the trauma this poetics deals with is as immeasurable in scale and scope as it is structurally resistant to easy notions such as closure? It is, therefore, this acceptance of the limitations of language in the face of traumatic legacies that gives rise to the strategies this poetic practice employs, which, when skillfully employed in creative combination, can conversely loosen those limitations.

"The personal is political" redux

A fervent introjectory and creative motivation is needed in order to write through the inescapable shame and fear of the secret—the ghostly or phantomic traumatic gap, which surfaces more distinctly in the case of the phantom and as more nebulous in its ghostly appearance. Wright's Sydney PEN lecture, "A Question of Fear," was delivered several weeks after *Carpentaria* swept up several prestigious awards (*Book Show* 2007). She spoke of her involvement in, and observations of, the fight of Indigenous people in the Gulf of Carpentaria to keep intact their profound spiritual and lived bonds with their land against the threats (still) posed by imperial forces in the form of government-sanctioned multinational mining companies. Referencing the underhanded deeds of successive governments she said that in May 2007 the Northern Territory government "enacted legislation in the dead of night" to green light a mining development sure to devastate native land. It seems certain that her personal connections to areas affected by contested mining operations directly informed the narrative of *Carpentaria*.

She spoke too of the trauma of the death of her father and her childhood fears and phobias and their roots in the impact of colonialism:

> I felt that a lot of fear did live in our house, through my mother's personal crises that was as much to do with the effect on my family of a colonising history as it had to do with her hard efforts as a widow to raise my sister and myself in a world she felt was without sympathy and unjust. (*Book Show* 2007)

So it is that the "personal crises" that beset so many of her Indigenous characters stem, at least in large measure, from such "colonising history." Wright's personal experience working with the government in advocacy roles directly influences the arc of her narratives, and the many insights within them. It is evident too that this childhood experience of fear and grief informs her work at its deepest strata. In expressing a sense of guilt around her privilege in taking time out to write novels and the pressure she felt to produce a work worthy of that privilege, Wright touches on a point Adamson and Clark note in their introduction to *Scenes of Shame: Psychoanalysis, Shame, and Writing*, when they describe shame in relation to writing as the "painful feeling of exposed vulnerability" (1999: 28). Acknowledging the dangers of writing, Adamson and Clark go on to state, "Writing, precisely because it allows one to hide and reveal oneself at the same time, also allows for an intimacy and trust to be established with another or others, perhaps, in a way that no other situation provides" (Adamson and Clark 1999: 28). Elsewhere they identify "shame as the primary negative affect involved in 'empathic failure'" (20). It is the capacity of writing and literature to create a context of "dangerous exposure," along with its invitation to empathic connection that summons the hauntological spirits.

In the poetics of transgenerational trauma a writer does this intentionally and mindfully, in much the same way the atmosphere of a séance is carefully created to intensify sensitivity and receptivity to the voices of the dead (whether the subsequent visitations and conversations are real, imagined, manufactured, or uncertain is not so much the issue). The function of family secrets and transgenerational traumatic tombs is the "preservation of a shut-up or excluded reality," which is what Abraham and Torok call "preservative repression." This involves a particular kind of repression that "seals off access to part of one's own life in order to shelter from view the traumatic monument of an obliterated event" (Rand 1994: 18). The writer of the poetics of transgenerational trauma must negotiate and pass through the shamefulness and prohibition of the phantom, and successfully doing so in the act of writing can act as a kind of initiation and reclamation, if not a final resting place. The writing and reading of the phantom can assist in gaining "access to part of one's life," or indeed culture, that has affectively exposed "the traumatic monument of an obliterated event." I am intimating that the operations of the phantom in the poetics of transgenerational trauma mean literary readers, critics, and theorists need not be limited to a choice between an Abraham and Torok–inspired detective-like interpretive zeal and a post-structuralist insistence on the "openness to what exceeds knowledge" (Davis 2005: 379). In its disruption of binaries that privilege logic and rationality over bodily knowing and relational intangibility, such writing constitutes a feminist practice that confronts any demand to obedient subscription to either position.

The usefulness in teasing out these distinctions between Derrida's ghost and the psychoanalytic phantom perhaps lies less in establishing conflict between them, or in reprimanding the sloppiness of critics, and more in collapsing the two approaches into a complementary amalgamation in relation to texts that testify to transgenerational trauma. In other words, I want to entertain a Derridean-inflected reading of the psychoanalytic phantom that subverts the impulse toward interrogation in favor of a kind of experiential witnessing, one that can relax the demand for outcomes and closure, while still accomplishing the work of introjection. In this way the secrets of phantoms can be viewed less as fixed and necessarily knowable—the slipperiness of trauma, in terms of meaning, access, and expression, being notorious in trauma theory—and more as fertile territory for literary testimony.

As Derrida says, sounding quite Abraham and Torok phantomlike: "The spectre is a paradoxical incorporation, the becoming-body, a certain phenomenal and carnal form of the spirit" (1994: 6). Neither simply soul nor body, or self nor other, yet all, it is that which gives to "the spirit its spectral apparition" but which, paradoxically, disappears in the apparition, "in the very coming of the *revenant* or the return of the spectre" [italics in original] (6). In the texts I interpret the process of introjection is not at odds with a revenant of the specter. I cast this as writing that draws from the depths, informed by a bodily knowledge that defies rationality, though it nevertheless involves a complex cognitive and emotional process of channeling and translation. In this way Derrida's "structural openness or address directed towards the living by the voices of the past" (Davis 2005: 379) becomes a portal for a "thinking through the body" (Gallop 1988: 1) feminist practice of writing that deals with trauma as a "personal is political" (reportedly Hanisch, 1970)[2] cultural operation.

Wright's identity as an Indigenous Australian and her engagement with the region is critical in the way this work achieves a seemingly impossible feat in presenting a nondidactic, undialectical, and highly literary treatise on the state of the nation. As Bernadette Brennan writes, "Australia lives in complacent peace and prosperity" (2008: 11). Dominated by a mainstream, increasingly middle-class, populace, it is the "fringe dwellers in our society" that are "hit hardest" as they are cast outside of "mainstream ease, mainstream safety, mainstream protection at law" (11). Wright herself puts it another way:

> I have a theory that *Carpentaria* was imagined from an Australian heritage that has created disconnected islands of individuals, families, races, regions, beliefs, just as the continent itself is an island disconnected from anywhere else. (Wright 2007: 16)

Carpentaria is a veritable bridge of testimony to that heritage and its affects/effects today. So it is that ghosts come forth to whisper, inaudibly, into the spaces between words and grammar, and phantoms spill their secrets through the embodied affect of the writer, channeled and translated, dynamically entangled, and encountered through, and by, an affected reader. This is the power, experimental art, and potential of the radically spooked text. This is its gift in guiding us to undead losses, its mode of helping us understand so that we may, in the words of Jacques Derrida, "learn to live" (1994: xvii). The writing and reading of a spooked text such as *Carpentaria* allows us to, through the *medium* of literature, engage with the ghosts and phantoms with whom we pass the days, so that we may, against all odds, emerge from this dance with death more alive.

4

Family Snapshots to Big Picture: Cyclical Haunting

War and its traumas have transformed and proliferated in radical ways since the First World War began over a hundred years ago. Its consequences are no longer confined to national warfare with mass combatant, and minimal civilian, casualities, and economic hardship in warring nations. Today war comes in the guise of "shock and awe" rapid dominance strategies, drone strikes, and targeted killings with higher civilian impact. The rise of global terrorism propagated by al-Qaeda and now the self-described "Islamic State of Iraq and Syria" (ISIS) has introduced a deadly randomness and reach into the lives of civilians. ISIS armies hold whole communities hostage in Syria and Iraq, encouraging "lone wolf" attacks in the West via the radicalization of mentally ill and/or socially lost or disadvantaged individuals, themselves often made vulnerable to that process due to traumatic personal histories. "Asymmetric warfare" is now just as likely to take out a carefree young woman attending the show of a favorite metal band or a retired couple enjoying a meal at an outdoor table on a cool autumn night in Paris as a frightened young soldier persuaded to his death by a sense of moral or national obligation or the promise of eternal glory. Ever since the Bush administration and its allies initiated the War on Terror, attacking Afghanistan and Iraq and further unhinging the geopolitics of the Middle East, a dreadful and paradoxical sequence of suffering has been enacted, a deadlocked lose/lose battle without end in sight. The public record of violent deaths in Iraq since the 2003 invasion is currently clocked at 242,000 (*Iraq Body Count* 2016), and it will have climbed considerably by the time these words are read. The Watson Institute of International and Public Affairs reports that around 92,000 people have been killed to date in the war in Afghanistan since 2001, more than 26,000 of them civilians. Those who have survived the ravages of war and remain in their country have faced innumerable ongoing crises and challenges, including injury, the destruction of homes and infrastructure, and increased disease (Brown University 2015). They carry on as best as they can despite loss, the deaths of loved ones, and the destruction of their culture, as they know it. And there are fresh (if related) hells. The crisis in Syria and the rumored interference of the Central Intelligence Agency (CIA), with its high-risk strategy of backing of insurgent groups, has further destabilized the region. Many Iraqis and Syrians live with violent oppression and in the cross-fire between regimes, insurgents, and terrorists.

The Syrian civil war is one of the most of the destructive conflicts in living memory, resulting in 4,597,436 registered Syrian refugees at the time of writing (UNHCR 2016). The lives of millions of people have been destroyed as nations around the world debate immigration policy or pull up the gangplanks and declare borders closed. The Australian government has done just that with steely resolve in implementing "Operation Sovereign Border." Prime Minister Malcolm Turnbull publically maintains that this is necessary to "stop the people smuggling racket and keep people safe from drowning at sea" (*7.30 Report* 2016), though the menacing and lurid "No Way: You Will Not Make Australia Home" public information campaign is an odd way to express concern about the safety of desperate people. This official, bipartisan obstinacy is an affective ploy calculated to soothe the anxieties of the electorate, whose fear of terrorism on Australian soil is only somewhat tempered by sadness and guilt over the estimated 1,000 lives of asylum seekers lost to shoddy, overcrowded boats in Australian waters since 2008 (Davies 2013). Others view the drownings as little more than a cynical excuse for xenophobia. Either way, it seems certain that being seen to protect its citizenry and to appease panic is at least part of the political motive.

The Australian Border Force meets those who flee their homelands and make their way to the Lucky Country by boat. They then turn their vessels around and force them back to Indonesia and an uncertain and often unsafe future. Others languish in offshore and indefinite detention in the substandard conditions of privatized facilities on Manus Island or Nauru, Papua New Guinea (Alexander 2014). The so-called "Pacific Solution" has, ironically, created more problems than it has solved, but the hard line remains, despite international criticism—

the immigration policy has been deemed by the United Nations to be an abuse of human rights and contravening international law (Millar 2015). Alleged human rights abuses include the accused murder of a detainee, 23-year-old Iranian Reza Barati, by guards (Doherty 2015), reported rapes, the detaining of unaccompanied minors, riots, enforced isolation, dubious hygiene, and inadequate medical and psychiatric care (Amnesty International 2013, 2015). Many health professionals, refugee activists, child and human rights advocates, and Australians consider the mandatory, indefinite detention of children to be inherent, institutionalized child abuse. In fact, pediatricians sent to investigate on behalf of the Human Rights Commission have declared that children who spent time in detention at Nauru were "among the most traumatised we have ever seen" (Hasham 2016). Doctors are risking legal prosecution for speaking out against the abuses they see in treating detainees (*7.30 Report* 2016), and conditions are so bad that leading academics have declared the centers "black sites" qualifying as enacting torture (Perera and Pugliese 2015). Following the alleged rape of a young Iranian woman, proceedings were brought to the Australian High Court to determine the future of Australia's offshore immigration detention centers. Though refugees and advocates held out hope the court's finding might lead to an end to offshore detention, the High Court ruled the Manus and Nauru centers lawful on the February 3, 2016 (Choahan 2016). The finding is technically correct, due to dubious legislation (Doyle 2015) pushed through to block the High Court challenge (Newman 2015) (though Manus Island Regional Processing Centre is set to close after Papua New Guinea's highest court ruled it illegal).

All of these people face the challenge of living with trauma of a scale and severity that is immeasurable and for most of us unimaginable. That trauma will not be contained. Millions of bodies are irrevocably changed by it, and become symptomatic. Interpersonal relationships become bound by it. Families fracture; many never mend. The many children among the survivors grow up with brains rewired by chronic shock and misery. There are other fights and horrors in other parts of the world: brutal drug lord empires in South America, black lives not mattering in the United States and here in Australia, Indigenous communities living in third-world poverty, sophisticated pedophile rings, "Ice" epidemics producing rampant methylamphetamine psychosis, and populating prisons. There will be consequences well beyond the personal, an unavoidable price that the social will be forced to pay. Herein lies the destructive movement of trauma I refer to as cyclical haunting.

Pat Barker's *Regeneration Trilogy* (1999), made up of the three novels *Regeneration*, *The Eye in the Door*, and *The Ghost Road*, is justly regarded as a classic of English literature due to its vital rendering of the trauma of the Great War. Its formal achievements as a major work of fiction have been widely praised, yet it is also a remarkable depiction of the affects/effects of familial trauma. As such, Barker's novels are illustrative of a cyclical operation of traumatic affect—meaning affect that is bound to, and by, trauma—which both informed and resulted from the First World War, and that informs and results from the more diverse manifestations of war today. Drawing a link between Barker's focus on the First World War and the contemporary moment may initially seem like an inexplicable leap, but cyclical haunting and the literary testimony of transgenerational trauma transmissions is not specific to one war, however major, or one type of war. They are, above all, about those circuitries by which trauma and affect proceed. This chapter is chiefly concerned with the currents of those transmissions, rather than with specific ways in which they are expressed in war and history in one epoch or another.

It may seem a curious move to proceed from the post/anticolonialism of Wright's hauntological witnessing to the *Regeneration Trilogy*, so I want to briefly clarify my use of Barker. There is a good deal already written on the trilogy, and I am aware this might lead to a reader expectation that I mean to converse with existing readings. This is an opportune moment, then, to reiterate that this book is not a work of literary criticism per se and nor is it primarily concerned with engaging in dialogue with other criticism. This chapter is not intended to add to the considerable secondary literature on Barker, but to, in keeping with my approach in other chapters, perform an interdisciplinary examination of complex cultural operations through the portal of selected texts.

Though Barker's trilogy may seem an odd choice, I view it as essential for my project. *Regeneration* is the only text in the book that wrangles with war in a way that is direct, sustained, and in-depth, demonstrating trauma transmissions between the micro and macro, the familial realm and the bloody theater of war. As such, these novels facilitate the teasing out of "cyclical haunting," a conception that is critical to the subsequent chapter.

I am aware too that there are those who view Barker's trilogy as a move away from the feminist agenda of her early work, but in my reading this is a matter of style; I see the trilogy as a more subtle expression of Barker's feminist agenda, rather than a departure. To my mind, it is no less a deeply feminist work for its focus on war, a world of men, and masculinity, and it is every bit as much a critique of patriarchy as her earlier works.

It is difficult to offer a brief account of the plot of the trilogy, since it weaves in and out different time periods and fictional and historical characters, suffice to say that it explores the experience of the First World War, of life in England during the war, and the personal histories of its protagonists. The main characters include Billy Prior, a young British man turned fighter, Siegfried Sassoon, the real-life celebrated poet, soldier, and antiwar protester, and Rivers, the doctor who attends them both. *Regeneration*, the first book, is the most famous of the three. A powerful and well-rounded account of life in and after the trenches, it is the hardest hitting in its depiction of the horrors of war. *The Eye in the Door* is a more nuanced and layered portrait of trauma, dwelling more on the childhood history and inner experience of traumatized soldiers at home. *The Ghost Road*, the final novel, continues Barker's exploration of trauma with a broadening into focus on Rivers's background and non-Western traumatic traditions such as the headhunting culture in the doctor's exotic professional past.

Barker seems to embed awareness of the challenge she has undertaken in attempting to testify to a cycle of suffering that involves so many shattered lives in a wonderful scene in which Siegfried Sassoon is visited in hospital by Rivers after returning from the trenches with a head injury. Sassoon is manic and enduring bad nights, tormented by internal conflict between the pacifist poet and the ruthless soldier. Telling Rivers about his calling to write about the trauma of war, he says:

> "I keep thinking how big it is, the *war*, and how impossible it is to write about, and how useless it is to get angry, that's such a trivial reaction, it doesn't, it doesn't do any sort of justice to the to the to the tragedy, you know you spend your entire life out there obsessed with this tiny little sector of the

> Front. I mean *thirty yards* of sandbags, that the war, you've no conception of anything else, and now I think I can see all of it, vast armies, flares going up, *millions* of people, *millions, millions*."
>
> Rivers waited. "You say you see it?"
>
> "Oh, yes, it just unfolds." A circling movement of his arms. "And it's marvellous in a way, but it's terrible too and I get so frightened because you'd have to be Tolstoy." (1994: 220) [Italics in original]

The "it" Sassoon sees suggests not just the war itself, immense and grueling as it was, but also the operation that called it, and every other war, into being. Barker obviously understood the enormity of her project, which is why she could approach it with no less than a hefty three books. But the most remarkable aspect of her achievement is the way the account and the language capture the scope of the war—that Benjaminian sense of futility before its vastness—*and* the intimate suffering of familial trauma.

It is notable and unsurprising that trauma studies came to prominence in the wake of war. Sigmund Freud advanced upon the early explorations of trauma by pioneering psychoanalysts following First World War, when the men Barker would later research and characterize returned from Europe with horrific injuries and debilitating "shell shock." Freud's work at that time popularized the basic understanding of psychic trauma that remains in usage today. Situating trauma within his theory of the unconscious, Freud considered it in economic terms, describing it as "an experience which within a short period of time presents the mind with an increase of stimulus too powerful to be dealt with or worked off in the normal way," the subsequent result being "permanent disturbances of the manner in which the energy operates" (Freud 1974: 315). Since then, this formative psychoanalytic perception of trauma has been expanded upon in various ways and disciplines, including Laplanche's engagement with affect as the bodily (and relational) representative of trauma (Laplanche 1999: 109), which facilitates my exploration of the autonomous force of structural trauma. The notion of cyclical haunting is immense both in scope and allusion, and while categorically proving and comprehensively itemizing the implications of this conceptual framework outweigh the scope of this book, I draw out several aspects from Barker's books, most exigent and relevant to the poetics of transgenerational trauma. Barker's portrayal of trauma as a structural force in her otherwise seemingly conventional (but surreptitiously experimental) text reveals the way historic traumatic affect feeds into subjective and familial experience, and in turn plays out past these interpersonal realms to enact and transmit trauma in networks beyond. In arguing that the trilogy confronts entrenched denial by exposing hauntological cycles of traumatic affect between familial life and historic events as they were played out upon a war-torn world stage, I show that transgenerational testimony warrants reading, and respect, as political account rather than being read in terms of genre, and as merely personal or fictional stories. To begin, I briefly introduce the main concepts that inform my interpretation before moving on to look at Barker's novels.

Discussing the "phenomenality of the political" in *Spectres of Marx*, Derrida refers to an element of public life that is "neither living nor dead, present nor absent," making the claim that such an element is that which "spectralises" (1994: 51). With his figuring of hauntology, Derrida seeks not to explore beingness and presence in the common understanding of the word, but to posit the figure of the ghost as a site of vacillating certainty and possibility. If Derrida toys with the commonplace understanding of "haunt" by utilizing words like ghost and specter, he remains adamant that his conception is not about ghost stories, or the simple remnants of the past in the present. Rather, he uses the word "hauntology" to supplant ontology: the specter does not require a belief in ghosts in the conventional sense and it cannot be known in the usual ways of knowing. In the previous chapter, I extended upon Colin Davis's contrasting of Derrida's notion of the "spectre" (1994) with Abraham and Torok's concept of the "phantom" (1994). In the same disconcerting way that present-day maverick physicists suggest there is no such thing as "time," but rather the coexistence of simultaneous "nows" (Frank 2012), Derrida's hauntology casts into doubt the sequence of one solid and comforting present seguing to the next in the way it seems to do when we experience time passing in a chronological order. Hauntology questions the supposed border between the "actual or present reality of the present, and everything that can be opposed to it: absence, non-presence, non-effectivity, inactuality, virtuality, or even simulacrum in general" (Derrida 1994: 39). In other words, hauntology speaks to the unreliability of what we think of as the past, present, and future. Though

Derrida's writing on hauntology does not explicitly feature affect, it does imply it, revealing simpatico points between his specter and Deleuze (1988, 1992, and in Bennett 2005) and Massumi's (1996, 2002) work on the autonomy of affect. Jean Laplanche's psychoanalytic view of trauma as a kind of ontological condition also aids my exploration of the way trauma operates as a structural force that troubles imagined notions of subjective experience as confined to an individual body.

Affect theory, as a polysemic, multidisciplinary and often interdisciplinary field, comprises affect in many definitions and theoretical configurations. I understand affect to be a biological and energetic response inherent to all sentient beings (the systems and expressions of which may differ between species) and more poetically, as Gregg and Seigworth put it, "the passage (and the duration of passage) of forces or intensities" and the "visceral forces beneath, alongside, or generally other than conscious knowing, vital forces insisting beyond emotion" (2010: 6–8). Massumi, working from a Deleuzian conception of affect as bodily capacity, fosters an understanding of the autonomy of affect as escaping subjective containment in virtuality operative beyond particular bodies. Describing such affect as intensity unqualified, not ownable or recognizable (by or to a given subject), Massumi casts emotion, conversely, as intensity owned and recognized (by a given subject) (1996: 221). I define traumatic affect in cyclical haunting as affect that bears the characteristics of trauma comprising both these forms of intensity, more or less distinctly or entwined on a circular, or feeding back and forth, continuum. Massumi's positing of affects as virtual synesthetic perspectives anchored in what embodies them is compelling for its potential for thinking about the blending of sensual modes of transmission, that is contagion via smell, language, tone, vision, touch, etc.

When Derrida's notion of the virtual/simulacrum as hauntologically spectral is given a Deleuzian inflection, Derrida's virtual lends itself to inference as the space in which transgenerational trauma occurs across assemblages, from minor ones, such as a singular subjectivity, to major ones, such as a nation. So it is that Deleuze's and Massumi's work on the autonomy of affect resonates with the Derridian specter. The very notion of autonomy of affect and virtuality conjures up visions of ghostliness. Though they represent distinct and different philosophical and ontological positions, both theories bring to mind a plane beyond that of the flesh and outside what can be seen with the naked eye, but which nevertheless might still encompass the flesh and the eye as well as the emotion registered by the flesh and evident in the eye. How might the specter be felt or marked if not through affect and language? The operations of cyclical haunting come into view in Barker's tour de force trilogy about that greatest of spectral legacies: world war. A legacy of this scope, we might pause to remember, is not only of the past, but also potentially in the making. Some commentators believe the beginnings of the Third World War may already be upon us (Pilger 2016, Singer and Cole 2015, Ghitis 2015).

Regeneration's cyclic suffering

The *Regeneration Trilogy* is not as obviously experimental as the other texts surveyed and it is not memoir (though Barker does have significant personal and familial connections to the First World War and the works are scrupulously researched and peopled by a mix of fictional and real-life historic characters). Its prose is orthodox, if skillfully crafted. It does not share the same strikingly original edifice of the other works generally considered to represent trauma, such as Alain Resnais's trailblazing cinematic masterpiece *Hiroshima, Mon Amour* (1959), based on the Marguerite Duras screenplay, or Duras's *The Lover* (1992), another of my surveyed texts. As discussed in Chapter 1, that text alternates between first and third person, present and past tense, subjective shifts of intimacy and distance, and times that proceed in a nonlinear manner capable of crossing continents, seas, decades, and narrator selves. All this is carried along by an experimental fervor that makes Barker's work seem comparatively conventional. Yet, I am not quite prepared to discount it as such.

Even if Barker's trilogy exhibits a less overtly traumatic structure and language, it cunningly demonstrates the poetics of transgenerational trauma by means of a subtle yet insightful cultural exposé. Tracking back and forth across time, and in and out of the worlds of characters, these novels show the ways in which trauma circulates from its most individual experience to its most global enactment. The novels testify to the trauma of masculinity on a number of levels: masculinity as traumatized, masculinity as traumatic, and masculinity as traumatizing. The trilogy has been much praised for its description of the trauma of the First World War, and rightly so, but it is a more multilayered representation of trauma than has previously been acknowledged. I highlight the way Barker reveals the multigenerational familial transmission of trauma at the heart of war. The trilogy translates a complex web of personal, cultural, national, and global trauma, and as such it is a creative portrayal of cyclical haunting that shows how the autonomy of traumatic affect circulates in and between assemblages.

The transmission of trauma and affect are evident everywhere in Barker's three books. Billy Prior, the cynical, damaged, and damaging protagonist, was troubled and traumatized well before he went to war. Sexually assaulted by a priest as a child, he acts out of trauma throughout his life through a propensity for sexual addiction and sexual violence. He grew up witnessing domestic violence and was emotionally abused by his father. *The Eye in the Door*, the second in the series, gives most focus to Prior's familial history. It also attends to the inner experience of traumatized soldiers in the messed-up climate of "home." The two themes converge in a striking scene in which Prior visits his hometown in an effort to help Beattie, an old family friend and conscientious objector unjustly jailed. Staying with his parents, Prior is confronted with the childhood memory of chanting "PIG PIG PIG" to himself and punching his fist into his other hand on the steps overlooking the lounge room while witnessing his drunken father beating his mother. Barker writes:

> Obviously, his present attempt to understand his parents' marriage was more mature, more adult, more perceptive, more sensitive, more insightful, more almost anything you cared to mention, than PIG PIG PIG PIG, but it didn't content him, because it was also a lie: a way of claiming to be "above the battle." And he was not above it: he was its product. He and she—elemental forces, almost devoid of personal characteristics—clawed each other in every cell of his body, and would so until he died. (1999: 90)

This moment is, in a sense, the beating heart of the trilogy. Here Barker suggests that this is what calls war into being, the "lie," the "claiming to be above the battle" of facing and addressing individual and collective trauma, and that dooms us to acting it out. For all the terrible, unspeakable horror witnessed and experienced in France this image of Prior's parents clawing each other in every cell of his body till the day he dies is perhaps the most horrific of all. Later in *The Eye in the Door*, the link between Prior's war and childhood trauma is made even more overtly when he starts to dissociate into an alter personality and Rivers, his psychologist, makes the connection and observation that this traumatic splitting didn't begin in France as the alter claimed, but way back in the time of PIG, and that it was an existing subjective splitting that was triggered and intensified by a particularly traumatic war event. Even supposedly "normal" characters in the trilogy embody transgenerational trauma. Rivers, the anthropologist/shell shock doctor who features in all three novels, treating the men returning shattered from the trenches, is also disturbed, having been traumatized by his father at the age of four, beaten for crying during a haircut before being shown a portrait of an ancestor of the same name as an example of manhood, who had withstood the amputation of a leg with no anesthetic without making a sound.

The transmission of trauma and autonomy of affect, then, challenge the boundary between the past and present, and the very presumption of a reliably discernable distinction in Barker's trilogy, even though the past and the present are, in a literary sense, apparently clearly demarcated. Hence the *Regeneration Trilogy* is a hauntological text in which Barker channels a generation long past. As Anna Gibbs asserts, the body writes rhythmically and musically as much through cognitive thought, with "sensory and affective knowledges which are not secondary to thought" (2005: 7). The process of writing cyclical haunting might be viewed as the conjuring of an intensity-rich and atmospheric environment in which virtual spectral affect is anchored in the materiality of writer, text, and reader. But what of the events themselves? What role does traumatic affect play in their formation? Any process of contagion would likely involve many variables, assorted modes, and circulations within families, cultures, and communities, and different degrees of vulnerability, collectively and individually, depending on a range of factors, including age, previous traumatic history, power relations, gender and other social conditioning, the presence or not of violence and/or physical danger, etc.

Gibbs draws on the affect theory of American psychologist Silvan Tomkins in teasing out the relationship between cognition and affect in contagion, suggesting ways in which politics and social issues may become affectively and traumatically embodied. Gibbs states, "Just as cognitions take on an affective colouring, so too does affect call forth certain ideas and attitudes with which it has become associated in the inner world of the individual" (Gibbs 2001). She goes on to cite Tomkins's claim: "Prolonged unrelieved distress is an innate activator of anger" (Tomkins 1991: 200–01). Due to social prohibition on expressions of anger, this anger may bind with shame (for Tomkins, Gibbs explains, some affects are innate activators of other affects), resulting in a tendency toward contempt for the self and/or others, all of which takes place "internally and automatically," outside of conscious awareness. And all of which, presumably, would be operative in the interactions and interpersonal relationships of the afflicted subject, whether that subject happens to be an airport cleaner or the president of the United States of America. This has particular implications in the case of familial transmission and in the staging of political conflict. We see this anger/shame/contempt being acted out by Billy Prior both behind closed doors and in the theater of war. In private, he enacts a misogynistic attitude that finds its affective expression in sexualized rage, and as a soldier, he is bloody-mindedly driven, returning again and again to what will become iconic battlefields. As a child chanting "PIG," Billy was in the process of absorbing transmissions, in addition to experiencing his own organic affect/emotion.

As I have conferred elsewhere, the process of transmission within families and in subject-social-political relationships involves manifold, highly complex movements difficult to speak to, and at this stage almost certainly impossible to scientifically or otherwise definitively prove. Any discussion of it is, therefore, necessarily hypothetical in nature. The question of whether trauma and memory *can* be transmitted is a controversial one, and I do not mean to suggest that, assuming it can, the process is a literal one. Following on from her discussion of maverick psychiatrist R. D. Laing, who spoke of relational dynamics in terms of knots, fankles, and impasses, Lisa Blackman describes him as gesturing toward an "energetic exchange that is felt within an affective register, and which is not easily available for conscious deliberation," exchanges suggestive of the complexity of the "relationship between energy, transmission and rhythm" (2012: 101). Affect or emotion is not, she stresses, "simply 'caught' or transmitted between subjects." It is more a case of subjects getting caught up in a force field of relational and affective dynamics. Blackman elsewhere proposes an operation of "embodied hauntology" that involves a "mediated form of perception, which is simultaneously somatic, psychic, technical, and historical, and which can animate, stage and, importantly, allow one to 'see' what might usually exceed conventional modes of perception" (2015: 26). Though Blackman's focus is on embodied hauntology as a methodology pertaining to research-led examinations of affect, it also grafts onto literary and practice-based modes of production.

What Barker's work suggests, and what I propose in this chapter, is that there appears to be some kind of process of transmission that defies what Ernst van Alphen calls "indexical memory" (quoted in Hirsch 2008: 109). In a move compatible with Ruth Leys's approach, van Alphen argues against the transmission of trauma between generations, insisting that memory is fundamentally indexical in terms of continuity between event and recall and that this is inherently the property of the individual and cannot be transferred (van Alphen 2006: 485–86). As Marianne Hirsch observes, this objection only holds if you view memory as a purely cognitive indexical operation. "Postmemory" is Hirsch's term for memory that encompasses bodily and affective memory, which can be transmitted and carried as affect and body memory. Postmemory is, for Hirsch, "not identical to memory: it is 'post,' but at the same time, it approximates memory in its affective force" (2008: 109). In this sense Prior is a "carrier," who takes his childhood trauma to the front, and brings it back home with added war trauma. Hirsch's statement that "nonverbal and non-cognitive acts of transfer occur most clearly within a familial space, often in the form of symptoms" (112) describes precisely the experiences of Prior's childhood, though of course intentional speech (words themselves, but also tone, volume, pitch, and gender) is a primary mode of traumatic transfer too. My understanding of cyclical haunting testimony in the poetics of transgenerational trauma is in keeping with Hirsch's assertion that "postmemorial work" endeavors to "reactivate and re-embody more distant social/national and archival/cultural memorial structures by reinvesting them with resonant individual and familial forms of mediation and aesthetic expression" (111).

As Gibbs points out, transmitted attitude and affect intertwine in an impossibly complex manner. This complexity both stems from, and results in, "learned affective sequences" that have roots in "emotion memory," a form of memory that does not involve conscious content. Manifested by nonverbal, noncognitive means, such as "dreams, body memory, vague and particular dreads, moods, overreactions, and repetitive behaviours" (Orange 1995), this is the kind of nonrepresentational memory Hirsch contemplates, the kind active in psychosomatic conditions, in which traumatic and affective memory produces physical symptoms without the involvement of indexical memory and outside of conscious awareness. Informing attitude-affective sequences within an individual, this memory may then be transmitted affectively, in ways that have been varyingly hypothesized by various contemporary theorists, including, most notably and compellingly, Teresa Brennan (2004), Sara Ahmed (2004), and Gibbs. For Tomkins, this takes the form of "redintegration," which describes a kind of transmission less to do with mimicry and identification (though they too have a place in Tomkins's view), and more by way of a volatile process that challenges "notions of inside and outside" (Gibbs 2001) of a subjective containment and an external "out there." Citing Massumi, Gibbs suggests that the focus need shift from "the concept of cause" and instead take up the question of, in Massumi's words, "effects," "interweavings," and "syndromes," affective contagion being one such syndrome. We might think of cyclical haunting as another, interrelated, syndrome, one that continually transmits the affective interweavings of trauma unless or until there is sufficient discernment enabling mediation and some mitigation of its negative effects.

Barker's trilogy deals with the first worldwide instance of traditional warfare. Conventional wars and armed conflicts are still active in numerous locations around the world, including Afghanistan, Iraq, Syria, Turkey, Yemen, Libya, South Sudan, Nigeria, etc. There are also new faces of war: one is depersonalized and technologically advanced, symbolized by the drone bomber and cyberattacks, the other very much bodied (though also employing sophisticated uses of technology) and on the ground (figuratively speaking), epitomized by the figure of the suicide bomber. With roots in guerrilla warfare and the perennial conflict between Israel and Palestine, the political violence known as "terrorism" announced a new order on 9/11 when it went global, targeting civilians by increasingly violent means, planning, and where possible executing elaborate, coordinated, international attacks. Like war, terrorism means to ideologize, kill, and traumatize. Its effects are not just the stuff of textbooks and memorials; they are emotional, psychological, and contagious, and the bodily memory never quite fades, no matter how distant the events become.

Based in Manhattan in the early 2000s, I left my Upper East Side apartment for my workplace in Midtown just before the first passenger plane hit the north tower of the World Trade Center. By the time I reached the building where I worked, in the shadow of the Empire State Building, the south tower had been hit, both buildings were on fire and black smoke rose up from the downtown skyscape. Soon after, Flight 77 crashed into the Pentagon, and I left work and headed uptown, first on foot, and then on a free bus, along with thousands of other stunned and terrified New Yorkers. To say it was, for those at relatively close quarters to the attacks, a day of heightened affect would be an understatement. To say it was traumatic, especially for those at ground zero, and those with histories of chronic trauma, would be stating the obvious. It was nothing less than a catastrophic day for those on the planes and in the buildings who lost their lives, or survived with great trauma and injury, and for their loved ones, but it was also a day in which traumatic affect—primarily fear and sadness, but also anger—seemed to speed around the world instantaneously, transmitted electronically via television coverage, Internet exchanges, frightened, grieving bodies in proximity, and the force field of somatic and psychic energy itself. It was also a day in which the personal (subjective experience of the event, wherever one was physically located) smashed headlong into the political, into decades-old struggles, a culmination of centuries of war, imperialisms, and micro and macro traumas in the lives of individuals and families.

Those of us on the island were still absorbing the visceral shock, walking past fire stations covered with flowers, photos of fallen firemen, and mini flags, and living in lockdown, when, only hours and days after the towers fell, commentators and self-appointed pundits around the world started trying to make sense of it. The reprisals began, in political rhetoric and unfortunate, misguided mob-think in which would-be vigilantes responded by beating men with black beards in turbans to a pulp or spitting on women wearing the hijab. One notable common view emerged from the ubiquitous upset in the aftermath in Western nations, particularly among those on the Left: an understanding that for all their horror and recrimination, the attacks of 9/11 were not an isolated event. They did not emerge out of a vacuum. They were the consequences of US foreign policy, and of British colonialism before it, the "comes around" in a what goes around comes around cycle of suffering ordained in the political arena with high-impact fall-out in daily life, body blows to actual lives. What was new was that it was now not only those enlisted or conscripted to fight who paid the price of policies past and present, but civilians who simply had the misfortune of being in the wrong place at the wrong time. It is as if an informal acknowledgment of cyclical haunting already existed, a sense in which many a layperson comprehended, instinctively, that the trauma of one life necessarily informs other lives and that the breeding and circulation of traumatic affect propagated by acts of war and imperialism exacts a price, a price that was now, shockingly, being paid by Western countries and people. Yet at the same time comprehension eludes us. In one scene in *The Eye of the Door*, Charles Manning uses the word "ungraspable" when attempting to describe the war to Rivers, explaining that even though he was there he can't grasp it: "I can't get my mind around it" (Barker 1994: 169). Likewise, though we are, to varying degrees, depending on location and privilege, caught up in it, and may instinctively and affectively sense, even rationally perceive, this cyclical suffering, at some crucial cognitive level it confounds us because it is so colossal, and so traumatic. Some individuals develop an affective sequence that includes the age-old reasoning that the ends justify the means of violence. When such an individual is empowered and armed within an assemblage, whether that assemblage is a government, a terrorist cell, or the patriarchy itself, the stage is set for another round of traumatic transmission.

Affect and assemblage

Massumi's view of the autonomy of affect as "participation in the virtual" lends itself to the idea that traumatic affect might be transmitted autonomously between assemblages, such as families, organizations, nations, and wars, *and* play a part in the formation of such assemblages. This is because just as "no man is an island" (Donne 1624), no assemblage in which humans participate can exist in energetic and psychic isolation. Affect is, Massumi declares, "autonomous to the degree to which it escapes confinement in the particular body whose vitality, or potential for interaction, it is" (1996: 228). This is a fascinating possibility, particularly in relation to family and societal dynamics, if one that has attracted criticism (most notably from Ruth Leys, whose objections will be considered later in the chapter). In this vision of autonomy, affect is captured perceptually and cognitively via circuitries of connections or closed off by blockages. Emotion, claims Massumi, is the most intense, the most contracted "expression of that capture," a sign that "something has always and again escaped" (228). If this process is considered in relation to Manuel DeLanda's theory of assemblage, a sense of traumatic affect as a social force in circulation becomes palpable.

There are, predictably, strong germinal connections between the notions of affect, autonomy, and assemblage. Deleuze and Guattari's *A Thousand Plateaus* was the inspiration for Manual DeLanda's assemblage/network theory (2006). DeLanda acknowledges these connections by beginning his book with a nod to Deleuze and Guattari's framing of assemblage and the historical processes that create and stabilize "a wide variety of wholes constructed from heterogeneous parts" (3). Noting that Deleuze and Guattari only focused on the idea of assemblage for a few pages in *Plateaus*, hardly constituting a theory proper, DeLanda maintains that the concepts used to describe the characteristics of assemblages in those few pages, such as "territorialization", are omnipresent throughout the body of work. DeLanda goes on to cast his understanding of assemblage as being a whole characterised by properties that emerge from the interactions between parts. For example,

> Interpersonal networks and institutional organizations are assemblages of people; social justice movements are assemblages of several networked communities; central governments are assemblages of several organizations; cities are assemblages of people, networks, organizations, as well as of a variety of infrastructural components, from buildings and streets to conduits for matter and energy flows; nation-states are assemblages of cities,

> the geographical regions organized by cities, and the provinces that several such regions form. (5)

Assemblage (or network) theory makes possible an alternative model of social ontology to traditional individual/social and personal/political dichotomies. In basic terms, DeLanda's neoassemblage theory is sociological in the sense that it is interested in the way institutions operate. It rejects both essentialism and social constructionism in addressing the "problem of the link between the micro—and the macro—levels of social reality" (4). He claims that entities big and small, from atoms to entire ecosystems (or galaxies for that matter) form assemblages that are "products of historical processes" (3), and that assemblage theory can in turn be applied to the societal sphere. While the idea of assemblage is useful, it comes with a proviso: the parts of an assemblage do not equate to a seamless whole.

This thinking on assemblage has implications for the fields of trauma and affect, and specifically transgenerational transmission within and beyond the family. Considering the properties emerging from the interactions between entities (bodies, institutions) as being traumatic affect, that is, affect generated by trauma, and as emerging and transmitting in an autonomous manner, avoids both solipsistic tendencies in thinking trauma and the abstraction of affect and trauma, and locates the poetics of transgenerational trauma in lived individual and social experience.

Among affect theorists such as Denise Riley (2005), Teresa Brennan (2004), Deleuze, and Massumi, affective autonomy and transmission is hinted at as everything from a kind of subjective demonic possession to an impersonal cosmic dance. I take the position that the autonomy of affect operates on a number of levels and in ways that make different theoretical views of it useful. For example, Riley insists that the intentionality of language is informed, overwhelmed, and at times driven by affect, most especially the kind Spinoza casts as "the passions" (Spinoza 1996: 130). Riley describes the way the raging speaker [a common mode of familial transmission] is not himself or herself speaking so much as being spoken by rageful affect (2005: 16). Most people don't set out to abuse and traumatize others. Many parents unwittingly transmit traumatic affect to their children, more or less unconsciously, or on a conscious–unconscious continuum, and even where there is consciousness or apparent intent, the force of traumatically driven affect can make responsible personal choice and reasoning difficult, if not impossible. As Hirsch says, post[traumatic] memory is transferred via symptomatology (2008: 112).

If traumatic transmission can function somewhat independently of an agent, that is to say independent of will or intention, it may be that it surfaces as the restless site of a denied subjective/collective splitting/death, giving rise to all manner of deathly processes, such as addictions (including process addictions, such as work and gambling), suicide, all forms of child and animal abuse, misogyny and violence against women, homophobic violence, racism, turbo-capitalism (Lattwak 2000), and a host of obsessive, compulsive, and damaging behaviors. It may be akin to what twelve-step fellowship recovery programs, such as Alcoholics Anonymous, refer to as the "disease," perhaps at worst a malevolent force and at best an insidious one, constantly disturbed and disturbing. It may be the Moloch in "HOWL," savaging the best minds of Ginberg's generation, heralded by him as the death within life that has the potential for rebirth and reincarnation: "Wake up in Moloch! Light streaming out of the sky!" (1992).

Traumatic affect rumbles, spills, bursts forth, erupts, leaks, emits, fumes, whispers, screams, and acts from its restless grave, because at the deepest level it seeks recognition. It demands witnessing and memorial and it haunts until it gets it. It is the crime (or imagined crime) that wants to get caught; the perpetual cry for help that plugs its ears to the sound of its own cry. Every time it appears, in any form, every time it is transmitted, in any way, to any degree, it is begging for "living attention" (Brennan 2004: 32), which means, for Brennan, something like a cross between love, the life drive, and what she terms "discernment," a kind of mindful sensing that serves as a threshold of emotional response. The transmission of traumatic affect takes place with routine and endemic gravity, often with serious consequences, and that is why the poetics of transgenerational trauma is so vital an interpolation. In its concentration on familial transmission and cultural operations and its revelation of trauma as a structural force such literature hails from the most intimate areas of personal experience while extending well beyond to encompass cultural and collective history.

Barker's trilogy makes clear who among us, in terms of lived individual and social experience, is most susceptible to the transmission of traumatic affect and the violence often associated with it. Another of Prior's most haunting childhood memories involves walking near the cattle pens while cattle were being driven to slaughter and finding that a cow had broken loose and was following him:

> He backed away from the noise and commotion, ran up a back alley between the high dark walls, then realized that, as in a nightmare, a cow was following him, with slithering feet and staring eyes, and men chasing after her. More men came running from the other end of the alley. They cornered her, closing in from both sides, and the terrified animal slipped in her own green shit and fell, and they threw heavy black nets around her and dragged her back to the herd, while all along the alley housewives whose clean washing had been swept aside erupted from their backyards, shouting and waving their arms. . . . The sight of the cow in the net stayed with him. Many a night he dreamt about her and woke to lie staring into the swirling darkness. (1999: 106)

This passage evocatively conveys the tragedy of trauma under the oppressive assemblage of capitalist patriarchy, in which nonhuman animals, children, women, the socially disadvantaged, the disabled, and those discriminated against by race, age, sexual orientation, or gender identification, are the most at risk of traumatic transmission. Barker's description of the real-life scene as "as in a nightmare" hints at the way the event becomes, for the young boy, a recurring nightmare, a representation perhaps of all the trauma, injustice, and powerlessness he witnesses and experiences all around him. Regrettably, this does not prevent Prior from himself becoming an actor in capitalist patriarchal oppression.

Structural/historic/Historic trauma

The proposition of transgenerational traumatic assemblage calls for consideration of two significant notions within trauma theory referred to as "structural" and "historical." Laplanche's reworking of Freudian psychoanalytic theory (1999) offers a productive model for conceiving structural trauma and its transmission. His theory of "primal seduction" describes a process whereby the unconscious material transmitted by the [m]other undergoes a kind of metabolic development in which the transmitted material is absorbed, digested, or undigested by the child and in the process broken down into some refigured entity. Here the dependence of the child is the foundation of transmission. This can result in pathological patterns, but it is also the means by which the fundamental infant psychic self comes into being, the process that enables "the construction of the unconscious and the psychical apparatus in general" (Fletcher 1999: 10). In other words, for Laplanche, the development of subjectivity is itself a traumatic operation that depends upon familial transmission. Laplanche also seems to hold that there is no affect in the unconscious, and that enigmatic messages operate as unrepresentative and thinglike, or as "internal foreign bodies" (Laplanche 1999: 109). However, this assertion that affect is not operative in the unconscious does not amount to a dismissal of affect. Laplanche describes affect as the manner in which the ego and body are affected and that therefore affect is the way in which the unconscious speaks itself in the body via the ego. Thus, he insists, he is merely relocating affect topographically, rather than ruling it out of trauma transmission (109).

By contrast, small "h" "historical" trauma might be thought to function as trauma that comes to pass in the life of the subject after the formative mother-child transmission has taken place, that is, trauma experienced in environment, nurture, and culture, whereas capital "H" Historical trauma denotes collective traumatic experience of historical import such as war or ecological extremity. Dominick LaCapra (1999) addresses both structural and Historic trauma in his examination of notions of objectivity and constructivism in the writings of critical historians. Arguing for a distinction between the two, LaCapra contends they involve differing modes of mourning and challenges to writing, positing structural trauma as a subjective transhistorical absence that is part of the human condition. Though experienced by all individuals, regardless of cultural difference, structural trauma may manifest in diverse ways across ethnicities and different time periods. LaCapra configures this lack as originating in separation from the maternal, the entry into language, culture, and interpersonal relations, a traumatic, melancholic loss constitutive to the formation of subjectivity (722).

On the contrary, Historic trauma, as epitomized by the Holocaust, is a specific occurrence to which only those with direct experience of it can reasonably testify (722). This creates an ethical dilemma for nonsurvivors writing about it, with unavoidable temptations to problematic empathetic and subjective identifications an inevitable pitfall. Crucially, LaCapra writes:

> One may even argue that it is ethically and politically dubious to believe that one can overcome or transcend structural trauma or constitutive absence to achieve full intactness, wholeness, or communal identity and that attempts at transcendence or salvation may lead to the demonization and scapegoating of those on whom unavoidable anxiety is projected. But historical traumas and losses may conceivably be avoided and their legacies to some viable extent worked through both in order to allow a less self-deceptive confrontation with transhistorical, structural trauma and in order to further historical, social, and political specificity, including the elaboration of more desirable social and political institutions and practices. (727)

If *The Eye in the Door* most embodies structural and small "h" historical trauma, *Regeneration*, the first in the series, best illustrates capital "H" Historical trauma, presenting a powerful and well-rounded account of Britain in battle during the Second World War. Focusing on the relationship between Rivers and Sassoon, the poet and antiwar protester, with Prior as a lesser but still significant character, *Regeneration* features many distressing scenes that zero in on the often insurmountable challenge of attempting to work with, and through, trauma that is frequently a combination of structural, historic, and Historic trauma. It highlights ill-conceived medical and psychiatric attempts to treat trauma and the danger of their resulting in further traumatization in the problematic quest for a "cure." This is the case in a scene in which a doctor whose brutal methods differ from those of Rivers tortures a patient. Yealland, witnessed by a mortified Rivers, applies electric shocks and verbal abuse until a mute patient talks. Barker writes: "Rivers had felt that he was witnessing the silencing of a human being. Indeed, Yealland had come very close to saying just that. 'You must speak, but I shall not listen to anything you have to say'"

(1999: 238). Rivers, it turns out, is not only outraged by Yealland's extreme methods, but also disturbed about the nature of his own, though undoubtedly more benign, methods. Barker continues,

> Just as Yealland silenced the unconscious protest of his patients by removing the paralysis, the deafness, the blindness, the muteness that stood between them and the war, so, in an infinitely more gentle way, he [Rivers] silenced his patients; for the stammerings, the nightmares, the tremors, the memory lapses, of officers were just as much unwitting protest as the grosser maladies of the men. (238)

Being a good man, conscious of his ethical duties, Rivers is torn between his desire to help the men and serve his country in its hour of need and his doubts about the war and the reality of what serving his country actually means. In plain terms, Rivers's task is to render the stricken soldiers functional so that they can be returned to the trenches for further traumatization: "His patients might be encouraged to acknowledge their fears, their horror of the war—but they were still expected to do their duty and return to France" (45).

And so, the cycle continues well beyond the point where Barker stops writing. The men who ultimately survive the war return home ineffably traumatized, expected to resume civilian duties, and to provide for the families they make with the women left behind, many of whom have also been traumatized by bomb raids, economic hardship, and the loss of fathers, brothers, partners, and friends. As with most wars, there were also the forgotten "others" of war, the rape victims, the doctors and nurses, and the nonhuman casualties, most often dogs and horses. And so, in due course, the structural/historical/Historical divisions previously noted are collapsed or, rather, the usefulness of distinguishing between them is affirmed ahead of the recognition that they inevitably cross over into one another. Cyclical haunting describes a spectral cycle in which the big picture Historical trauma of patriarchy, with its political, religious, racial, and gendered violence and oppression, as visited upon an individual life or certain culture, feeds into and out of formative and subjectively historical trauma, generating an impossible-to-categorize state of flux between bodies within any given assemblage.

In a case of the proverbial chicken and egg dilemma, historical/Historical trauma is transmitted to, and within, families, and this is in turn transmitted and acted out beyond the family in social and historical contexts and relations—not in some linear, cause and effect, predictable fashion, but in myriad, chaotic, continual, and often imperceptible movements of circulating affect. The feedback loop of traumatic affect shapes subjectivity and, by extension, family and culture, which also shapes subjectivity—in tension and relentless dynamic with the positive and transformative power of love and living attention. How, then, might a text embody this collapse? According to Massumi, social constructionism has hit a wall due to its denial of nature. This proves a fatal mistake in that discounting nature means missing the emergence of culture and its transmissions:

> Ideas about cultural or social construction have dead-ended because they have insisted on bracketing the *nature* [italics in original] of the process. If you elide nature, you miss the becoming of culture, its emergence (not to mention the history of matter). You miss the continuum of interlinkage, feed-forward and feedback, by which movements capture and convert each other to many ends, old, new, and innumerable. (2002: 12)

If nature includes affect, which as an involuntary biological function it surely must, cyclical haunting may be seen as a continuum of interlinkages between traumatized subjects and the broader culture they inhabit, of networks of feeding forward and feeding back, by which "movements capture and convert each other to many ends, old, new, and innumerable." The concept of cyclical haunting enables consideration of the ways transgenerational trauma might function socially, and even independently of the intentionality or consciousness of an agent, making it possible to broaden and deepen the connection between trauma, affect, and writing. The idea of trauma functioning socially may seem counterintuitive given the way trauma is so routinely figured as resisting representation and the fact that subjects who suffer from posttraumatic stress so often struggle to communicate their experience to those around them, or even to conceive of their experience satisfactorily in thought themselves. But by zooming out to the panoramic view, one that acknowledges multi- and intergenerational transmissions passed down the line unconsciously, we see an array of symptomology and energetic dynamics capable of communicating the affect bound to trauma without need of its linguistic record or permission by the agent.

It is worth mentioning that some propositions around affect and its autonomy I consider useful in regards to the transmission of trauma and the subsequent writing of it, have come in for harsh criticism, most notably from Ruth Leys (2011), whose preoccupation with intention and signification favors a cognitivist inclination toward the operations of affect and emotion. While I concede that intentionality and cognitive involvement are vital concerns, I view her damning of the rise of affect theory in the humanities and her claim that notions of autonomy necessarily conceptualize affects as "inherently independent of meaning and intention" (450) as problematic. The detail of Leys's critique centers on methodology, and most especially studies attempting to establish a "neuroscience of emotion" (434). This is a legitimate investigation, and her meticulous analysis is persuasive when it comes to some of the finer details of methodologies like those employed by the likes of Tomkins and Massumi. But while Leys seems to privilege neuroscience, readily dismissing the words and works of affect theorists who rely on faulty studies or who admit to their proposition being more or less speculative, I maintain the validity of nonscientific knowledges of affect. We might also reasonably question the suggestion that neuroscience is necessarily more "truthful" than what interdisciplinary scholars have to say, given that conventional wisdom in that field seems to radically change every few years (faster, even, than the theoretical trends that sweep through the humanities). Leys's critique was predictably contentious and has elicited a number of papers in response (Connolly 2011; Frank and Wilson 2012; Altieri 2012), to which Leys, in turn, replied (2011, 2012). Leys raises more pertinent points worthy of reply than I can address given that weighing into the debate with an exhaustive response to her charges is not a priority, or the primary purpose, of this book, but I am not sufficiently convinced by her conclusions to disregard the promise and potential of engaging with several of the theorists in her sights.

While I appreciate Leys's scholarly demand for discipline in discussions and claims around affect, I do not think we should shy away from attempting reasoned understanding of the ways in which affective processes might inform the dire realities this chapter has called forth simply because their convoluted and often indiscernible movements cannot (yet) be empirically proven. Does Leys actually believe individual and contained affectivity and intentionality can account for the entirety of these realities? Leys casts the cultural critics with whom she wants to engage as promoting affects as "autonomous processes that take place below the threshold of conscious awareness and meaning" (2011: 437), as if the two—the unconscious and meaning—were mutually exclusive, and she appears to view the desire of these critics to use affect to understand its relation to discourse (in the Foucauldian sense) and political consequences as worthy of castigation. Leys also pits Tomkins against Freud, associating the former with "affects as non-intentional bodily reactions" and the latter with a view of emotion as "embodied, intentional states governed by our beliefs, cognitions, and desires" (2011: 437). Though there are, to be sure, notable differences between their affective frameworks, those differences don't, for Freud, exclude openness to, and interest in, the transmissive and autonomous potential of affect. Massumi and Freud would make for strange bedfellows, and I do not claim a direct correlation between their thinking on affect or the possibility of its autonomy. Freud does not address affective autonomy explicitly at all in his exploration of the historical operations of trauma. Yet it seems clear that he views transgenerational transmission as not only possible, but constitutive of culture, at least when it comes to Jewish religion and society, and that he views affective contagion (in this case guilt) as at least one of the ways that it takes place.

As Caruth points out in her essay on Freud's *Moses and Monotheism* (1939), Freud himself conceived of an operation in which the "historical power" of trauma's latency can be identified "not just that the experience is repeated after its forgetting, but that it is only in and through its inherent forgetting that it is first experienced at all" (Caruth 1996: 18). This book was Freud's last completed manuscript, and he began writing it as an old man on the eve of the Second World War, when suffering and strife around Judaism, Jewish culture, and Jewish persecution was once again at the fore in public life. As an Austrian-Jew based in Vienna these concerns would have been very much on Freud's mind in private. But with this project he was grappling with something particularly contentious: the proposition that the phenomenon of Judaism was a traumatic "reaction formation." The insightful move of thinking of religion in these terms has at times been lost in indignation over the book's numerous controversies, including the sacrilegious (and to many minds unhelpful, considering the circumstances) claim that Moses was murdered by a mob of resentful Jews, leading to transgenerational guilt that found its expression in avid commitment to the monotheistic religion Moses established. I do not take a position on claims of this nature, but his radical overall casting of religion as a posttraumatic strategy educes something similar to the cyclical haunting I have formulated, with affective and traumatic transmissive delay evoked in passages like the following:

> It has long since become common knowledge that the experience of the first five years of childhood exert a decisive influence on our life, one which later events oppose in vain. Much could be said about how these early experiences resist all efforts of more mature years to modify them, but this would not be relevant. It may not be so well known, however, that the strongest obsessive influence derive from those experiences which the child undergoes at a time when we have reason to believe his psychical apparatus to be incompletely fitted for accepting them. The fact itself cannot be doubted, but it seems so strange that we might try to make it easier to understand by a simile; the process may be compared to a photograph, which can be developed and made into a picture after a short or long interval. (Freud 1939: 202–03)

This would seem to be a process in which intention does not, certainly on the part of the child or adult child, seem to figure. The experience, Freud suggests, hovers somewhere outside cognitive processing, and yet remains active, poised to come into view, by means so mysterious it can only be referenced by way of allegory, at a later date (and quite probably, one assumes, in illogical or seemingly nonsensical exhibitions). Further, Freud's vision of the unconscious seems to admit the possibility of autonomy operative beyond, but also involving, subjective containment and conscious awareness.

> It is not easy to translate the concepts of individual psychology into mass psychology, and I do not think that there is much to be gained by introducing the concept of a "collective" unconscious—the content of the unconscious is collective anyhow, a general possession of mankind. (1939: 212)

Evoking Derrida's hauntology, Freud goes on to say in no uncertain terms that the "mental residue of those primeval times [when Moses lived and died] has become a heritage which, with each new generation, needs only to be awakened, not to be re-acquired" (212). It would appear that the entire thesis of Freud's book rests upon an argument for the transgenerational transmission of traumatic affect. If this transmission does not take place via indexical memory and conscious cognition, is accounted for in language, and need only be "awakened," not "re-acquired," as Freud suggests, how then might it be relayed? Might we not fairly view it as proceeding by way of a combination of precognitive, mother-to-baby transmission (structural), symptomological contagions in familial and communal contexts involving all of the senses, speech, body language, and affective transfer, both conscious and unconscious (historical), and cataclysmic, collective life changing/threatening events (Historical)? Might not each contain sites of potential capture and blockage of shared circulations of traumatic affect within a virtuality that connects them? If this sounds outlandish, let's not forget the wise words of Shakespeare's Hamlet when he reminded Horatio that there are more things in heaven and earth than are dreamt of in our philosophies (1604: 28). "Spacetime," for example, was first theorized by Einstein in the early twentieth century, and though physicists still don't know what it is exactly they are increasingly convinced it exists. Spacetime has been described as referring to "whatever external reality underlies our collective experiences of the space between things and the time between events" (Perez-Giz 2015) and as a "fabric" that moves and changes shape in relation to matter (Greene 2005). Scientific understanding of the workings of sentience within spacetime, with possible implications regarding traumatic and affective transmissions, seems some way off in the future.

Venturing even further out on the proverbial limb, Max Tegmark, a Swedish-American cosmologist and professor at the Massachusetts Institute of Technology, recently published a paper that builds on the work of neuroscientist Giulio Tononi in arguing that consciousness is a state of matter (2015). All matter is made up of particles called atoms, and quantum physicists have announced that a proposition as incredible as entanglement and spooky action at a distance—the phenomenon by which one particle becomes entangled with another particle exhibiting correlating properties no matter how far apart they are, even when the distance between them is arbitrary or light years—has now been established (*Phys.org* 2015). The implications are vague and distant, suffice to say that in fifty or a hundred years' time we might have a scientifically demonstrable understanding of transmission that is unthinkable in the current paradigm.

Elsewhere, Leys notes that the motivation behind the multidisciplinary trend toward affect in the humanities is a misguided conviction that the role of reason, rationality, and logic in theory, politics, and public life has given rise to "too flat" or "disembodied" accounts (2011: 436). Well, yes. Leys goes on to say that these erroneous theorists rest their endeavor on the assumption that "philosophers and critics have largely neglected the important role our corporeal-affective dispositions play in thinking, reasoning, and reflection, then it seems to follow that an account of affect and its place in our lives and institutions is called for" (436–37). Well, yes. Though I have some sympathy for the general concerns regarding responsibility that imbue Leys's work, in my reading her critique of affect neglects to substantially address gender politics and feminist theories that largely, or at least in part, informed those convictions, and this is a significant shortcoming. Leys seems to miss or dismiss the feminist project intrinsic to the embrace of affect theory amid insistence on scientific verification. Though she does succeed in casting doubt on certain neuroscientific methodologies previously employed and the logic of certain specific arguments based on them, I find her concluding position to be a black and white verdict brought to bear on deliberations of shades of gray. Leys's ultimate assertions foreclose complexities and potentials of affect and its operations that, unlikely to be wholly accounted for by intention and logic, warrant exploration, even if conclusive proof remains tenuous.

I stand by my decision to bring the theoretical filaments of hauntology, affective autonomy, and assemblage together in my reading of Barker's trilogy, confident that though cyclical haunting cannot be irrevocably confirmed in the ways Leys demands, my reasoned critical interpretation has been cogent. A final word about affect and its theorization as knowledges somewhat outside of those traditionally ordained by the academy: in their introduction to "Philosophy and the 'Affective Turn,'" a special issue of *Parrhesia* (2011), editors Marguerite La Caze and Henry Martyn Lloyd tease out the possibilities of a less dichotomous approach within the humanities. Describing the agenda of the affective turn as a "turn away" from "rationalist traditions of philosophy which are often characterized simply as 'Cartesian'," toward somatic phenomenon, they propose that rather than reveling in "bodies simpliciter," contemporary affect theorists might instead "celebrate non-dualist accounts of the self" (6). I do not see why this might not also apply to those mysterious spaces in between selves, to the mingling of interpersonal energies so palpable between bodies, even in disembodied communications (as anyone who has ever been embroiled in a social media spat knows). While Leys stresses language and statements used by certain theorists that suggest an outright separation between affect and cognition, La Cruz and Lloyd acknowledge that many working with affect are far from "disdainful of the concept of the mind." To the contrary, as I discussed in Chapter 2, Spinoza (a major inspiration for Deleuze and others) sees both mind and body as proceeding autonomously and in parallel, and affect and cognition as fundamentally indivisible (Hardt 2007: x). Without doubt authorial intention is evident in Barker's trilogy—we can only imagine the strength of character, fierceness of intellect, keen attention to detail, and painstaking patience that researching the books alone must have required. Building upon my assertion that traumatic affect operates as a social force that upsets assumptions of subjective containment, and that challenges and extends upon standard readings of certain texts, I echo LaCapra's appeal for understanding of the operations of h/Historic trauma institutionally, socially, and politically.

In conclusion, Leys serves as a tempering influence, one that reminds those working with affect not to lose sight of embodied accountability and justice, but it would be a mistake to ignore the potency of this cycle and affect's role in it, since effective intervention in part depends upon it. In *The Ghost Road*, the final installment, Barker ends the trilogy with a prime example of the feeding-forward and feeding-back loopings of cyclical haunting. Prior's structural/historical trauma in part informs his suicidal voluntary decision to return for a fourth tour in answer to the deathly call of the grave that is the Historical trauma of the trenches, where he is tragically killed in a futile battle only days before Armistice. Prior's ultimate demise reads as an inevitable outcome. Short of a revolution in Billy's consciousness and in culture, Barker's troubled antihero seems doomed to play out the sum of the h/Historical parts that circulate in affective currents between subjectivity and society. His death may herald the end of the trilogy, but it is not the end of his story. The trauma of the millions fallen in war—108 million estimated in the twentieth century alone (Hedges 2003)—reverberates on in a nameless, timeless spectrality, lying dormant and emerging in new generations, informing new incarnations of often age-old conflicts, and every now and then this resonance is brought to life on the page. The poetics of transgenerational trauma is literature that tells the stories and charts the topography of interlinkages and movements of intensities within assemblages inhabited by a given subject, family, and society. This is what Barker attests to in the *Regeneration Trilogy*, her profoundly layered and epic witnessing to the cyclical haunting of war, both familial and nationalistic.

In this way, the poetics of transgenerational trauma witnesses and testifies not only to trauma, but also to the work of recognizing traumatic gaps within the self and culture and reinstating life within those gaps through the acts of witnessing and living attention. Accepting this individual and artistic responsibility hardly absolves a writer or reader from advocating in more grassroots ways in the material world and the social and political realms, but literature of this kind serves a crucial role in illuminating the structural and historic underpinnings of History, thereby calling individuals to discernment. Such testimony is achieved not so much in prescriptive, literal, representational terms as by way of diverse, affective, and creative embodiments. Furthermore, this literature stands as a multigenerational political–ethical account. When Barker speaks in the *Regeneration Trilogy*, she speaks through her affected body as well as her cognition; she speaks out of the memory of her culture and the spectral bodies within it "sustaining sensation" (Bennett 2005: 38).

War narratives abound. They are always tragic, always thematically traumatic. The focus on the familial transmission of trauma in these novels is key, since the family is the primary and frontline assemblage that links the subject to assemblages beyond—institutional, social, national, and global. In the poetics of transgenerational trauma, micro–macro traumatic memory is written as a ghostly presence and an affective feeding backward and forward. It is a creative process that converts distance—or the unknowability of trauma in the instance of its occurrence—into intensity artfully expressed in language. This is literature as political act, as covert, yet formidable political activism. Early on in *Regeneration*, Barker writes:

> Sassoon's determination to remember might well account for his early and rapid recovery, though in his case it was motivated less by a desire to save his own sanity than by a determination to convince civilians that the war was mad. . . . He [Rivers] thought that Sassoon's poetry and his protest sprang from a single source, and each could be linked to his recovery from that terrible period of nightmares and hallucinations. (1992: 26)

Barker's commitment to creative remembrance and witnessing can be likened to Sassoon's. Just as the poet and antiwar protester's determination is an act of love, dissent, and literary testament born of trauma, so too is Barker's.

Until humanity adequately grasps the intimate connections between structural, historic, and Historic traumatic experience in assemblage the "elaboration of more desirable social and political institutions and practices" LaCapra calls for cannot be made manifest.

5

Provocations Beyond the Human

There is nothing modern about injustice and trauma, which have dogged human civilizations since great apes stood on two legs and initiated the sophisticated use of tools. Likewise, struggles for justice and social revolutions. Nevertheless, there have been crucial developments over the last two centuries that have seen the concept of individual rights gain global and political status, and which have given rise to numerous world-changing social justice movements. The Enlightenment paved the way for a multitude of sociopolitical activisms to gain mainstream momentum, becoming shifts of consciousness and challenges to practices that upon reaching "tipping point" brought about radical change, or at least its beginnings. Anticolonial nationalist independence movements, unionism, antislavery and the civil rights movement, Indigenous rights, disability rights, child rights, animal rights/protection, and multiple feminisms all sought to address and redress systemic traumas and injustices rooted in patriarchy, imperialism, and capitalism. This chapter looks at, and beyond, contemporary human culture through the lens of "intersectionality," which seeks to identify shared underlying structures between some of these injustices and traumas.

Each of the aforementioned movements represents innumerable lives and indignities. The experiences these movements embody need, and deserve, to be communicated and addressed specifically, in accordance with their particular orders of suffering. At its best, intersectionality does not attempt to replace that specific focus or to dilute it, but rather to build upon it in order to more effectively challenge the stranglehold of the patriarchal, imperialist, and capitalist power base. It is in this manner and spirit that I employ this framework in my final chapter on the poetics of transgenerational trauma.

Avtar Brah and Ann Phoenix describe intersectionality, which emerged from the work of African American feminists dissatisfied with the ways in which (white) Western feminism failed to reflect their experience, as "signifying the complex, irreducible, varied, and variable effects which ensue when multiple axis of differentiation—economic, political, cultural, psychic, subjective and experiential—intersect in historically specific contexts" (2004: 76). In part, my decision to use this framework comes down to this: just as patriarchy, imperialism, and capitalism have thrived on the overlapping oppressions and discriminations around gender, race, class, species etc., so too must the restitution of such oppressions, discriminations, and traumas involve an introjectory intervention aware of intersected injustices and their transgenerational impact.

In May 2014, *The Guardian* published an article titled "The novel is dead (this time it's for real)" in which Will Self declared that advancing technology has made redundant a form that "should have been laid to rest at about the time of *Finnegans Wake*." Self's article speaks to the technological and cultural evolution upon us to ends we may only ponder and predict. To that degree, it is hard to argue with him, but I was left wondering how, exactly, (yet more) assertions about the "death of the novel" serve us in an epoch of global crises. If ours is an era of heightened trauma, and therefore of testimony, as the prominent trauma theorist Shoshana Felman (1992) proposed, a more compelling focus might be to explore the role of the novel vis-à-vis testimony in such crisis. We might rather ask: Can large-scale intersected injustices and looming global crises be represented in literature? And if so, might this contribute in some way toward moving people to enact and demand necessary change?

When Ursula K. Le Guin accepted the Medal for Distinguished Contribution to American Letters in November 2014, she made a germane observation, stating that hard times are coming:

> I think we need writers who know the difference between production of a market commodity and the practice of an art. . . . We live in capitalism. Its power seems inescapable; so did the divine right of kings. Power can be resisted and changed by human beings; resistance and change often begin in art, and very often in our art—the art of words. (Arons 2014)

Alexis Wright, known for her "difficult" novels, is that sort of writer. Discussing the revolutionary speeches of Sojourner Truth, the nineteenth-century African American ex-slave, abolitionist, feminist and activist, Brah and Phoenix note that despite being illiterate she managed a "devastating critique" of the culture of her times. They add that Truth had the "sensibilities of a poet" and a decolonized open mind (2004: 77). Alexis Wright, from Waanji country in the highlands of the Gulf of Carpentaria, has that kind of mind, and she has created two books that disprove Self's obituary on the novel, *Carpentaria* (2006) and *The Swan Book* (2013).

Wright's work reveals contemporary reality and its burdens as an intersected condition, both embedded in trauma and furiously producing it, bound and circulated by affective transmissions. Such testimony is, as Le Guin suggests, vital to fostering resistance to seemingly inescapable and overwhelming power. As this chapter demonstrates, *The Swan Book* serves as a timely witnessing to traumatic injustices around gender, race, species, and the environment and a warning of where we may be headed in these early decades of twenty-first-century patriarchy. It is not an easy story to summarize, largely because its potency precedes less by way of plot and logic and more by way of affective-driven imagination. In stripped-back terms, it tells the story of Bella Donna, an old woman and refugee of the climate change wars in the Northern Hemisphere, who rescues a mute Aboriginal girl called Oblivia, severely traumatized following a gang rape. After Bella Donna's death, Warren Finch, a magnetic Indigenous hero, risen to the rank of deputy president of Australia on the back of mining deals, kidnaps Oblivia, believing her to be his promised wife, and imprisons her in a southern city, from which she eventually escapes to be reunited with her country and the swans that populate the book from the title to the final page.

Critics praised *The Swan Book* as a development of the singular writing style Wright established in her 2006 novel *Carpentaria*. Noting her "linguistic dexterity, mashing words and phrases from high and low culture, from English, Aboriginal languages, French and Latin," her "fierce political purpose," her "genre bending" gift for the multifaceted layering of stories (Gleeson-White 2013), and pronouncing it a "bitter, lovely, and tragic book" (Webb 2013), reviewers were effusive in lauding its poetic experimentation. The book matters because it speaks poetically and profoundly to many pressing concerns in twenty-first-century society. In Wright's hands, violence against women, child abuse, racism, neocolonialism, climate change and the well-being of the environment, unethical corporatism, the exploitation and suffering of nonhuman animals, and reprehensible immigration policies and practices are woven together, along with love and the fleshed goodness of human beings and their many idiosyncrasies and eccentricities. The result is a lyrical and inspired text that works upon the imagination and emotions at depth and with surprising nuance to reveal connections between trauma and injustices at several junctures, including gender, age, and race.

Intersectionality I: Gender, age, and race

In Chapter 3 I considered the spectral legacy of colonialism in relation to *Carpentaria* (Wright 2006), which involved the colonial occupation of Aboriginal land and sustained attacks on the sovereignty of the Indigenous peoples of Australia. In Chapter 4 I explored cyclical haunting and transmissive loops between intimate assemblages, such as families, and Historic assemblages, such as war, via Pat Barker's *Regeneration Trilogy* (1999), which chronicles the horrors of the First World War. I ended that chapter echoing LaCapra's (1999) call for a remedy to undesirable social and political institutions and practices. In this section, I explore some of those undesirable social and political institutions and practices through the lens of intersectionality and via *The Swan Book*, but a brief introduction to my intersectional approach is in order before advancing.

Patricia Hill Collins, one of the first scholars to write on intersectionality in the 1990s, explains intersectionality as a framework that allows examination of the ways in which gender, race, class, etc. "mutually construct one another" rather than treating them as "distinctive social hierarchies" (1998: 62). While some intersectionality-oriented academics work with a particular set of issues and concerns in their definition and focus, others attempt to identify and address the almost limitless array of them. Intersectionality unsettles identity politics in that it questions a feminism that ignores race, or lesbian, gay, bisexual, transgender, queer and nonbinary, intersex or asexual activisms. In turn, intersectionality challenges a critical race position that enact ableism, or a class politics and union activism that fails to consider ageism, and so on and so forth. Its central tenet is that working on one category of inequality or discrimination without acknowledgment and the intention to address others, is ineffective and unethical. This view maintains that each manifestation of social injustice and oppression is based in the same fundamental process: a dominant assemblage refuses the rights and interests of certain individuals or minority assemblages by classifying the other as inferior or morally bankrupt, or by objectifying the other in such a way as to enable and justify discrimination and oppression.

At its most hard line, intersectionality is a position that calls this elementary process, as well as specific issues and instances and the intricate webs they form, into account, submitting that participating in, or turning the other cheek in relation to, any injustice equates to a condoning of, and colluding with, the entire schema. The adoption of an intersectional stance does not mean distinct focus can no longer be given to a particular issue, but it does mean that issues need be addressed with at least implicit awareness and advocacy regarding the other intersecting issues. There are currently many debates and tensions at play within the intersectionality movement, in both its scholarly and grassroots realms, and between it as a field of study or advocacy approach and various issue- and identity-based movements. It is not my intention to move into these or to reconnoiter intersectionality in all its nuances and possible assemblages. Rather, I use it as a productive context through which to pass my reflections on *The Swan Book* and the subjective and social realities it epitomizes.

Profoundly illogical and affective in equal measures, *The Swan Book* is a novel that hardly makes any sense, and yet it makes perfect sense. More uncompromising than *Carpentaria* in its poetic experimentation and imagination, it is nevertheless grounded in unbearable realities. It is a text that resists textual analysis, hence my intention to not so much interpret it as to converse with certain aspects of it. While *Carpentaria* highlighted masculinity, *The Swan Book* engages more with the feminine (and the feminist) via the figure of the central protagonist Oblivia, a "living wound" (Webb 2013), left for dead, forsaken by her family, and saved by Bella Donna, the deranged and kindly white survivor of environmental Armageddon, who adopts her after finding her in the hollow of a gum tree. As Webb (2013) points out, *The Swan Book* projects the preoccupations of *Carpentaria* (2006)—"environmental degradation, deracination, poverty, violence, and lack of empathy"—into the future: the resulting fictional apocalypse predicts the traumatic endgame of eons of patriarchy, several centuries of industrialization, and the corporatized capitalism that took root mid-twentieth century.

Embodying the wounded political, social, and economic system of a modern-day Western nation, *The Swan Book* depicts Australia in a way that is a lament for the past, an agitation for the present, and an indictment for the future. In its vision, the continued "intervention" in the Northern Territory—rebranded as the Stronger Futures policy in 2012 by the Australian Labor Party with a view to tempering bad press, expanding geographical reach, and extending the policy timeframe by ten years—has progressed into a countrywide military-operated police state in which Indigenous communities are open-air prisons. The world, post climate-change hostilities and battles for diminishing habitable land, is an ongoing warzone blighted by cultural and environmental devastation and populated by severely traumatized beings in various kinds of exile. A prime example of the poetics of transgenerational trauma as postmodern allegory, *The Swan Book* is a textual tapestry whose warp and weft work madly over the page leaving loose threads dangling. The result is a spectral saga whose qualities mimic the reverberations of traumatic experience in flashing neon. It is by turns disturbing, confounding, mournful, elegiac, compelling, intense, shocking, relentless, confronting, demanding, and testing. It is a long novel, especially for one so steeped in poetic and surrealistic abstractions, so disdainful for the conventions of narrative drive. It is a book of vital importance in its expression of imperialist cyclical haunting and this is apparent on the first page, when a nameless narrator speaks:

> Upstairs in my brain, there lives this kind of cut snake virus in its doll's house. Little stars shining over the moonscape garden twinkle endlessly in a crisp sky. The crazy virus just sits there on the couch and keeps a good old *qui vive* out the window for intruders. It ignores all of the eviction notices stacked on the door. The virus thinks it is the only pure full-blood virus left in the land. Everything else is just half-caste. Worth nothing! Not even

> a property owner. Hell yes! it thinks, worse than the swarms of rednecks hanging around the neighbourhood. Hard to believe a brain could get sucked into vomiting bad history over the beautiful sunburnt plains [italics in original]. (Wright 2013: 1)

On the pages that follow the virus is also described as "nostalgia for foreign things" (3) and a "sickness developed from channelling every scrap of energy towards an imaginary, ideal world with songs of solidarity, like *We Shall Overcome*" [italics in original] (3). Furthermore, the virus "sings with a special slow drawling voice, like an Australian with *closed door syndrome*" [italics in original] (3). The "closed door syndrome" can only be read as a swipe at the hard line governmental policies around undocumented asylum seekers that have been in place since former prime minister John Howard's reign, and which have prompted accusations of human rights abuses. In other words, this reference to viral "nostalgia for foreign things" begins as an allusion to the traumatic heritage and cyclical haunting of the colonial inhabitancy of a land radically altered by Anglo settlement, and ends with a critique of the paradoxical and increasingly ruthless defense against those seeking to now immigrate.

These opening pages from the inside voice of the silent, speechless protagonist, Oblivia, conclude thus: "The virus thinks I want what it wants—to hide in a dark corner of its lolly pink bed, where it dreams, in my diseased mind" (5). Following an interview promoting *The Swan Book*, a member of the audience asked Wright what the virus represented to the author, and what it meant in relation to the character of Oblivia. Wright replied that Oblivia is a "damaged character" who "feels she doesn't have control about what's happening in her world" (The Wheeler Center 2013). The idea, Wright continued, of having sovereignty over your own mind, even if you can't have sovereignty over the land is prominent in Indigenous communities and runs through both *Carpentaria* and *The Swan Book*. "With the character of Oblivia that's not happening," she said. "She's having a struggle to regain control of her own mind. She's got something else happening there." That "something else" might be thought of as a critical mass of transmitted and intersected traumas.

The "dark corner of its lolly pink bed," the position from which the narrating "diseased mind" dreams, suggests that this virus, this something else, is not a neutral, nongendered operation (as if anything could be). In terms of vulnerability to abuse and trauma, Oblivia's gender is significant, as is her race and age. As a female, she is born into certain conditions that have been identified and documented by feminism, the proliferation of which has drastically altered the way female experience is perceived. For example, domestic violence and rape were once viewed as private aberrations, but are now commonly acknowledged as manifestations of "a broad-scale system of domination that affects women as a class" (Crenshaw 1991: 1241). Oblivia is also Aboriginal, and as such she is affected in ways not addressed by mainstream feminism. Indigenous activism might represent her in terms of human rights, land rights, and racially discriminatory policies, practices, and attitudes, but it would not necessarily address the specificity of her *Aboriginal* experience *as a woman*. As Kimberlé Crenshaw (1991) says, "The intersection of racism and sexism factors into Black women's lives in ways that cannot be captured wholly by looking at the race or gender dimensions of those experiences separately" (1244).

Age also needs to be taken into account, and this is a task neither feminism nor Indigenous activisms, in their current forms, are equipped to do justice to. If Oblivia were a real world girl, social justice advocacy and legislation around child's rights may have come into play in relation to her youth. But any construction or representation of her in those terms would inevitably fail to comprehensively address other aspects of her being and experience—her femaleness and her Aboriginality—with all their lived nuances and realities. Nura Taefi (2009) cites tensions between discourses on the rights of children and women in United Nations Conventions, stating, "Girls are marginalised within the category of children as female, and within the category of women as minors" (345). Gender, race, and age each mark Oblivia as vulnerable to injustice, oppression, and abuse.

Just as traumatic affect feeds back and forth spectrally in cyclical haunting, challenging the boundary between the past and present in Barker's trilogy, so too its intersected movements are embodied in Wright's work. And just as Barker charts virtual currents connecting the small "h" history of Prior's troubled family to the big "H" catastrophe of world war, so too Wright illuminates the currents of spectrality circulating from Aboriginal history before colonialism, through the devastation of invasion, to present postcolonial conditions and beyond into the future within intersectional configurations of trauma and transmission.

Oblivia was raped by a gang of petrol-sniffing Aboriginal youths—young men themselves traumatized to the point of madness. It is not only numb, dangerous boys that perpetrate this rape; it is also the expression of an imperialist (and as such patriarchal) nation. In Bella Donna's telling, Oblivia is "joined with the *undoable*" as a result of "having been gang-raped physically, emotionally, psychologically, statistically, randomly, historically, so fully in fact: *Your time stands still*" [italics in original] (Wright 2013: 82). In other words, the *undoable* equals trauma. It is not only the overwhelming shame of the boys themselves that is transmitted to Oblivia in this act of (literally) unspeakable violence, but also the shame of a nation. Discussing the mechanisms by which women of color in the context of the United States are "frequently the product of intersecting patterns of racism and sexism" (1991: 1242–43), Crenshaw states that intersectionality facilitates a mapping of "the ways in which racism and patriarchy have shaped conceptualizations of rape, to describe the unique vulnerability of women of color to these converging systems of domination" (1265–66).

It may initially seem surprising that Bella Donna is not exactly hailed a savior by the community for rescuing Oblivia from her slumber in the hollow of a tree, until the realization hits that Oblivia is a site of shame for the community who had long ago denied her: "*Why can't she stay lost? All this searching and searching,* they claimed, *and the only thing discovered was shame*" [italics in original] (82). Only Bella Donna, the eccentric white immigrant, commits to Oblivia understanding, as she does:

> The girl has never recovered from being raped. But feeling and knowing are two different things: she retaliates all the same, and like any other long-standing conflict around the world, one act of violation becomes a story of another. (Wright 2013: 19)

Bella Donna alone seems to grasp Caruth's point that history *is* the way in which we are implicated by one another's trauma (Caruth 1996: 18). Oblivia's muteness is, likewise, more than a subjective condition. As with Barker's

First World War vets, Oblivia's wordlessness is a symptom of individual trauma *and* of a traumatic operation that exceeds a given individual or interpersonal relationship. Silent ever since "the last word she had spoken when scared out of her wits, the day when her tongue had screeched to a halt with dust flying everywhere, and was left screaming" (Wright 2013: 19), Oblivia's inner world is conveyed through the fractured and disjointed, the *undone*, experimental narration, which reflects the embodied reverberations of trauma and the way it tends to be experienced as a subjective fracturing. And yet, there is a palpable impulse toward communication and restoration. Just as imperialism and patriarchy involve systematic constructs of oppression, injustice, and trauma, restitution requires a multifaceted intervention. *The Swan Book* is testimony to the power of testimony, celebrating the sustaining of life in story and poetics in the face of extreme hardship. In particular, it honors the initiative, character, and agency of Aboriginal peoples and communities, as well as showing, unflinchingly, the need for healing.

Toward the end of the novel Oblivia's traumatized passivity begins a process of transformation. Having been kidnapped and taken to the city of refugees to live, locked up, in the People's Palace, she escapes to save the "fallen swans" (Wright 2013: 254) that gravitate to her. Her relationship to Bella Donna and her stories continue well after the death of the old woman who "must have left her voice behind after she died" (90). Bella Donna's great gift to Oblivia is story, and it is this gift that directs Oblivia out of her imprisonment into the "panicky night" (300). In a brave, bold move, Oblivia flees the palace and the city. "Goodness poor heart" writes Wright, "the ghost walk. There are those who will warn anyone making this strange solitary journey, and will say: *You have got to take enough to make it through*" (300). Out there, alone, "entangled in the vortex of a thunderstorm dizzily spinning over many kilometres in the higher strata of the atmosphere" she walks "without any thought" of where she is headed, nor of life or death (300), when suddenly "the sky is blanketed by black swans in the cold night" and Oblivia realizes she has found "her swans" from the swamp:

> They had found each other's heartbeat, the pulse humming through the land from one to the other, like the sound of distant clap sticks beating through ceremony, connecting together the spirits, people and place of all times into

> one. These were her swans from the swamp. There was no going back. She would follow them. (303)

Following her black swans, Oblivia makes tentative contact with the land that is, like her, wounded, but which has been her people's life-sustaining heritage for eons. Although she is in some ways a waif, Oblivia has a deep communion with nonhuman animals and a belonging to country that provides grounding in the hostile environment in which she dwells. These are moments of beauty in an otherwise bleak scenario. Oblivia is, fundamentally, the metaphoric product of what Wright refers to as Australia's "history of wanting to lock people up. . . . We had reserves for Aboriginal people for years where people were locked up" (The Wheeler Center 2013). Though she is held hostage and imprisoned, the manner in which Oblivia is locked up is primarily psychic. Hers is traumatically conditioned passivity, an embodiment of Australia's history of locking up, in terms of gender, age, and race. This brings me to focus on Wright's refusal of easy, pat psychologizations in relation to racial trauma.

Layering tropes and motifs with staggering density, Wright's characterizations and bizarre storylines form a veritable map of suffering and spirit that defy what Stef Craps and Gert Buelens describe as the typical, limited individualistic focus on psychology that "ignores and leaves unquestioned the conditions that enabled the traumatic abuse" (2008: 4). In rejecting the customary "psychologization of social suffering," Wright questions the idea that recovery from the traumas engendered by colonization rests in the main on a given individual coming to understand and speak their pain, thereby releasing the past (4). While such individual healing is doubtless an essential aspect of post/anticolonial recovery, the tendency to ascribe personal responsibility to the most traumatized individuals is problematic and all too convenient, denying or minimizing as it does the accountability of government and the relations between individuals, institutions, and communities.

The suspect notion that those traumatized by colonialism need simply, in effect, to get over it, was the premise of Howard's steadfast near decade-long rejection of the call to apologize to the "stolen generations." In essence, Howard, an archconservative, was refusing responsibility for a long-standing policy that involved the forced removal of Aboriginal and Torres Strait Islander children deemed "half-caste" from their families by the government, and their subsequent placement in white homes. The policy was enacted at least in part with an agenda to breed out "full-blood" Aborigines, and for this reason many view it as a policy of genocide. While debate continues around this point, the publication of *Bringing Them Home—Report of the National Inquiry into the Separation of Aboriginal and Torres Strait Islander Children from Their Families* in 1997 left no doubt as to the traumatic legacy of the policies that saw such removals enacted. The official refusal to apologize continued until 2008, when Howard's successor Kevin Rudd made a formal national apology as his first act of office after the Labor Party won the 2007 election.

Though this most divisive chapter of the so-called "history wars" or "black armband debate"—disputes around to what degree Australia's colonial history has been unfairly and inaccurately cast in positive or negative terms—concluded with that welcome gesture, "The Apology" now stands as a disappointing symbol of inadequate follow through. It offers little more than public, collective recognition in lieu of substantial reconciliation and "reparation or restitution and, more broadly, the transformation of a wounding political, social, and economic system" (Craps and Buelens 2008: 4). This is a salient point given that the United Nations has accused the Australian government of human rights abuses. Following a two-week tour of Aboriginal towns and communities in response to concerns around racial discrimination and the "intervention" launched by Howard's government in 2007, Professor James Anaya, UN special rapporteur on Indigenous human rights, announced that health conditions were "even worse than in some Third World countries" (Sharp and Arup 2009). He also deemed the intervention "overtly discriminatory."

The question of race regarding the poetics of transgenerational trauma is a crucial one, because as Stef Craps and Gert Buelens (2008) state, it has been somewhat absent from the founding texts of trauma theory, outside a focus on the persecution of Jewish people extending from traditional trauma theory's roots in Holocaust studies. The seeming intention of the theorists at the forefront of the trauma turn was to re-engage "real world" ethics through textualist examinations of trauma following the proliferation of abstracted post-structuralist theories. The Holocaust, as the catalyst for this development, was featured in early investigations, which understandably led to a dominance of European experience. As Craps and Buelens suggest, that resulted in an unfortunate trend in which non-Western experience was routinely sidelined. Caruth, Felman, LaCapra, and others positioned testimony as "a bridge between disparate historical experiences" that ensures that "listening to the trauma of another can contribute to cross-cultural solidarity and to the creation of new forms of community" (2008: 2). This was obviously a noble and welcome aim, but the overlooking of non-Western experience significantly compromised the very project trauma theory set out to advance. Craps and Beulens go so far as to state that the works of these theorists are "almost exclusively concerned with traumatic experiences of white Westerners and solely employ critical methodologies emanating from a Euro-American context" (2). I align myself with Craps and Buelens when they say "Western traumatic histories must be seen to be tied up with histories of colonial trauma for trauma studies to be able to redeem its promise of ethical effectiveness" (2008: 2).

More recent works are rectifying this problem. Craps's own book *Postcolonial Witnessing: Trauma Out of Bounds* (2013) is a text that commits to the examination of marginalized, non-Western testimony and traumatic histories, thereby lessening the gulf of understanding between the West and other cultures. Gabriele Schwab's 2010 book *Haunting Legacies: Violent Histories and Transgenerational Trauma* is perhaps most closely aligned with my examination of transgenerational trauma and its literary testimony. Schwab's figuring of haunting legacies as tenacious, traumatic, and transgenerationally transmitted memories that prove difficult to remember or recount (Schwab 2010: 20) draws, as do I, from the writings of Abraham and Torok, and Derrida. Though her focus is more decidedly on the experience and aftermath of violent and catastrophic trauma, such as war, torture, and rape, there are substantial resonances between Schwab's view of textual testimony, in a range of forms and genres, and mine. In particular, my exploration of the ways in which affective and bodily knowings are inscribed in literary trauma testimony shares some ground with Schwab's thinking on the ways "unthought knowledge" informs transgenerational testimony. Though Schwab, like Marianne Hirsch, focuses on second-generation Holocaust testimony, she expands her interdisciplinary consideration of transmission to non-European and postcolonial contexts, attempting to show intersections and interdependencies between traumatic histories.

In my reading of Wright, I seek to join these ranks in theorizing "postcolonialism as a post-traumatic cultural formation" (Craps and Buelens 2008: 2). In challenging the aforementioned Eurocentricism, it is crucial to challenge the established clinical and theoretical emphasis on individualistic experience. This is not to say that individual experience is no longer important, but an expansion of attention is vital to addressing the sly forms of trauma that result from structural persecution and assemblages of subjugation. Such slippery forms of transmission can be explored through an intersectional approach and increased awareness of non-Western understandings of traumatic experience. For example, Aaron Denham (2008) conducted ethnographic research on the transmission of resilience strategies in an American-Indian family intergenerationally affected by Historic/historic trauma, concluding that it is not only traumatic events and history that need to be taken into account, but also individually and culturally varied responses to them. Denham stresses that discussion about the consequences of colonialism frequently "illustrate the strengths expressed by individuals and communities, as powerful stories, songs, histories and strategies for resilience" that often "present behind the realities of inequality, injustice and poverty" (392).

Bella Donna's stories and Oblivia's books in *The Swan Book* may indeed be construed as successful "strategies for resilience." These are significant achievements in the face of overbearing oppression. Denham reports that the teachings of "specific family ancestors are of central importance to the current identity of living family members, as individual identity is primarily experienced as a continuing lineage as opposed to an individual ego" (Denham 2008: 400). This finding also pertains to Australia's First Nations. The spans of time that have traditionally informed Indigenous identity in relation to the land are mind-boggling to most non-Indigenous Australians. This is evident in *First Footprints* (2013), a documentary series about the history of Indigenous people in Australia prior to invasion. In a particularly touching scene exploring the cultural boom that took place after the end of the ice age, Sylvester Mangolamara, of the Wunambal Gaambera people, joins anthropologists at the site of the Gwion Gwion figures, painted on an ancient rock formation in the Kimberley region of Western Australia. This rock art is dated at 12,000 years old and is considered the oldest representation of ceremony anywhere in the world. Approaching the rock, Mangolamara gazes up at the figures and intones loudly in his native tongue:

> "Gwion it's me, Mamajii."
> "Gwion do you know who I am?"
> "Do you know who I am?"
> "It's me, Mamajii."

His relationship with the ancestors who painted the figures is plainly not one of distance, not a relation of the present looking back at the past. Mangolamara is, as Jacques Derrida (1994) advises us to do, encountering the ghost, engaging with the "spectre" in a relationship that is very much alive and present and that tangibly informs his sense of self.

Deprived of such tender ties by colonialism, isolated in her posttraumatic condition, caught between two worlds, and victimized in both, Oblivia is, in Wright's words, struggling to "regain control of her own mind" in a "big story of that ghost place" (Wright 2013: 334). Attesting to the unbearable realities that "do this to children" (300), the novel's ending hints at a glimmer of hope for Oblivia. Even so, the big picture remains decidedly grim and Oblivia is, from beginning to end, an orphan, the embodiment of Indigenous trauma. Yet, returning to Denham's point, despite her handicaps (her muteness and lack of worldly resources beyond those bequeathed her by Bella Donna), Oblivia maintains an integrity and bond with the land and its multitude of beings that Warren Finch and his entourage have, in their adoption of Western mores, lost. As Wright says, in conversation with Sophie Cunningham, Oblivia is the "rage in the Aboriginal world, the silence that came out of the Howard years and leading into the intervention and the continuation and reinforcement of the intervention" (The Wheeler Center 2013).

The "intervention" Wright and Cunningham discussed is the official response to the *Ampe Akelyernemane Meke Mekarle: "Little Children Are Sacred" Report* (Wild and Anderson 2007), which proved an unwitting catalyst for a federal policy that involves the presence of the police and army, along with other government representatives, in remote Aboriginal communities.

Winding back Aboriginal land rights under the NT Aboriginal Land Rights Act, the policy enforces health checks for Aboriginal children and oversees the quarantining of welfare payments in 73 Aboriginal communities (Reconciliation Action Network 2008). Formally known as the Northern Territory National Emergency Response, the intervention of *The Swan Book* is this contemporary penal, paternal control taken to its extreme end.

Wright renders the intervention as an ongoing neocolonial suppression in which the consequences of continued colonial thinking and methods are dire. Most vehement opponents agree that definitive measures need be taken to address the tenacious problems documented in the "Little Children" report, but many dispute the pedophile ring and sex slavery claims as a media beat-up and the heavy-handed government tactics in play. Its questionable success on both a practical and political level and the protracted ineffectiveness of leadership in relation to Indigenous communities are founded in denial and ignorance. Both major parties in Australian politics fundamentally fail to grasp the gravity of the pandemics of traumatic transmission resulting from colonization and fail to comprehend the nature and severity of the subsequent Complex Post-Traumatic Stress Disorder. In other words, the government attempts to exert control over a social reality that exceeds its capacity and desire for understanding, empathy, and responsibility.

The intervention targets towns peopled by individuals who can expect to die roughly 6–11 years sooner than a non-Indigenous Australian (Australian Bureau of Statistics 2013), who for the most part live in inadequate housing, who are routinely plagued by ill health—and who were not even counted in the census until 1967. High incarceration rates and deaths in custody continue in startling disproportion to that of non-Indigenous Australians. Traumatic transmissions are also routinely acted out in variably raced families (including white families) in cities, as well as in Indigenous families and communities in the outback. In exclusively targeting remote communities (and asylum seekers) with punitive policies, the government displays an unconscionable irresponsibility around the ways trauma is transmitted down ladders of hierarchical power structures. It is little wonder, then, that the plight of nonhuman animals barely even registers on the governmental/legal radar.

"*Welcome to the dystopia of dysfunction*," Wright writes in italics (2013: 140), ahead of a breathtaking passage about the postcolonial condition in the form of the mutated and advanced intervention:

> Isn't that right that we have been waiting for somebody to turn up here and tell us how we are going to fix this crisis? We need someone to tell us how to run the community store, the health center, get the bums on seats at the school, fix up all the violence, alcohol, petrol-sniffing, criminality, overhousing, maintenance, tell mothers how to have babies, healthy babies, pretty babies, clean babies, immunised babies, and to implement Canberra's policy to teach these people how to love their children, and while I am mentioning health, to rid the place of diabetes, heart disease, kidney disease, mental health, eye, ear, nose disease and dogs; not to mention training people for work, to go out and be useful to society, to drive a bulldozer, build houses, be electricians and plumbers, grow and cook their own food, feed it to the children, and then to lift a box and bury themselves in a box. (140)

Postcolonial, cyclically haunted and intersected assemblages of structural and h/Historic trauma will not be undone by force. Nor will they respond positively to prohibition. Just as war does, the intervention, as it is currently conceived and carried out, seems set to breed more traumatic affect, more Billy Priors and more Oblivias, failing some promising turn of consciousness and events.

Colonizing notions of family are central to governmental thinking in its blunt response to the crimes identified in the report and in official justifications for the strategies employed. The idealized Western family ideal is one in which the functional family is imaged as caring for the interests of all its members, from the most to the least powerful (Collins 1998: 64). The tragedy of pervasive child abuse in Indigenous communities exposes the schisms between Australia's ideal, actual, and "naturalized" conditionings and hierarchies within families relating to gender, wealth, age, sexuality, race, ethnicity, etc. (64) and the reality of traumatic transmissions in these remote communities. Further, a nation state "conceptualized as a national family with the traditional family ideal providing ideas about family" (66) necessarily ostracizes people whose traditional customs and traumatic adaptions ensure that they diverge from the norms of mainstream society, or whose trauma symptoms present more visibly or extremely, minus acknowledgment of the intersected constructions and histories underpinning such differences. Here we see a cultural contrast between Barker's intervention into the nation-making mythology of the First World War and Wright's prophesying of national, subjective, familial, societal, and environmental catastrophe in the making. The world Barker re-creates is a pre-multicultural British homeland at war with nationalized others. It is a world in which the nation state is more readily conceptualized as a national family with traditional family ideals, and which Barker upends in her rendering of historic and Historic loops of traumatic transmission. The postcolonial, cross-, and multiculturally intersected world Wright envisions is impossibly complex. And this weighty complexity necessitates innovative modes of storytelling capable of honoring an Indigenous heritage that predates and evades the confines of white prescription and practice as well as testifying to the damage done to Aboriginal people in "recounting a world where no one has a place any more" (Webb 2013).

Regardless of a lack of acknowledgment, traumatic intersections of all shapes and sizes are routinely acted out, in white-skinned families in cities as well as in brown-skinned families in rural and remote communities. There are those, too, whose trauma and suffering is all but socially and politically invisible. Craps and Buelens refer to marginalized people and communities who "often fly under the trauma-theoretical radar because of the fact that current definitions of trauma have been constructed from the experiences of dominant groups in Western society" (2008: 3). At this point I want to expand my reflections on *The Swan Book* and my thinking on intersectionality to configure the idea of "minority beings" as those whose lives are deemed the least grieveable (Butler 2010). If trauma and injustice can be thought of as operative via intersected junctures of transmission, it does not stand that those junctures form on an even playing field. A friend of mine, working for the United Nations, was based in East Timor in the 1990s, during the occupation of the Indonesian military forces. He once recounted an experience that had a profound impact on him. He described watching, incredulously, a scene in which a Timorese family interacted and the way abuse was literally passed down the line in a domino effect: the father, possibly traumatized by Indonesian soldiers, acted out on the mother, who acted out on the oldest child, who acted out on the youngest child, who acted out on the dog. This image of the nonhuman animal as the final figure of a hierarchy of power relations brings me to contemplation beyond the human.

Intersectionality II: The many among us not human

> *My sweet Lord, they only see what they want to see. They are blind, not stupid. They see, but they are blind.* [italics in original]
>
> (Wright 2013: 21)

Until recently, mainstream society rarely gave focus to nonhuman animals. Even though there have been marked and welcome developments in terms of public consciousness of abuses and injustices relating to nonhuman animals, many people still barely acknowledge the systematic suffering of animals. Wright was already paying mind to animals in her writing back in *Carpentaria* (2006). When Norm and Bala return to the post-cyclone flattened ghost town of Desperance on the second-last page in that novel, the only living beings they encounter are dogs:

> He was met by the bony, hollow-ribbed, abandoned dogs of the town that had run to the hills and back again after the cyclone. Now, having appeared from nowhere, they roamed along streets that no longer existed, searching for their owners. They did not bark or howl. The shock of the cyclone had left them like this: speechless, dumbfounded, unable to crack a bark. Unable to emit a sound out of their wide-opened mouths. (518)

This scene of dogs stripped of voice, abandoned by humans, and traumatized by the effects of possible human-induced climate change is painfully affecting, and Wright is unusual among writers for both her sustained interest in nonhuman beings and her inventive representations of them.

Nonhuman animals figure so significantly in Wright's fiction that when Sophie Cunningham posed a question beginning with, "At what point did Oblivia, the main character . . ." she stopped and corrected herself with "the main *human* character" [italics added] (The Wheeler Center 2013). Later, when Cunningham points out that animals "have as much authority" as human characters in *The Swan Book* (2013), Wright replied: "I've always liked animals, since I was a child, but also in the Indigenous world everything is sacred and animals are sacred and have stories." She went on to recount the wondrous, perplexing, and sad discoveries she made while researching the demise and disappearance of swans from their habitat and their recent appearances in odd numbers and places.

The Swan Book tells a story that so often goes untold: that of the nonhuman animals for which both contact with humans and human-influenced environments are a traumatizing catastrophe. Wright's extraordinary ability to bring an Indigenous conception of animals alive in stories set in the contemporary world reveals the involvement of nonhuman animals in the traumatic cycles of, and beyond, humanity. Consider the following passage, which recounts a routine scene of horror, testifying to the traumatic effect of human civilization on animals as collateral damage:

> A crescendo of dead—the carcasses of splattered or bloated bullocks and native animals lay over the sealed or unsealed corrugated roads, where the eyes of dingoes and curlews gleamed in the headlights. . . . The girl watched as they collected those still with a trace of life: small rodents, mangled rabbits, various marsupials, broken-back snakes, a bush turkey, a smashed echidna. (165)

This is the work-a-day world divorced from the land it plunders, disconnected from hearth. It is also writing against what David Brooks (2013) has called "saturation capitalism," which he defines as consumerism driven by the "deep wound" and "ontological distress" (47) at the divide between head and heart and human and nonhuman animals.

The controversial ethical philosopher Peter Singer (1975) popularized the term "speciesism" in his seminal book *Animal Liberation*. It refers to the assumption of human superiority and the relegation of nonhuman animals to the status of things and property leading to systematic dominance and exploitation. Speciesism is widely considered among many scholars working in critical animal studies, and activists at large, to be a feature of patriarchal culture, along with sexism and racism (and other bigotries). With roots in patriarchal history, attitudes, and customs, speciesism is now implicated across a diverse range of academic fields. The term "critical animal studies" (CAS) is itself an example of the way in which the concept of speciesism is embedded in a broader political critique of culture. The Institute for Critical Animal Studies (ICAS) website states that the term was coined in 2007, after much consultation between animal rights/liberation academics and activists around the world. The intention was to denote an interdisciplinary field "dedicated to establishing a holistic total liberation movement for humans, nonhuman animals, and the Earth." This was deemed necessary in order to address speciesist tendencies within the higher education sector by bringing diversely disciplined scholars together "under one common field of study, similar to that of other marginalized fields of study (e.g., Women's Studies, Ethnic Studies, Latina/o Studies, Native American Studies)" (2014).

Indeed, an exciting and eclectic array of (often interdisciplinary and intersectional) scholarly approaches to critiquing interspecies relations between humans and nonhuman individuals is now emerging. For example, Piers Beirne, a professor in criminology, begins his call for a "nonspeciesist criminology" by evoking the British feminist Mary Wollstonecraft and her "attempt to establish animal abuse as an antecedent of female abuse" in her pioneering treatise on women's rights (1999). New Zealand researchers, who published an article titled "Vegan Sexuality: Challenging Heteronormative Masculinity through Meat-Free Sex" in *Feminism and Psychology* (Potts and Parry 2010) explore social media aggression and trolling by heterosexual men toward those identifying as "vegansexuals" (vegans for whom a commitment to cruelty-free consumption extends to sex and who only have sex with other vegans). While in the *Journal for Critical Animal Studies* Erika Calvo discusses the "gendering of agricultural animals" in an article cleverly and evocatively titled "Most Farmers Prefer Blondes: The Dynamic of Anthroparchy in Animals' Becoming Meat" (2008). It is within this multi- and interdisciplinary development that I stage my own critical intervention around speciesism within trauma and literary theories. It stands to reason that language and representation are, as the means by which shared meaning and culture is made (Hall 1997), at the very heart of speciesism.

For philosopher Jacques Derrida, as well as for Brooks, disregard for nonhuman animals has its foundation in language, in the manner in which we conceive and then speak about "us" and "them." In a video interview (2008), Derrida declared a dislike for talking of "animals in general" because "when one says 'animals' one has already started not to understand anything and has started to enclose the animal into a cage." Pointing to the irreducible specificity of "radically different organisms of life," he adds: "To say 'animal'," thereby putting all living things that aren't human into one category, is "a very violent gesture" and a "stupid gesture," as well as "theoretically ridiculous." Derrida sees this oversimplification as the origin of the "very real violence that humans exercise toward animals that leads to slaughterhouses, their industrial treatment, their consumption." Wright (2013) presents us with this divide and its demands for ethical response in part by dealing with nonhuman animals in their specificity. Swans are literally everywhere. There are also owls, parrots, cats, rats, cows, sundry road kill, snakes, a monkey called Rigoletto, brolgas, and many more. On a grand scale, Wright confronts the "Anthropocene"—the proposed geological era marked by the dominion of human activity.

Wright was already working this territory back in *Carpentaria*. In a chapter titled "Norm's Responsibility" she recounts a scene in which a groper has been winched out of the water onto the beach by a four-wheel drive. The groper dies a slow, agonizing death as "white fishermen from the mine" (2006: 249) hack the flesh off its live body blow by blow. This rendering of what the neoliberal, corporatized Anthropocene and its henchmen do to animals turns out to have been something of a precursor for the near future Wright leads us into in *The Swan Book*.

In tackling both the singularity of being as well as its comprehensive sweep in terms of trauma, Wright challenges what Hill Collins (1998) describes as the tendency to analyze "one or more hierarchies as being socially constructed while continuing to see others as naturalized" (67). Exposing the inner workings of saturated capitalism for women and girls, Indigenous peoples, nonhuman animals, and the environment, *The Swan Book* poignantly portrays the industrialized corporate dominance of the Anthropocene as callously traumatizing:

> This was the place where the mind of the nation practiced warfare and fought nightly for supremacy, by exercising its power over another people's land—the night-world of the multi-nationals, the money-makers

> and players of big business, the asserters of sovereignty, who governed the strip called *Desperado*: men with hands glued to the wheel charging through the dust in howling road trains packed with brown cattle with terrified eyes, mobile warehouses, fuel tankers, heavy haulage steel and chrome arsenals named *Bulk Haul, Outback, Down Under, Century, The Isa, The Curry, Tanami Lassie*, metal workhorses for carrying a mountain of mining equipment and the country's ore [italics in original]. (2013: 165)

The "brown cattle with terrified eyes" enduring crowded road trains are destined to become "meat," the production of which takes place out of sight and out mind for the vast majority of people. The naturalization of human uses and abuses of nonhuman animals facilitates industry secrecy as to the processes that turn them from sentient beings, with their own affective and relational capacities and ties, into a product for human consumption. As well, the willing collective ignorance of human individuals and communities ensures endemic cruelty and killing of animals on a scale that dwarfs, in terms of sheer numbers, the highest toll of human genocides and persecutions on historic record. Yet denial of the glaring ethical concerns around the mass production and consumption of meat remains firmly entrenched despite eyewitness video and audio evidence obtained by activists confirming the pain and suffering of nonhuman animals in factory farms.

Considerations around trauma and its transmissions are therefore highly relevant to the experiences of nonhuman animals and their relations with human beings. Addressing such considerations comprehensively exceeds the scope of this book, but there is already sufficient evidence that trauma transmission is applicable to nonhuman animals. Between the 1950s and 1970s a series of notorious, torturous, and misguided experiments were conducted by researchers from the Department of Psychology Primate Laboratory and Regional Primate Research Center at the University of Wisconsin (Hansen, Harlow and Sealy 1962, Harlow, Dodsworth, and Harlow 1965, Harlow and Suomi 1971). What is perhaps most tragic about these experiments is the fact that the researchers were essentially attempting to understand the effects of familial trauma and propagation of social problems, a phenomenon they could have studied in human families and society (albeit radically different methodologies would have had to be developed). The results of these studies confirm what common sense dictates: that primates are not only capable of being severely traumatized, but that the effects of traumatization are transgenerational. Though research conducted on animals does not usually use the term "trauma" (the more oft-used word is "stress"), they repeatedly show what can only be described as traumatic symptomology in animals. Monkeys traumatized as infants exhibit abusive behaviors when they become mothers. Traumatic adaptions and symptoms are evident when mothers and infants are forcibly separated and forced into isolation. Isolated infants grew up to display sexual dysfunction, to be "highly fearful," to act out "suicidal aggression," and to tend toward "aggressing against infants" when put into a social group (Harlow, Dodsworth, and Harlow 1965: 96). More recently, a 2014 article described the transgenerational effects of painful husbandry procedures in farm animals. Researchers conducted the experiment on sheep and concluded that there were "long-term and trans-generational effects" relating to pain responses (Clark et al. 2014). Those like myself, who cohabit with a nonhuman animal that had traumatic beginnings (having taken in a disturbed stray kitten, for example, or an animal previously tormented by humans or attacked by other animals), often daily observe for themselves a stubborn degree of posttraumatic symptomology, somewhat comparable to that in humans. Wright's momentary depiction of the "howling" road trains with their terrified-eyed cargo reminds us to ponder what philosopher Theodor Adorno might have meant when he said, "Philosophy exists in order to redeem what you see in the look of an animal" (Adorno and Horkheimer 2011: 71).

Though Wright's writing is most overtly powerful when propelled by the heat of anger as it homes in on the ignorance and damage of contemporary life, it is at its most sorrowful and poignant when it turns to the swans. The last chapters of *The Swan Book* focus on Oblivia's bid for freedom following the death of Bella Donna and Oblivia's abduction. Her escape and the swans' drought-stricken fight for survival are brought together in an interwoven affective relation. In a lyrical depiction of what Teja Brooks Pribac (2013) calls the "neural substrates for conscious and affective states humans share with other species" (83), Wright enacts a requiem for the shared attachments, needs, and grief between humans and nonhuman animals. In her own words, Oblivia and the swans are "caught in the winds of a ghost net dragged forward by the spirits of the country" (Wright 2013: 326). In the final passage of the novel, ahead of the epilogue, the swans meet their demise as the earth heats to an inhospitable degree:

> In hotter skies, their wings beat faster in desperation until finally, they become completely disoriented. They lose faith in their journey. They lose each other. The remaining swans fly in every direction in search of the last drying water holes. They stand on baked earth and hiss at the sky they cannot reach, then the time arrives when no more sound comes from their open beaks. The weak, feather-torn necks drop to the ground, and eventually, with wings spread they wait for the spirit flight. (327–28)

Maneesha Deckha (2008) argues for the urgency of a posthumanism that addresses institutionalized speciesism, racism, sexism, etc. as "the residue of imperial discourses; particularly social Darwinist views about the value of different cultures, races, and human beings" (250). This is not a claim that injustice and oppression began as late as the nineteenth century, but an attempt to explain how the stage was set for the saturation capitalism that prevails today. "As racial, cultural, and gendered others proved themselves more or less civilized under an imperial gaze," says Deckha, "they were seen as correspondingly more or less human" (252). Nonhuman individuals, considered the least human of all, are, therefore, the most vulnerable sentient beings in virtually every country and culture. Viewed as voiceless, and largely unrepresented in law, human mistreatment of nonhuman individuals is endemic.

Millions of nonhuman animals are held captive and perish in the mass production of meat and dairy foods alone, and that's just the tip of the (melting) iceberg. One would have to add the live export of animals, the use of animals in medical and scientific experimentation, racing, circuses, and other animal-centered entertainments, zoos, and breeding, to even begin to approach a thorough inventory of the many cultural uses and abuses. Unable to testify in language humankind can, or will, understand, their position on the lower rungs of the hierarchical ladder is thoroughly naturalized, with the most human-like (such as primates) ranking above the less human (crustaceans and ants). Meanwhile, politics and advocacy regarding gender, race, species, and the environment often remain divided and even at odds. Even those most negatively impacted by patriarchy, imperialism, and capitalism are not necessary sufficiently sympathetic or empathetic toward the plight of nonhuman animals to make life changes or advocate on their behalf. Kimberlé Crenshaw (1991), a prominent critical race theorist and founding intersectionality scholar, points out that subordinated groups often face problematic contradictions in responding to violence and oppressive conditions.

Ingrained speciesism has precluded serious consideration of nonhuman animals in relation to other injustices and traumas. This is likely due to a combination of the naturalization of speciesism and an uneasy sense that giving focus to nonhuman animals in this way would somehow negate or devalue human trauma and distress. Deckha suspects that the main objection to including nonhuman animals within a broader framework of social concerns is the "threat 'animal rights' and posthumanist pleas for deconstructing the animal/human boundary are seen to pose to still fragile human subjectivities [like, say, the Aboriginal subjectivities Wright characterizes]" (259). I sympathize with such concerns; but I view them as mistaken and bound in precisely the tiered thought and practice that produce those "fragile human subjectivities." As Deckha says so concisely: "A species hierarchy is always already racist and colonial" (259–60). Wright understands and demonstrates this in her fictional performance of a comeuppance doomsday, and it is this, even more than her passionately innovative use of language, that makes hers a pioneering testament.

If this plea for posthumanist potential at first appears to be built on the shaky foundation of utopianism, it, in fact, rests on a surprisingly pragmatic supposition. As Deckha concedes, an evaluation that renounces the animal/human boundary might seem impossibly radical, implying as it does legal and economic revolution. But, as she maintains, a thorough revision of the way we do culture may be indicated "irrespective of animal concerns such that what is required to realize justice for animals may not seem so extreme or starkly different in comparison" (263). *The Swan Book* confirms the need for such a revision. In her paradoxical and ethical task of speaking in human language on behalf of human and nonhuman individuals, Wright's work attempts to break the speciesist imperial trance. Pushing past our ingrained human-centric view leads to some tough questions, such as: How and to what extent does human usage harm and traumatize nonhuman animals? How significantly do our abusive relations with nonhuman animals become a source of human trauma? And how might the traumatic affect of humans and nonhumans feed back and forth in transmissive loops? As Brooks Pribac (2013) points out, speciesism involves a number of questionable assumptions, not the least of which is the privileging of the "arguably exclusively human" neocortex over affect and emotion conceived of in Western discourse as "something inferior to logic," a bias that has "to date kept the Cartesian divide alive" (69). This rift has governed psychiatry and psychology to the obvious disadvantage of nonhuman animals and the less obvious disadvantage of human life and community, consolidating a "conceptual divide between humans and other animals, a divide which is progressively losing theoretical and empirical ground" (69).

This divide is also progressively losing ground in literature. The potential for witness and testimony regarding nonhuman animals and the environment in the poetics of transgenerational trauma is intriguing. While many writers touch on this potential in passing (the evocative scene in Barker's trilogy, in which the young Billy Prior is traumatized by witnessing cattle driven to slaughter is but one example), but few devote themselves to witnessing to speciesism and the trauma of nonhuman animals to the degree Wright does. While I am unsure of Wright's political intention regarding speciesism and its surrounding activism, *The Swan Book* is a welcome example of what I have elsewhere referred to as "animal poetics" (Atkinson 2013: 114). Wright's novels reveal an exigent interspecies ethical crisis in which connections between disparate beings are rendered in a pointedly affective and creative way that highlights intersections of injustice and traumatic transmissions in such a way as to challenge them.

In Wright's fiction, nonhuman animals are, much like her Aboriginal characters: resilient, traumatized, broken, beautiful, funny, lost, and found. And again, much like her Aboriginal characters, they live in the long shadow of the privileged, prevailing white human, be it government, the owners of the means of production, or the "average Australian." In these pages, animals are remarkably drawn: unique yet bound together in their struggle for survival. They are central to Bella Donna's stories. As the old woman declares:

> I have become an expert on music made from old bones, and I saw it could be from swan bones, or bones of drowned people, or of drought-stricken cattle, imitating the scores of Mozart's fingers racing across the ivory. (Wright 2013: 46)

This poetic description demonstrates a writer encountering transgenerational transmissions beyond the human. Evoking the "bad weather" (21) of global warming and climate change, it depicts the havoc anthroparchy has wreaked, is wreaking, and will almost certainly continue to wreak, on nonhuman animals.

The intersections of suffering and survival between human and nonhuman animals in Wright's fiction are too numerous to cover exhaustively, though some connections between women and nonhuman animals and Indigenous people and nonhuman animals can be readily identified. Nonhuman animals are beloved, mistreated, and slaughtered, knowing, spiritual, and prophetic by turns. *Carpentaria* (Wright 2006) features a white seer cockatoo called Pirate who lives with Norm Phantom and is considered "more than holy" (103) by the Phantom clan. Nonhuman animals appear as predictably damning social commentators as evidenced in a description of a "large flock of resident cockatoos, thousands of them, flying over the town, screaming in a spectacular, uncoordinated chanting, *What are you doing youse bastards?*" [italics in original] (104). They can also become humorously human in surprising yet meaningful ways, such as when Pirate

> screamed repeatedly at the sleeping white dog Dallas, who unlike the Jimmy Dale Gilmore country and western song he was named after, had never been to Dallas on a DC9 at night. The dog was such a big fan of country and western music, it had no time to listen to Norm's stories, as it lay with its back on the dirt floor, piebald belly belly-up, showing its fleas. (104)

That the dog has a penchant for country and Western music is not insignificant; it is perhaps the genre of popular music most favored by Indigenous Australians. Nonhuman animals are even more ubiquitous in *The Swan Book* and they are represented in inimitable ways. As Patrick Condliffe has asserted in his reading and defense of the work of B. Wongar (later outed as Serbian immigrant Sreten Božić), the distinction between animals and humankind in Indigenous cultures is made very differently and less completely than in non-Indigenous cultures. "In terms of representation, symbolism, and totems," he writes, "the animal and the human are considered part of the same spiritual and creative order" (2013: 186). There are many examples of interspecies affective communications and transmissions, such as in the reference to the cuckoos and cockatoos hearing "every single thing and, it might be, their nervous flinching and tapping of beaks on wood were imitating insecurities in the hearts of the children" (Wright 2013: 51).

Condliffe proclaims that B. Wongar's "Kafkaesque narratives" challenge the "colonial language of racism by making corporeal and spiritual identity a liminal thing that shares, at least within the human mind, something of the same space as animality" (2013: 184). This might also be extended to Wright, although *The Swan Book* not only deals with a history of racism in which "taxonomies of descent" ascribe "differentiation between groups" between "those with voice and rights and those without" (Condliffe 2013: 189), but also tackles the history of imperialist anthroparchy as it plays out across a range of intersections. It is the sheer depth, breadth, and complexity of Wright's vision that led Gleeson-White to christen *The Swan Book* "the first truly planetary novel" (2013). This is because it not only addresses existing intersections of injustice and trauma in relation to gender, age, race, and nonhuman animals; it also encompasses the environment as a living entity. Wright seems to be alerting us that failing sufficient immediate action, the consequences of global warming and climate change are poised to be the ultimate insult of (corporatized, globally capitalized) patriarchal imperialism.

Postscript on intersectionality

If intersectionality is a useful framework in which to rethink traumatic affect and transmission, it is also a potentially tricky one. I am aware that in speaking to intersectionality in Wright's "Aboriginal realism" (Leane 2015), I am, as a white woman, treading precarious ground, and that despite the promise and productivity of taking an intersectionalist view there are possible objections. As I gestured toward at the start of the chapter, one crucial concern centers on the question of whether categories of the oppressed can be rightly subsumed into one great "other," and the subsequent risk of dilution. As Toril Moi warns, "Simply to equate woman with otherness deprives the feminist struggle of any kind of specificity. What is repressed is not otherness, but specific, historically constructed agents" (1988: 12). I have also already hinted at another hitch in the intersectional project: if all "others" were indeed unified they would be equally committed and united in advocacy across sites of injustice. Plainly, a given individual can identify in one oppressed category while actively participating in the oppression of another "other." An animal rights activist is not necessarily a feminist. A feminist may not have a commitment toward the liberation of animals. Being an Aboriginal is not a guarantee against perpetrating sexism or misogyny. Yet, as a female scholar engaged in cultural critique, the oppression of women, children, Indigenous peoples, nonhuman animals, and those disadvantaged by an increasingly industrialized, corporatized, and globalized economy, are all evident in my reading of Wright.

How then to frame this paradox? There is no avoiding a certain tension between two truths. Specific struggles warrant their own platform and primary representation by those affected, but it is also compelling and productive to examine the ways in which oppressions and injustices intersect, even if some compromise is inevitable in terms of pointed focus. There is also a danger of equating gender and race (or any other category of injustice with another). For example, reading Hélène Cixous on Africa and "darkness" (1981), it might be tempting to relate her metaphoric conception of "feminine space" to Aboriginality, but such a move is problematic to say the least. While Cixous might stake claims for the usefulness of evoking binary systems that structure gender in relation to those that inform imperialism in order to critique said structures, she has been much challenged on this point by feminists of color. For example, bell hooks states emphatically, "I am waiting for them [white scholars, feminist thinkers] to stop talking about the 'other,' to stop even describing how important it is to be able to speak about difference" (1990: 343). hooks goes on to outline the ways in which our speaking of the other conceals white privilege, declaring it "a mask, an oppressive talk hiding gaps, absences, that space where our words would be if we were speaking, if there was silence, if we were there" (343). The failure of "Western" feminism to appreciate and incorporate the different ways Aboriginal women view and organize themselves around women's issues is articulated by Jackie Huggins when she says that "black women" have been unimpressed by "white feminism" because it has failed to consider the specific needs of Aboriginal women. It is, she says, largely ignorant of the effects of colonialism, particularly in relation to the behavior of Aboriginal men in families, and she takes aim at its tendency toward elitism and inability to appreciate that many Aboriginal women view their primary struggle as being around race rather than gender (1998: 118).

Aileen Moreton-Robinson (1999) points to another weakness in Cixous's attempt to identify a binary structure using an equation of darkness (unconscious) with the feminine and lightness (selfhood) with the masculine. For Moreton-Robinson, such connections can only be made from a position of whiteness that is itself unconscious of whiteness as a specific race and culture; in other words, from a position that assumes that whiteness is itself consciousness and that inherently casts nonwhiteness out into the shadows of otherness. Objecting to what she perceives as the use of Indigenous people and other nonwhite peoples as mere objects, Moreton-Robinson charges white scholars with using Aboriginality as a means to an end in which their theories are developed by drawing on other white scholars. The result is that Indigenous academic work continues to be marginalized. This is a predisposition in which "different knowledges are not applied as tools for thinking about and theorising the human condition. The effect of such theorising is thus to recenter whiteness" (Moreton-Robinson 1999: 3–4). If the dissatisfactions voiced by hooks, Higgins, Moreton-Robinson, and others, have to a certain degree been addressed with some restitution made by white scholars and institutions over the past decade or so, it is safe to say there remains reason for serious concern and for caution.

For my part, I have endeavored to write about Australian transgenerational trauma in a manner that does not reduce Indigenous peoples to the objects of white scholarship. If I am guilty of continuing to draw theoretically on largely non-Indigenous scholars, I have also included Indigenous voices and views. I have given a great deal of focus to the work of Alexis Wright, a pioneering Aboriginal author and activist, to show the ways in which her fictional testimony reveals cultural and political operations of critical importance and urgency. And I have foregrounded Wright's own reflections in my explorations and meditative readings of her texts by drawing on essays and interviews in which she reflects on her work, process, and country. While the argument for viewing colonized people of color as occupying the same space of otherness that women occupy is not convincing, there is no escaping the fact that to be an Aborigine in Australia is to be marginalized and that to be a woman is to be socially constructed and conditioned in ways that involve marginalization in certain respects. I maintain intersectionality is a productive notion for conceiving of the ways in which these experiences cross over in Wright's testimony, and that there is a marked difference between the way I have employed it and the kind of metaphoric, structural, dualistic analysis Cixous performed.

Despite this awareness of these pitfalls, I align myself with Huggins when she says, "To say that [white people] writing about Aboriginal people is too hard is a great cop-out" (1998: 125). As Toni Morrison also notes, "To enforce its invisibility [the issue of race] through silence is to allow the black body a shadowless participation in the dominant cultural body" (1998: 926). This is precisely the point Craps and Buelens (2008) raised regarding the underrepresentation of postcolonialism and race in the works of the star theorists of the trauma turn. In short, I did not deem it adequate, ethical, or responsible to attempt to address the matter of transmissive and transgenerational cycles of traumatic affect in an Australian context without significant inclusion and discussion of Aboriginal experience. And though it was my intention to give due attention to the postcolonial transgenerational traumatic realities of many Indigenous people and communities in Australia, I have aimed to show Aboriginal marginality as more than a site of deprivation, to identify "the site of radical possibility, a space of resistance" (hooks 1990: 341) within Wright's work and within Australian society. I have no doubt that were Australia under the kind of governance that could satisfactorily, empathically, and compassionately facilitate healing of postcolonial transgenerational trauma, this nation would find much to learn from Indigenous Australian leadership and community.

Finally, I am aware too that my inclusion of nonhuman animals in the intersectional matrix in relation to transgenerational trauma will likely attract charges of anthropomorphism. The question of anthropomorphism is not so nearly compelling for me as is the systematic and profound suffering of myriad species at human hands. If I were to spend time engaging with this question it would be in the service of challenging its supremacy. As Brooks Pribac (2013) says, the stalwart belief in the concept of anthropomorphism is a convention that "favours an unwarranted, highly separatist view in regard to different others" that has, through its negative connotations and exposure over time, induced a knee-jerk fear of being associated with it. Even though as Brooks Pribac observes, "Occam's razor is still a first principle," the emergence of critical animal studies and human-animal studies means the dogma of anthropomorphism has come under scrutiny in contemporary Western academic discourse, drawing strong criticism for "engendering reductionist views" (76). I am allied with David Brooks (2013) when he insists that rather than being wary of the capacity for empathetic affect to inform our view of, and relations with, nonhuman animals, we should rather embrace it. We must, he says, "develop, articulate and amplify" the feelings we experience in engagement with the world. We must sensitize ourselves to it, experience and relate to it the only way we can, "which is to extend our senses into it, and guard ourselves against—consider most carefully—any voices which would have us turn our backs on it" (52). If I am culpable of charges of anthropomorphism it is my hope that mine is "an anthropomorphism that serves to remind us of anthropomorphism's inadequacies" (Finlay 2013: 75). When it comes to the "immense question of pathos" that Derrida summons (2002: 395), I stand with the "minority, weak, marginal voices, little assured of their discourse, of their right to discourse and of the enactment of their discourse within the law" (395) in advocating on behalf of nonhuman animals. I experience no shame regarding my vocal and affective championing of nonhuman animals, only in the perpetration and "organized disavowal" of their subjugation (395), for which my own species is wholly responsible.

The Swan Book suggests that the stories we tell ourselves, and each other, are implicated in the injustices we participate in, allow, and remain willfully blind to. Wright's work also suggests that the stories we tell ourselves and each other are central to rectifying and redeeming those injustices, and that we "need new stories for our new age, the Anthropocene" (Gleeson-White 2013).

The Swan Book has rightly been hailed as just such a story (of stories) and I hope to have done it justice in my deliberations.

Climate change: Planetary PTSD?

In 2014 I attended an environmental humanities conference where Professor Will Steffen charted a natural science history of climate change, demonstrating that the perilous turning point was the year 1950. The graphs showed a spectacular escalation: global warming rose dramatically in the mid-twentieth century and has continued its ascent ever since. When one of the respondents stated enthusiastically that time will prove the big story of the twentieth century to be not women's rights, or civil rights, but this anthropocentric impact on the earth's ecology, I wanted to interject and proclaim that at some fundamental level those stories *are not separate stories*, but rather major plot twists in a founding master narrative. Nor are they the only stories we are called to bear witness to. Hence, I once again summon the "spectre" (Derrida 1994) of intersectionality in adopting the term "anthroparchy," which Erica Calvo (2008) coined to describe the way in which the history of patriarchy meets and informs the anthropocentric age. Since my encounter with Steffen as a member of a conference audience, he has gone on to publish his findings in updated form (Steffen et al. 2015). In explication of the term "Anthropocene," Steffen et al. write that

> the Great Acceleration marks the phenomenal growth of the global socio-economic system, the human part of the Earth System. It is difficult to overestimate the scale and speed of change. In little over two generations—or a single lifetime—humanity (or until very recently a small fraction of it) has become a planetary-scale geological force. (93–94)

The authors go on to conclude that the question of whether or not acceleration will be slowed in time to avoid inhospitable and catastrophic ends will be answered by 2050 (94).

There is now almost universal acceptance (influential vocal denialists notwithstanding), based on the recorded statements of many scientists, governments, and the United Nations, of the existence of "man-made" global warming or climate change. In this section, I speculate around climate change, trauma, intersectionality, and cyclical haunting, beginning with acknowledgment of the fact that global warming is now unequivocally linked to natural disasters negatively impacting communities. This is scientifically suggested in some cases and apparent in the public consciousness in others. What is evident is that climate change is increasingly cited as a potential security problem and source of unrest (Barnett and Adger 2007). The role of speciesism in environmental destruction and the suffering of nonhuman animals in relation to climate change is a concern that emerges hand in hand with questions around the fate of human societies should acceleration continue on the trajectory established in the mid-twentieth century. Likewise, the postapocalyptic suffering of humans, nonhuman animals, and the environment itself appears unavoidably interconnected in Wright's fiction, as it surely will be in lived reality should such unthinkable outcomes eventuate.

The Swan Book (2013) quite literally takes up where *Carpentaria* (Wright 2006) left off. At the end of *Carpentaria*, extreme weather has wiped out the town of Desperence. When Will Phantom, son of the main protagonist Norm, returns home post cyclone, he is humbled by the power of the earth to undo the vast works of imperialism and capitalism:

> It was at this point he realised how history could be obliterated when the Gods move the country. He saw history rolled, reshaped, undone and mauled as the great creators of the natural world engineered the bounty of everything man had ever done in this part of the world into something more of their own making. (492)

When Wright returns with *The Swan Book*, this extreme weather has become full-blown climate change, which has already destroyed the Northern Hemisphere and is working on what remains. Wright cites the character of Bella Donna as both symbolic of the good that struggles to survive the brutality of twenty-first-century life and as a cautionary figure warning us against this outcome:

> Where's the sense of decency in all this? We are capable of being good; if you look at the poetry of the world just in terms of the swan you see all

> these beautiful thoughts and sentiments that come from people all over the world. What we're doing here is so wrong and mean and nasty; Bella Donna is a representation of the heritage, the world where a lot of the decision makers come from and it's saying, "this can happen to you." (The Wheeler Center 2013)

Bella Donna, as prophet, presages that there will be a price to pay, finally, for the sped-up escalation and globalization of cyclical haunting that has occurred over the past few hundred years, and not just the price that has always been paid by those with less power, status, and capital, as I addressed in the last section. This price, she tells us, will be paid by all, some more than others, but no one will escape its dreadful toll.

The Swan Book is set in just such a world, a world in which "brain-damaged, toxic-fume-sniffing addicted kids" (Wright 2013: 31) rule the swamp surrounded by the Army sent to "intervene and control the will, mind and soul of the Aboriginal people" (47). This is Oblivia and Bella Donna's Australia. Like everyone, they make do in a country-turned-dangerous-dust-bowl, alternatingly prone to flooding cyclonic downpourings. It is an ominous landscape of litter, pollution, degradation, and extremes in which all sentient beings struggle and hurt:

> Wild dogs lay in over-crowded burrows in the soil; and in the grasses, up in the rooftops, in the forests of dead trees, all the fine and fancy birds that had once lived in stories of marsh country, migrating swallows and plains-dancing brolgas, were busy shelving the passing years into a lacy webbed labyrinth of mud-caked stickling nests brimmed by knick-knacks, and waves of flimsy old plastic threads dancing the wind's crazy dance with their faded partners of silvery-white lolly cellophane, that crowded the shores of the overused swamp. (Wright 2013: 18)

Wright's swamp life is a creative rendering of what Berry, Bowen, and Kjellstrom (2010) discuss as the limits of human capacity to adapt to the extremes of climate change. Citing a range of studies establishing the link between human PTSD and acute disasters such as major floods, fires, cyclones, earthquakes, and heat waves, they note there is little research on the long-term effects of these events. In other words, we have no way of knowing as yet what the transgenerational impact of climate change may be. Wright offers some intimation. In recounting Bella Donna's reaction to questions about what annihilated her North American homeland, sending her south to Australia, the narrator explains that the swamp people seek to understand what "devil, not a person, but a freak of nature, went to war on her people" (2013: 25). In response, Bella Donna:

> Looked startled, as though she had been asked to describe the inexplicable, of what happened to people affected by the climate changing in wild weather storms, or the culmination of years of droughts, high temperature and winds in some countries, or in others, the freezing depths of prolonged winters. (25)

Barnett and Adger (2007) seem to support Wright's foretelling of ensuing climate change wars. "In certain circumstances," they state, "these direct and indirect impacts of climate change on human security and the state may in turn increase the risk of violent conflict" (651). Studies suggest intensifying occurrences and severity of adverse weather events are set to affect us in several ways, including the known PTSD outcomes of acute disasters. In addition, a rise of injury and physical and mental health problems are predicted. The threat to ecological and social environments on which people depend for livelihoods and well-being is noted, as is the possible unreliable availability of natural resources such as drinking water and hygiene measures that prevent vector-borne disease (Berry, Bowen, and Kjellstrom 2010).

These are the miseries that plague the futuristic landscape of *The Swan Book*, in which sentient beings either die or survive severely traumatized. As Barnett and Adger state, "There is every reason to worry" about the impact of climate change "given that the rate of change is unprecedented in the past 10,000 years, and that climatic variations have triggered large-scale social disruptions in the past" (2007: 640). Unsurprisingly, these ill effects are expected to fall disproportionally on those most vulnerable: Indigenous people, those living in developing countries, and nonhuman animals. Wright bears out the researchers' apprehension about the Indigenous populations being among those most vulnerable: everyone in *The Swan Book* feels the effects of a planet irreversibly altered by climate change, but few feel it more than those living in the swamp.

As a hypothetical exercise, I want to consider the persistence and near global domination of patriarchal and imperialistic culture in terms of traumatic acting out and cyclical haunting. There is a clear question driving my desire to tease this out. History has shown that governments and the owners of the means of production are more than willing to allow devastating consequences to befall those under their domain. But what can possibly be driving the continued commitment to zealous, unchecked corporatized capitalism now that the evidence is stacking up that it is simply unsustainable, both financially and environmentally? What kind of operation permits a denial that can be upheld in the face of scientifically proven dire risk to human civilization? Observation of the behavioral characteristics of the appointed and clandestine (read corporate) political leaders indicates a range of attributes commonly associated with addiction: denial, minimization, rationalization, justification, obsession, and compulsion (in the form of monetary greed, political power, prestige, etc.). I suggest that these are the cognitive-affective dysfunctions at play in political, economic, and commercial assemblages that enable and fuel engagement in the unethical environmental destruction perpetrated by multinationals and big agribusiness, and facilitated by many governments around the world.

This possibility hints at another aspect and potential of cyclical haunting, which Wright obliquely envisions in *The Swan Book*. In this formulation, the acting out of traumatized *and* privileged individuals within corporatized and globalized assemblages generates climate change, which in turn generates further trauma by way of catastrophic weather events that have a devastating impact on individuals, families, communities, and nations. As discussed in Chapter 4, this familial and communal trauma inevitably feeds back into collective acting out in the form of violent conflict and Historical trauma. If I have been arguing in part that social and often intersected disadvantage makes a body (individual or collective) more vulnerable to trauma and its transmissions, what does it mean to attribute trauma to the perpetrators of injustice, to those who benefit most from conditions as they are and as they have historically been? It means that if we "describe as 'traumatic' any excitations from outside which are powerful enough to break through the protective shield" of the psyche (Freud 1991: 301), present privilege is not a protection against trauma or traumatic legacy, especially if one takes the long view of trauma as a significant aspect of the foundation and history of culture, as do Freud and Caruth. What privilege, power, and capital do mean is that the person who possesses these advantages is positioned to, through their individual and assemblaged acting out, be high-level and high-impact transmitters of traumatic affect. Such transmissions are, as I have argued, operational in interpersonal realms and assemblages like the family, community, or business by way of circulations of affect, as produced and spread through discourse. Foucault outlined discourse as that which constructs and promotes knowledge and practices in relation to a given topic, theorizing that it is represented and organized institutionally and materially as well as linguistically and textually (2006). Politically, structurally, and financially empowered and assemblaged transmitters can in addition send trauma down the line by institutionalized discursive means: through legislation, public policy, law enforcement, and public health programs (or the lack/inadequacy of them).

Ascribing traumatic acting out to bodies of privilege does not amount to a defense. Nor does it excuse acting out behavior that has overwhelming or potentially life-threatening consequences for others (including nonhuman individuals). It is not my intention to absolve responsibility with this speculative contemplation, or to explain all human character and endeavor as essentially traumatic, the latter being something of an occupational hazard for those working conceptually with trauma. Returning to Spinoza, who I consulted in Chapter 2, I propose that the more power a body has—individual or collective—the greater the attendant ethical responsibility to address traumatic symptomology and reduce acting out. Spinoza refers to "man's lack of power to moderate and restrain the affects" as "bondage" (1996: 113). Remember that Spinoza does not define power as the kind of power I have been discussing in relation to high-impact transmissions. Power for Spinoza is not a power over, domination, or status, but an expansion of beingness that is not necessarily associated with financial or political privilege. Rather, it is the outcome of healthy affective-cognitive functioning. In Spinoza's view, a lack of such power means the failure to live "according to the guidance of reason" (135)—reason being the result of a process of conscious affect, perception, discernment, and understanding that I have elsewhere referred to as "introjection." Spinoza's treatise on ethics also emphatically holds that, conversely, one who lives according to the guidance of reason (which he sees as an affective and bodily process as well as a cognition one) cannot fail to advocate for the greater good. Where a lack of internal power and reason (in Spinoza's terms) manifests as narcissism and is coupled with external influence and political, social, and financial control, we end up with a Napoleon, a Saddam Hussein, a Donald Trump. We might think here in terms of a *privileged bondage*. This describes a privileged subject or assemblage that ensnares less privileged others into a societal bondage reflective of the motivating affective bondage. In this way, power—of the kind of the common understanding to do with domination and entitlement—is shored up as a substitute for power in the Spinozan sense of the word.

Here, I pause to ponder the denied affect that blocks the process of understanding and reason. Though this is doubtless a matter of some enormity not possible to address in these few sentences, I want to gesture toward an area of research that deserves closer attention. Elspeth Probyn (2014) has suggested that shame might be ethically productive in regard to the human impact on the Anthropocene, animals, and the environment. This echoes an idea put forth by pop psychologists like John Bradshaw (1988), who configures two types of shame: "toxic" shame, which is overwhelming, unproductive traumatic shame, and "healthy" shame, which he casts as the essential capacity to experience the limits of subjective engagement and power (in the non-Spinozan definition). The question of shame and the Anthropocene is an interesting one. Unethical behavior on the scale of the Anthropocene is not just guilt producing, it is shameful, and at the same time it is shameless. This is because our damaging dominance is about more than just what we humans do; it goes to the heart of who we are in the world in relation to the earth and nonhuman animals. In refusing their own introjectory process and taking refuge in privilege, wealth, and power plays, those at the top tier of privileged bondage enact the intersected injustices Wright is witness to. "Trauma the infection," writes the Australian poet Robert Adamson, in concluding his wonderful poem about trauma, "carried on the breath of the man who repeats his orders: 'At ease. Attention. Pull yourself together'" (2015: 52).

I wonder, too, if awe (or the lack of it), as an aspect of love and the expansion of beingness Spinoza configures as power, might not also prove a productive line of enquiry. This may be especially pertinent in relation to human relationships to nonhuman animals and nature. Teresa Brennan states that love is not a simple affect, and cannot be conceived of or discussed in the same way as can an affect such as anger or fear. Love is "different in that it directs positive feelings toward the other by attending to the specificity of the other (rather than seeing her or him through idealizing or demonizing projections)" (2004: 32). Love can also, presumably, direct positive feelings toward, and attend to the specificity of, the self, rather than seeing oneself through idealizing or demonizing projections. Love, then, as the impetus of introjection, is not just, or even, a feeling or state, but that instinct or practice that frees unconscious material and repressed libido. As such love can be denied, dampened, and refused or encouraged, encountered, or embraced. Introjection is desirable and healthful. It is the work that psychotherapy facilitates, but living itself, and all relationship, art, language, and literature also aids (or hinders) it. At the upper echelons of privileged bondage, love and introjection are substituted with wealth and dominion.

Returning to my thoughts on traumatic acting out, it may be that repetition compulsion could, at least in some measure, underpin the often sadistic, and at this point potentially suicidal, impulses evident in the persistence and growth of the relentless and ruthless saturation capitalism agenda. In his provisional theory of a death drive, Freud (2011) posited that conservative, organic instincts leaning toward the restoration of an earlier state—the "inertia inherent in all organic life" (308)—are, by virtue of their obligatory relation with life instincts, destined to present with a "deceptive appearance of being forces tending towards change and progress, whilst in fact they are merely seeking to reach an ancient goal by paths alike old and new" (310). In his tentative conclusion, Freud later states that any hypothesis of death instincts must necessarily be bound up at the source with life instincts and that such an admission leaves us with "an equation with two unknown quantities" (30–331).

It may be these "unknown quantities" of life and death instincts are highly variable in individuals and communities, and that their ratio, their "will to power" in Nietzsche's terms (1968), may fluctuate depending on numerous possible factors. These may include the development and/or governance of the neocortex over the "reptilian brain" (which is influenced by trauma, among other things) and the degree of successful introjection or lack thereof. If such a scenario held true, politically, financially, and socially powerful and privileged bodies, under the influence of trauma and death instincts (often masquerading as productive and life enhancing), may be manifesting destructive acting out of projections and compulsions leading to mass and Historic cultural transmissions.

I do not mean to infer by this conjecture that it is only powerful and privileged bodies that participate in cyclical haunting or that ethical obligation is theirs alone. Participation in unethical operations is unavoidable at this point of Western civilization unless one chooses to live off the grid, cut off from mainstream society. But the degree to which we participate, can, and crucially must, be reduced. There is pressing need to explore the traumatic consequences of human-induced climate change as well as the possible traumatic contributing factors. I am not sufficiently versed in the natural sciences to speculate as to whether the earth might be thought of as having its own affective system, of which the weather and other operations of ecology are figuratively comparable to the sentient psyche. Even so, it may not be too far-fetched to suggest that the earth could be experiencing something similar to the subjective shock and disturbance that occurs in the experience of trauma of sentient life forms, a kind of PTSD if you will. If this seems too conceptually problematic to state as an outright claim it at least orients us to the kind of thinking outside the box that consideration of trauma beyond the human entails.

I am aware that the ways in which I have described circulations of traumatic affect as informing the multilayered rampant consumerism of contemporary saturation capitalism will strike some as eccentric. But the time is upon us to ask, and attempt to answer the question: What else but some form of trauma-induced addictive collective acting out explains the high-risk, high-casualty present-day practices of humanity? As Caruth (1996) says, in a "catastrophic age," a thorough comprehension of trauma could facilitate a bond between cultures, a bond based not on simple knowledge of the pasts of others, but on respective lessons learned from the "traumas of contemporary history" and on a mutual "ability to listen through the departures we have all taken from ourselves" (11).

It may seem as if I have drifted from consideration of the transgenerational in this chapter, but intersected experiences and histories are inherently intertransgenerational. Transgenerational transmissions of all kinds—affective, attitudinal, linguistic, and lived practices—are extant in all I have sought to address. To the degree that intergenerational lineages are marked by intersected injustices and losses, so too testimony to, and introjection of, traumatic transmissions is necessary. Duras's testimony centers on gender, race, and age; Bechdel focuses on gender, age, and homosexuality; Cixous explores gender, age, and the specter of anti-Semitism; Barker deals with gender, nationality, and war; and Wright speaks to gender, race, age, speciesism, and the environment. Wright is a visionary in confronting networks of injustice and oppression in the mode of literary testimony. Her work shows us that far from being "dead," new forms of the novel are kicking with life in response to the deathliness of pervasive trauma and suffering as a result of neoliberalism, neocolonialism, and capitalism. Exhibiting the qualities admired by Le Guin, Wright deftly calls attention to the soon irreparable damage being done to sentient life, the earth, oceans, and climes, reminding us of our own liability and susceptibility.

Experimental and poetic work of this kind helps reconnect us to subjectively and collectively suppressed affect. As Spinoza (1996) argued in *Ethics* over three centuries ago, affect is indispensable to reasoning and ethical action. Literary encounters with affect unsettle the entrenched and historical denials patriarchal imperialism and saturation capitalism depend on. In this way, its misogyny, racism, speciesism, and other discriminations are confronted and destabilized. Such literature—working as a social and political force—may not single-handedly change the world, or indeed change anything at all directly or externally. But this writing and reading does constitute an opportunity to listen through the most costly "departures we have all taken from ourselves." And what we hear is a desperate plea to transform the anthroparchy before it's too late.

Conclusion: Becoming Trans-formed

> *Fortinbras: "Now that your shame is understood, kind ghost, and everyone knows your secret, you may take your rightful place in the company of good men."*
>
> —Nicolas Abraham, from "The Phantom of Hamlet or The Sixth Act: Preceded by the Intermission of 'Truth'," *The Shell and the Kernel: Renewals of Psychoanalysis* (1994: 202)

This has been a book concerned with bodies and with the ways energy bound to trauma passes through, and between, them. These are physical, material bodies: human, nonhuman, environmental, textual, communal, institutional, and national, and they are psychic, encompassing the enigmatic realm where mind and body work as one. In my exploration of the operations of transgenerationally transmitted trauma as it manifests in lived experience and literary testimony, I have made claims as to the political potency of the writing practice I call the poetics of transgenerational trauma. Positioning this writing at the nexus of trauma and affect theories, I outlined a range of features via a selection of diverse literary works. I defined its strange-bodied feminism in relation to conceptions of feminine writing. I proposed the affect-ethic of this literary testimony, distinguishing it from more conventional trauma accounts on the basis of its cultural critique and introjectory potential, and I discussed its illumination of spectral operations that challenge Western notions of family and time, exposing traumatic feedback loops between familial and social/Historic assemblage in cyclical haunting. And I looked at intersected injustices as sites of trauma, considering some of the ways in which cyclical haunting exceeds the human in its effects/affects in regards to nonhuman animals and the environment. Yet, even nearing the end, I am struck by the still shimmering possibilities and beckoning nuances. There remain connections to highlight and new conceptual junctures to note.

In writing this book, I have been mindful of the problematic nature of hyperbolic claims as to the work literary testimony can do in light of trauma, and I have addressed this in various ways throughout, aiming to push against misguided notions of writing as a cure-all while presenting assertive claims as to the political nature and social importance of the poetics of transgenerational trauma. I realize I walk a fine line at times, but arguing for this writing and testimony as a political act is different from arguing for miraculous or unrealistic capacities. Therefore, it is not my intention to romanticize the potentials of this literary testimony, but to show how they might help us understand complex cultural operations regarding trauma, affect, and transmission.

I have done my best to navigate through the enormity and complexity of what is raised by summoning forth an interdisciplinary enquiry on this scale, and I hope this book serves as a multilayered and multifaceted work that substantially pulls through the questions it raises and the territory it maps. In a final contemplation, I want to reiterate, and expand upon, my claim that the poetics of transgenerational trauma is an innately feminist practice. I also want to give further focus to ethical issues in terms of introjection, integrity, and a generosity toward the unknown, the different, the traumatic.

In Chapter 1 I presented the poetics of transgenerational trauma as a complication of écriture féminine, a departure associated not with "woman" per se, but with the strange body, one with specific qualities and preoccupations (chiefly transgenerational trauma transmissions and testimony). It follows that its ethical properties, as I outlined in Chapter 2, are inherently affective-feminist in that this writing ruptures the conventional tendency to privilege externally coded logic over affect as a source of reasoning, and scientific or factual evidence over somatic and experiential knowing. In doing so, this kind of testimony unsettles the status quo of a collective denial around transmission of trauma in heightened association with that realm traditionally cast as feminine—namely affect—which has been customarily repressed and undervalued by Western societies on the one hand and unconsciously acted out of in micro to macro assemblages of bondage on the other. Testifying to both denied trauma and to the repression, undervaluing, and assemblaged acting out of traumatic affect, the texts I have surveyed enact a feminist intervention, without necessarily any recourse to explicit feminist statements, allegiance, or content.

There are linkages too between this strange-bodied writing and the theories of hauntology examined in Chapters 3 and 4. For example, Abraham and Torok's conception of the phantom marks the site of transgenerational transmission, and the manner in which the shame-bound traumas of one generation are carried by an unwitting subsequent generation, while Derrida's specter does "not belong to the order of knowledge" (Davis 2005: 373). These socio-psychic spaces are distinctively encountered through the strange-bodied writing showcased in this book, which hovers between presence and absence, unnamable and unknowable in the (phallocentric) order of knowledge. This unique witnessing and testimony enables introjection of more than subjective trauma, introjection being that life-affirming process in which all experience is endured, adapted to, worked through, and transformed through openness, awareness, and expression. As the works I have surveyed show, there is urgent need for increased introjection of carried and cyclically haunted trauma across most societies in our increasingly globalized and technologized age. While I do not claim this testimony can achieve the levels and scale of introjection that would facilitate positive social change and increased communal well-being necessary for a more harmonious future (or, perhaps, a long-view future at all), I do maintain that literature and art have a crucial role to play. I stand with Ursula K. Le Guin when she says that in the hard times that are coming we will need writers who "can see through our fear-stricken society" as "realists of a larger reality" (2014). I believe, as she does, that resistance and change often begin in the art of words, even if those beginnings are little more than an imperceptible shift of a shadowed perception toward the light of understanding.

The Rubik's cube of transmitted and trauma-bound shame, grief, and fear that the writer of transgenerational trauma writes out of in productive tension with love, charts a textually subterranean course that passes through liminal secrecy in the subjectively split and shame-bound traumatic sense of the word. And crucially, this secret does not have to be revealed factually or actually for introjection to be facilitated. As I have stated, it may instead be revealed imaginatively, metaphorically, and affectively, as unconscious knowledge and as unlying, in a relational process in which the intimate exchange between writer, reader, and broader society is intrinsic. In my conception, familial transmission is the fulcrum of transgenerational trauma, the site of an intergenerational record yet to be made (Felman and Laub 1992: 57). A writer who taps into cyclically haunted currents of traumatic affect morphs into a strange-bodied space from which a record may be made in literature using experimental techniques, multilayered narrative and/or a poetic generation of language, graphic elements, or some other multimedia modality. Such works are undertaken as an ethical response to the transgenerational transmission of trauma and cyclical haunting.

With these closing thoughts I want to expand the how and why of this writing in relation to the tacit suggestion throughout this book that trauma is not a static or entirely negative experience. The idea that along with wreaking havoc and causing distress, trauma comes with decidedly positive aspects and creative potentials is implicit in my argument—assuming trauma is sufficiently survived (physically and fundamentally psychically). Even when it is not survived, these positive and creative potentials exist for surviving others. In this expansion, I link Abraham and Torok's concept of introjection to the Deleuzian notion of "becoming," which is obliquely related to Deleuze's thinking elsewhere on the autonomy of affect. Deleuze and Guattari's writing on becoming (1988: 232–309) offers a compelling framework for considering how trauma shapes subjectivity in creative as well as destructive ways, including through writing. Though their thinking on becoming focuses on the human in relation to nonhuman animals (itself as an interesting challenge to speciesism), their conception of becoming also extends in other directions. I begin my consideration of the notion of becoming transformed by transgenerational trauma and its testimony by highlighting what becoming is not. Deleuze and Guattari do not understand becoming as aligned with resemblance, imitation, or identification (237). Nor do they view it as a linear movement in which change progresses or regresses logically. They are adamant that though becoming is not fantasy, neither is it literal (238). They favor the term "involution" over "evolution" in regard to becoming (238) because becoming is an internal operation that does not lead to *being*—it is itself leading only to more (or less) becoming. Becoming does not so much describe the shift from one state to another as a permanent flux in which states are less static than they seem. In other words, becoming hints at an affective, transmissive process. While for Freud involution describes a regressive movement in the direction of the inorganic (as an expression of the death drive), in Deleuze and Guattari's figuring it does not represent a movement of regression; quite the opposite, for Deleuze and Guattari describe a creative process (238). They speak too of becoming as "components of deterritorialization passing from one assemblage to another" (306) and the idea of becoming memory. Just as Derrida's hauntology challenges the reassuring order of presents, Deleuze and Guattari's concept of becoming challenges notions of fixed subjectivity, identity, and individual psychic-affective containment.

Nicholas Rand unwittingly hints at a nexus between Deleuze and Guattari's becoming, Derrida's hauntology, Abraham and Torok's introjection, and Brennan's living attention and discernment when he writes that Abraham and Torok's work shifts the focus of psychoanalysis from the Freudian Oedipal complex "toward the work of introjection or psychic opening and expansion, accomplished at any age and in the face of every sort of new experience" (Rand 1994: 10). This is perhaps a paradoxical proposition given that Deleuze and Guattari explicitly reject the psychoanalytic tradition that Abraham and Torok seek to advance in the belief that therapy intensifies introjection. This is one reason why Deleuze and Guattari's becoming cannot be likened to introjection as such. Rather than indicating semblance between these conceptions, this node of theoretical thought highlights a certain resonance between becoming, introjection, living attention, and discernment that suggests the possibility of mergings and overlappings. It is important to remember that Abraham and Torok's casting of introjection encompasses much more than the release of repressed affect or desire (Rand 1994: 8). It describes nothing less than productive subjective engagement with all experience. There are other differences between these theorists and theories. In challenging the Freudian obsession with notions of structural, sexualized, preconditioned, universal, and ahistorical formative traumas Abraham and Torok go some way in adapting traditional psychoanalysis to embrace both the effects/affects of history with a small "h" and History with a big "H" by focusing on the specifics of individual experiences, families, and contexts. While they do view introjectory processes as primarily taking place outside of the therapist's office they heartily promote the usefulness of analysis. Conversely, Deleuze and Guattari articulated critical and uncompromising views about psychotherapy.

Yet, each of these partnerships focuses directly on the introjectory and becoming propensities of literature. Abraham and Torok preshadow their focus on literary testimony in a beautiful quote in which they evoke a "divine right" in the work of being born unto oneself that "comes into being only if one asserts one's value, only if one succeeds in being acknowledged. Recognized, acknowledged by oneself to oneself before the whole universe" (Abraham and Torok 1994: 139). It may be that for some writers their readers represent the "whole universe" before which they are born unto themselves. Abraham and Torok's more pointed interest in literature is described by Rand as an appreciation of its capacity to deepen therapeutic understanding through the creative depiction of situations and experiences that lead to introjection (Rand 1994: 11). As I discussed in Chapter 2, the practitioner of the poetics of transgenerational trauma writes with creative, introjectory passion. Theirs is not the victim narrative, the straightforward sob story, the accusatory rant, or the sanctimonious declaration of survival. Theirs is a poetics driven and informed by a productive witnessing-testifying-introjecting drive.

Abraham and Torok speak of the phantom having been "unspeakable in words" in a previous generation. They state that reducing the impact of the phantom in the presenting generation involves reducing the "sin attached to someone else's secret." To wrestle this language away from its religious connotations, and to connect it more directly to the poetics of transgenerational trauma, I clarify "sin" as referring to shame. Voicing the secret involves expression that is able to deflect, defy, circumvent or placate our own and the phantom's resistance and denial in service to a "higher degree of 'truth'" (189). This is a dilemma I addressed in Chapter 3 and, though I affirm this statement, I cast my hypothesis of transgenerational testimony with a Derridian deconstructive inflection that tempers its emphasis and its insinuation of traumas as problems to be solved and as necessarily knowable in the conventional or cognitive senses of the word. The poetics of transgenerational trauma is unique in its capacity to reduce the "sin" (shame, suffering) attached to someone else's secret and in its ability to "defy" (write) and "circumvent" (introject) spectral trauma and one's own H/historic traumas, resistances, and refusals in service to a "higher degree of truth" (unlying a la Cixous).

Deleuze and Guattari also speak to something akin to Abraham and Torok's secret and Derrida's specter in ways that are compatible with my treatment, though typically, they do not locate it in the therapeutic context, nor do they advocate the therapeutic remedy. Their depiction of this idea sounds strikingly like a poetically rendered description of Abraham and Torok's phantom when they speak of a secret as content "too big for its form," or as content whose form has been replaced by a "simple container, envelope, or box whose role it is to suppress formal relations" (1988: 286). They elaborate with dramatic, metaphoric imagery: "Something must ooze from the box, something will be perceived through the box or in the half-opened box. *The secret was invented by society. . . . Every secret is a collective assemblage*" (287) [my emphasis]. These passages call to mind the charge and looping subjective-familial-cultural currents of circulating traumatic affect I have associated with the poetics of transgenerational trauma.

Deleuze and Guattari elsewhere evoke Cixous and Kristeva in their conception of "major" and "minor" literatures, which they describe as two different functions or practices of language (1988: 104). The practice of minor literature involves becoming, becoming other (man, woman, rat, etc.), becoming memory (as opposed to simply remembering a memory in readily accessible consciousness and language), a transformative process that makes "language stammer" and stretch in such a way as to draw out its wail, shout, and cry, in other words: affect, intensity. This has obvious resonances with écriture féminine and semiotic, revolutionary writing, but it most closely describes the queerness of the strange body. This minor literature Deleuze and Guattari conceive of is written by "only greats" and by "bastards" (interesting to consider this in relation to the semiotic rich writer as rejecting the Lacanian Name of the Father, or unlegitimized by patriarchal discourse in Butler's terms). "Minor" writers, in Deleuze and Guattari's meaning of the word, are bilingual and multilingual in their own language. They enact a writing practice that involves the "subtraction and variation" of the major as that which is the constant and the standard (105). This evokes the various experiments of the works in this book.

But despite the resonances there are clear differences. For Deleuze and Guattari, the question is less about whether one speaks as, or out of, one gender or another, and more about "the body they *steal* from us in order to fabricate opposable organisms" [italics in original] (276); any argument or practice that overtly and literally privileges one-sexed writing over another downplays this historical theft and the potential of becoming. In Chapter 1 I argued that despite appearances, Cixous does not fundamentally mean to do this in her conception of écriture féminine and for Kristeva revolutionary writing is a space and process that upsets this fabrication of opposable organisms. I also distanced myself from both écriture féminine and Kristeva's semiotic by positing the strange body via Butler's critique as the locus of the writing I have examined. In their work on becoming, Deleuze and Guattari cite writers and writing even more plainly than do Abraham and Torok. Echoing aspects of Derrida's hauntology—bringing to mind texts such as Kafka's *The Metamorphosis* (2001) and Spiegelman's *Maus* (1996)—Deleuze and Guattari speak of writerly becoming. "If a writer is a sorcerer," they say, "it is because writing is a becoming, writing is traversed by strange becomings that are not becomings-writer, but becomings-rat, becomings-insect, becomings-wolf etc." (242).

Recounting Virginia Woolf's dismay at the suggestion that she wrote "as a woman," they argue that "writing should produce a becoming-woman as atoms of womanhood capable of crossing and impregnating an entire social field, and of contaminating men, of sweeping them up in that becoming" (276). This conjures up Kristeva's strange body not as a site of asexuality or intersexuality so much as a continual flux of gendered becomings that can, and do, move along a continuum of possibilities in the process of living and writing. I want also to consider the possibility of thinking in terms of this writer (and reader) not only becoming-woman, becoming-man, or becoming-strange body, but also becoming-traumatic affect, becoming-specter, becoming-phantom, becoming-swan, becoming-weather, or becoming-generations past, in service to literary testimony and introjection.

It is also timely to take a moment to acknowledge the dark side of the potentials of which I speak: the less palatable becomings. There is always the possibility that the posttraumatic experience of becoming-traumatic affect might lead to what Spinoza calls bondage (Spinoza 1996: 113). In this case the autonomy of affect might be said to operate in a negative sense. Spinoza's bondage refers to affect unmediated (or insufficiently mediated) by the introjectory process. This becoming affect that does not facilitate perception, understanding, and ethical action is what Spinoza called "the passions." Of one thing we can be sure: individual and collective failure to sufficiently introject transgenerationally transmitted trauma and affect exacts a high price all over the planet. Spinoza stresses the necessity of coming "to know both our nature's power and its lack of power, so that we can determine what reason [understanding] can do in moderating affects, and what it cannot do" (124). In other words, it is advisable for a writer who would undertake a literary work such as those surveyed in this book, to ensure they are ready for the process.

I have stated that unlying—writing in the direction of what we call truth—is crucial to introjection and the poetics of transgenerational trauma, and that it can perhaps be thought of as similar to translation in that it comes with its own linguistic and creative reading of the experience of others. And I have argued for the validity of unlying informed more by affect and becoming than by indexical memory or factual account. I pause here to acknowledge an inherent doubt in this claim and the likewise validity of the question of how a writer might ensure that what they tell, and the modes of representation on which they rely, are as close to unlying as possible, and as far from traducing as possible. I have claimed that however fearless the poetics of transgenerational trauma may be in uncovering and exposing familial and cultural fault lines and the fractures, flaws, and failures of others, a defining characteristic of the poetics of transgenerational trauma is a refusal of individualistic victimhood, gratuitous violence, or familial denigration. What I mean by this is not that such writers are immune from the all-too-human shortcomings of resentment, self-pity, and the urge to revenge, but that it is the affect-ethical structure and fabric of the transgenerational testimony experiment that offers some protection from collapse into so prosaic a gesture as finger-pointing blame, though this testimony may be angry and does demand accountability: individual, societal, and political. As Marianne Hirsch says:

> Postmemory is not an identity position but a generational structure of transmission deeply embedded in such forms of mediation. Family life, even in its most intimate moments, is entrenched in a collective imaginary shaped by public, generational structures of fantasy and projection and by a shared

> archive of stories and images that inflect the transmission of individual and familial remembrance. (2008: 114)

This is the key difference between the poetics of transgenerational trauma and the so-called inspiration and misery literature discussed in Chapter 2.

In the former, a strange-bodied, experimental mining of circuitries of transgenerationally transmitted traumatic affect is performed in order to illuminate the cyclical hauntings that bind us all. In the latter traumatic testimony operates as an individualistic identity position, one in which the danger of vilification is much more present. Though Bechdel exposes her father's deceptions forensically it is her love for him and her grief around him that most palpably pervades these actions. Duras does not spare frank detail in describing the brother's reprehensible behavior and yet he is not so much a villain as a tragedy; a lamentable site of the failure of patriarchal, imperialist civilization. Barker researched her real-life characters tirelessly and rendered her diabolical fictional hero Billy Prior with compassionate candor. Cixous's self-reflexive and unsettlingly honest narration is preoccupied with holding the self to account first and foremost. And Wright staunchly refuses resentment and self-pity in the face of the incredible harm done to Indigenous people in her postmodern, postcolonial poetics, although her texts express a righteous fury and great sorrow.

Even so, ultimately there can be no sure, safe way forward and no guarantees. This writing is in the ethical sense, as well as in a literary and linguistic sense, experimental. I expect this is why only a certain kind of writer, at a certain point of life should, and can, tackle the poetics of transgenerational trauma. Such a writer must be moved to birth the self within the traumatic gaps of familial and cultural heritage. Such a writer accepts the daunting hazards of witnessing and testifying and is willing to negotiate the consequences. One aspect of this negotiation is the weighing up of the potential negative impact of writing on a given individual compared to the potential negative impact on many of not writing. As Schwab (2006) says, "The collective or communal silencing of violent histories leads to the transgenerational transmission of trauma and the specter of an involuntary repetition of cycles of violence" (100). This is not to say that consideration of the impact on individuals is not important, but rather, that such consideration should be undertaken in contrast with the bigger picture. Further, the writer poised to testify to familial transmissions has agency and a number of options. They can decide when to write the transgenerational trauma text, whether to publish, how to publish and present in terms of genre (i.e. as memoir, fiction, or other), whether to withhold publication so long as certain people are alive, and whether to discuss the work with potentially affected people prior to publication. It is to some degree a question of integrity and if there is any question as to the veracity of depictions of identifiable people in a given text, whether they are dead or alive, it is my view that the text should be presented as fiction, or at least not as conventional memoir, with its obligation to factual representation.

If I am unable to advocate any foolproof methodology for avoiding the dangers of the poetics of transgenerational trauma, I hope at least to have convincingly established that it is, along with certain other kinds of art, capable of unlying cyclical haunting, with its deeply entrenched, historical denials and refusals, in such a way as to pointedly challenge the dichotomies at the heart of anthroparchy (which cyclical haunting is bound to), thereby destabilizing its sexism, misogyny, homophobia, ageism, racism, and speciesism, etc. It is literary practice exercising the divine right of which Abraham and Torok speak—to the rediscovery of self and family, and the assertion of value in a quest to be recognized and acknowledged by oneself to oneself before the whole universe.

Such is the need to introject trauma, the fervor of the writer to write its transmissions and cycles, the urge of beingness to increase power by becoming. So it is that in becoming transformed by writing and reading, an optimal process of subjective and cultural introjection is expedited. Becoming trans-formed, one way or another, aids both personal and political revolution and restitution, and that is the most expansive and liberating traumatic becoming of all.

Notes

Chapter 1

1 Maria Torok's 1964 essay, "The Meaning of Penis Envy in Women," predated other feminist critiques of Freud. It was published with other collected essays by Torok and Nicolas Abraham in *The Shell and the Kernel: Renewals of Psychoanalysis.*

Chapter 2

1 This term appears in the title of a 1981 essay by Ann Rosalind Jones: "Writing the Body: Toward an Understanding of L'Ecriture Féminine" published in *Feminist Studies* 7, no. 2.

Chapter 3

1 Hosted by the Writing and Society Research Centre at Western Sydney University, May 26, 2010.

2 The phrase "the personal is political" is commonly credited to Carol Hanisch, the author of "The Personal is Political," in *Notes from the Second Year: Women's Liberation: Major Writings of Radical Feminists*, ed. Shulamith Firestone and Anne Koedt (New York: Radical Feminist Publications, 1970), but in an updated version of the essay that appears on her website, Hanisch states that it was not she, but editors Firestone and Koedt who came up with the title, http://www.carolhanisch.org/CHwritings/PIP.html (accessed December 27, 2012).

References

Abraham, N. (1994), "Notes on the Phantom: A Complement to Freud's Metapsychology", in N. T. Rand (ed.), *The Shell and the Kernel: Renewals of Psychoanalysis*, 171–76, Chicago: University of Chicago Press.

Abraham, N. and M. Torok (1994), *The Shell and the Kernel: Renewals of Psychoanalysis*, edited by N. T. Rand, Chicago: University of Chicago Press.

Acker, K. (1994a), *Blood and Guts in High School: A Novel*, New York: Grove Press.

Acker, K. (1994b), *Don Quixote: A Novel*, New York: Grove Press.

Acker, K. (1994c), *My Mother: Demonology*, New York: Grove Press.

Adamson, R. (2015), *Net Needle*, Melbourne: Black Inc.

Adamson, J. and H. Clark, eds (1999), *Scenes of Shame: Psychoanalysis, Shame, and Writing*, New York: State University of New York Press.

Addley, E. (2007), "So Bad it's Good," *The Guardian*, 15 June. Available online: http://www.guardian.co.uk/society/2007/jun/15/childrensservices.biography (accessed August 1, 2012).

Adler, H. G. (1955), *Theresienstadt 1941-1945: das Antlitz einer Zwangsgemeinschaft, Geschichte, Soziologie, Psychologie*, Tübingen: J. C. B Mohr.

Adorno, T. and M. Horkheimer (2011), *Towards a New Manifesto*, translated by R. Livingstone, New York: Verso.

Ahmed, S. (2004), *The Cultural Politics of Emotion*, New York: Routledge.

Alexander, C. (2014), "Meet the Companies that Run Our Immigration Detention Camps," 25 February. Available online: http://www.crikey.com.au/2014/02/25/meet-the-companies-that-run-our-immigration-detention-camps/ (accessed February 2, 2016).

Altieri, C. (2012), "Affects, Intentionality, and Cognition: A Response to Ruth Leys," *Critical Inquiry*, 38: 879–82.

American Psychiatric Association (2000), *Diagnostic and Statistical Manual of Mental Disorders DSM-IV-TR (Text Revision)*, 4th ed., Washington, DC: American Psychiatric Association.

Americans, Native (1998), "The Trauma of History," in R. Thornton (ed.), *Studying Native America: Problems and Perspectives*, 60–78, Madison, WI: University of Wisconsin Press.

Amnesty International (2013), "The Truth About Manus Island: 2013 Report," 11 December. Available online: http://www.amnesty.org.au/refugees/comments/33587 (accessed February 3, 2016).

Amnesty International (2015), "No More Secrecy: We Have a Right to Know How Our Government Treats People Seeking Asylum," 11 November. Available online: http://www.amnesty.org.au/news/comments/38392/ (accessed February 3, 2016).

Arendt, H. (1963), *Eichmann in Jerusalem: A Report of the Banality of Evil*, New York: Penguin.

Atkinson, M. (2013), "Animal Poetics: Singing the Scorched Tongue," *Southerly: Lyre/Liar*, 73 (2): 114–21.

Atkinson, M. (2015), "Carpentaria," *Copyright Agency: Reading Australia*. Available online: http://readingaustralia.com.au/essays/carpentaria/ (accessed February 10, 2016).

Australian Bureau of Statistics (2013), "The Health and Welfare of Australia's Aboriginal and Torres Strait Islander Peoples Oct 2010". February 17, 2011. Available online: http://www.abs.gov.au/AUSSTATS/abs@.nsf/lookup/4704.0Chapter218Oct+2010 (accessed May 15, 2016).

Australian Government (2013), "Australian Indigenous Cultural Heritage." Available online: http://australia.gov.au/about-australia/australian-story/austn-indigenous-cultural-heritage (accessed December 15, 2013).

Azam, M. (2014), "Alexis Wright: It Was Like Writing a Story to the Ancestors," *The Guardian*, 25 May. Available online: http://www.theguardian.com/books/australia-culture-blog/2014/may/25/alexis-wright-it-was-like-writing-a-story-to-the-ancestors (accessed March 24, 2016).

Bachelard, M. (2015), "High Tension in Papua and West Papua," 7 February. Available online: http://www.smh.com.au/good-weekend/high-tension-in-papua-and-west-papua-20150120-12uc2d.html (accessed March 22, 2016).

Ball, K. (2008), *Disciplining the Holocaust: Traumatic History as an Object of Inquiry and Desire*, Albany: SUNY Series, Insinuations: Philosophy, Psychoanalysis, Literature, SUNY Press.

Barker, P. (1992), *Regeneration*, London: Penguin Books.

Barker, P. (1994), *The Eye in the Door*, London: Penguin Books.

Barker, P. (1996), *The Ghost Road*, London: Penguin Books.

Barker, P. (1999), *Regeneration Trilogy*, Ringwood, VIC: Penguin Books.

Barnett, J. and W. N. Adger (2007), "Climate Change, Human Security and Violent Conflict," *Political Geography*, 26 (6): 639–55.

Bechdel, A. (2006), *Fun Home: A Family Tragicomic*, Boston: Houghton Mifflin.

Beirne, P. (1999), "For a Nonspeciesist Criminology: Animal Abuse as an Object of Study," *Criminology*, 37 (1): 117–48.

Benjamin, W. (1969), "The Task of the Translator," in H. Arendt (ed.), *Illuminations: Essays and Reflections*, 69–82, New York: Schocken Books.

Bennett, J. (2005), *Empathic Vision: Affect, Trauma, and Contemporary Art*, Stanford, CA: Stanford University Press.

Berry, H. L., K. Bowen and T. Kjellstrom (2010), "Climate Change and Mental Health: A Causal Pathways Framework," *International Journal of Public Health*, 55 (2): 123–32.

Bertlant, L. (2011), *Cruel Optimism*, Durham: Duke University Press.

Bertland, L. and J. Greenwald (2012), "Affect in the End Times: A Conversation with Lauren Berlant," *Qui Parle: Critical Humanities and Social Sciences*, 20 (2): 71–89.

Blackman, L. (2012), *Immaterial Bodies: Affect, Embodiment, Mediation*, London: Sage.

Blackman, L. (2015), "Researching Affect and Embodied Hauntologies: Exploring an Analytics of Exprimentation," in B. T. Knudsen and C. Stage (eds), *Affective Methodologies: Developing Cultural Research Strategies for the Study of Affect*, 25–44, Basingstoke, UK: Palgrave Macmillan.

Book Show, The (2007), [radio program], ABC Radio National, Sydney, July 6.

Bradshaw, J. (1988), *Healing the Shame That Binds You*, Tallahassee, FL, USA: Health Communications.

Brah, A. and A. Phoenix (2004), "Ain't I a Woman? Revisiting Intersectionality," *Journal of International Women's Studies*, 5 (3): 75–86.

Brennan, B., ed. (2008), *Just Words?: Australian Authors Writing for Justice*, St Lucia, QLD: University of Queensland Press.

Brennan, T. (2004), *The Transmission of Affect*, New York: Cornell University Press.

Brett, L. (1986), *The Auschwitz Poems*, Brunswick, VIC: Scribe.

Brett, L. (1990), *After the War: Poems*, Carlton, VIC: Melbourne University Press.

Brooks, D. (2013), "The Fallacies: Theory, Saturation Capitalism and the Animal," *Southerly: Lyre/Liar*, 73 (2): 47–60.

Brooks Pribac, T. (2013), "Animal Grief," *Animal Studies Journal*, 2 (1): 67–90.

Brophy, B. (1991), Foreword in *By Grand Central Station I Sat Down and Wept*, 7–13, by Elizabeth Smart, London: Paladin.

Brown University (2015), "Costs of War," *The Watson Institute of International and Public Affairs*, January. Available online: http://watson.brown.edu/costsofwar/costs/human/civilians/afghan (accessed February 3, 2016).

Buelens, G., S. Durrant, and R. Eagleston, eds (2014), *The Future of Trauma Theory: Contemporary Literary and Cultural Criticism*, New York: Routledge.

Butler, J. (1988), "The Body Politics of Julia Kristeva," *Hypatia*, 3 (3): 104–18.

Butler, J. (2010), *Frames of War: When Is Life Grievable*? New York: Verso.

Calvo, E. (2008), "Most Farmers Prefer Blondes: The Dynamic of Anthroparchy in Animals Becoming Meat," *Journal for Critical Animal Studies*, 6 (1): 32–45.

Cardinal, M. (1993), *The Words to Say It: An Autobiographical Novel*, Sydney: Allen & Unwin.

Caruth, C. (1991), "Unclaimed Experience: Trauma and the Possibility of History," *Yale French Studies* 79: 181–92.

Caruth, C., ed. (1995), *Trauma: Explorations in Memory*, Baltimore: Johns Hopkins University Press.

Caruth, C. (1996), *Unclaimed Experience: Trauma, Narrative, and History*, Baltimore: Johns Hopkins University Press.

Caruth, C. (2001), "An Interview with Jean Laplanche," *Postmodern Culture*, 11 (2). Available online: http://muse.jhu.edu/journals/pmc/v011/11.2caruth.html (accessed March 5, 2013).

Chang, J. (1991), *Wild Swans*, New York: Simon & Schuster.

Cho, G. M. (2008), *Haunting the Korean Diaspora: Shame, Secrecy, and the Forgotten War*, Minneapolis: University of Minnesota Press.

Choahan, N. (2016), "Iranian Asylum Seeker Faces Being Sent Back to Nauru 'to Face Her Rapist'" *Sydney Morning Herald*, February 3. Available online: http://www.smh.com.au/federal-politics/political-news/iranian-asylum-seeker-faces-being-sent-back-to-nauru-to-face-her-rapist-20160203-gmkuhp.html (accessed February 4, 2016).

Chute, H. (2012), "Visual Witness and Documentary Form: Nakazawa, Speigelman, and the Post-war Comics Field," paper presented at the 8th Biennial Conference of the International Auto/Biography Association (IABA), Canberra, Australia July 17–20.

Chute, H. and A. Bechdel (2007), "An Interview with Alison Bechdel," *MFS Modern Fiction Studies*, 52 (4): 1004–13.

Cixous, H. (1981a), "The Laugh of the Medusa," in E. Marks and I. De Courtivron (eds), *New French Feminisms: An Anthology*, 245–64, New York: Schocken Books.

Cixous, H. (1981b), "Sorties," in E. Marks and I. De Courtivron (eds), *New French Feminisms: An Anthology*, 90–98, New York: Schocken Books.

Cixous, H. (1991), *Coming to Writing and Other Essays*, translated by S. Cornell, D. Jensen, A. Liddle, and S. Sellers, 151–52, Cambridge, MA: Harvard University Press.

Cixous, H. (1993), *Three Steps on the Ladder of Writing, Wellek Library Lectures at the University of California, Irvine*, New York: Columbia University Press.

Cixous, H. (1998), *Stigmata: Escaping Texts*, London: Routledge.

Cixous, H. (2009), *Hyperdream*, translated by B. B. Brahic, Cambridge: Polity.

Clark, C., J. Murrell, M. Fernyhough, T. O'Rourke, and M. Mendl (2014), "Long-term and Trans-generational Effects of Neonatal Experience on Sheep Behaviour," *Biology Letters*, 10, July 2. Available online: http://rsbl.royalsocietypublishing.org/search/Long-term%252Band%252BTrans-generational%252BEffects%252Bof%252BNeonatal%252BExperience%252Bon%252BSheep%252BBehaviour%20jcode%3Aroybiolett (accessed February 20, 2016).

Clough, P. T., ed. (2007), *The Affective Turn: Theorizing the Social*, Durham: Duke University Press.

Collins, P. H. (1998), "It's All in the Family: Intersections of Gender, Race, and Nation," *Hypatia*, 13 (3): 62–82.

Condliffe, P. (2013), "Woman, Echidna, Man, Dingo: Bio-political Subjectivity and Ethics in the Animals of B. Wongar's Fiction," *Southerly: Lyre/Liar*, 73 (2): 183–94.

Connolly, W. E. (2011), "The Complexity of Intention," *Critical Inquiry*, 37: 792–99.

Cooke, J. (2011), "The Risks of Intimate Writing: Loving and Dreaming with Hélène Cixous," *Angelaki*, 16 (2): 3–18.

Craps, S. and G. Buelens (2008), "Introduction: Postcolonial Trauma Novels," *Studies in the Novel*, 40 (1 and 2): 1–12.

Crenshaw, K. (1991), "Mapping the Margins: Intersectionality, Identity Politics and Violence Against Women of Color," *Stanford Law Review*, 43 (6): 1241–99.

Cvetkovich, A. (2012), *Depression: A Public Feeling*, Durham: Duke University Press.

Davies, S. (2013), "Fact Check: Have More Than 1000 Asylum Seekers Died Under Labor?," *The Conversation*, July 23. Available online: http://theconversation.com/factcheck-have-more-than-1000-asylum-seekers-died-at-sea-under-labor-16221 (accessed February 4, 2016).

Davis, C. (2005), "Hauntology, Spectres and Phantoms," *French Studies*, 59 (3): 373–79.

Deckha, M. (2008), "Intersectionality and Posthumanist Visions of Equality," *Wisconsin Journal of Law, Gender & Society*, 23 (2): 249–67.

DeLanda, M. (2006), *A New Philosophy of Society: Assemblage Theory and Social Complexity*, London: Continuum.

Deleuze, G. (1992), "Ethology: Spinoza and Us," in J. Crary (ed.), *Incorporations*, 625–33, New York: Zone Books.

Deleuze, G. and F. Guattari (1988), *A Thousand Plateaus: Capitalism and Schizophrenia*, London: The Athlone Press.

Delvin-Glass, F. (2006), "Broken Songs and Ecology: Writing About the Gulf of Carpentaria," *TAIN* 44: 28–29.

Denham, A. R. (2008), "Rethinking Historical Trauma: Narratives of Resilience," *Transcultural Psychiatry*, 45 (3): 391–414.

Derrida, J. (1994), *Spectres of Marx*, translated by P. Kamuf, New York: Routledge.

Derrida, J. and D. Wills (2002), "The Animal That Therefore I Am (More to Follow)," *Critical Inquiry*, 28 (2): 369–418.

Destroy the Joint (2016), "Counting Dead Women." Available online: https://www.facebook.com/DestroyTheJoint/ (accessed April 11, 2016).

Doherty, B. (2015), "Men Accused of Reza Barati's Death in Manus Detention Center Stand Trial," *The Guardian, Australia*, September 21. Available online: http://www.theguardian.com/australia-news/2015/sep/21/men-accused-of-reza-baratis-death-in-manus-detention-center-stand-trial (accessed February 4, 2016).

Donne, J. (1624), *Devotions Upon Emergent Occasions*, Cambridge: Cambridge University Press.

Doyle, D. (2015), Licence to Kill? Australia's Migration Amendment Bill 2015, *Border Criminologies*, blog, May 12. Available online: https://www.law.ox.ac.uk/research-subject-groups/center-criminology/centerborder-criminologies/blog/2015/05/licence-kill (accessed February 4, 2016).

Duras, M. (1986), *The War: A Memoir*, translated by B. Bray, New York: Pantheon Books.

Duras, M. (1992), *The Lover*, translated by B. Bray, New York: Harper Perennial.

Edwards, N. (2012), "Christine Angot's Personal Archives," paper presented at the 8th Biennial Conference of the International Auto/Biography Association (IABA), Canberra, Australia, July 17–20.

Elmslie, J. and C. Webb-Gannon (2013), "A Slow-Motion Genocide: Indonesian Rule in West Papua," *Griffith Journal of Law and Human Dignity*, 1 (2): 142–65.

Felman, S. (1995), "Education and Crisis, or the Vicissitudes of Teaching," in C. Caruth (ed.), *Trauma: Explorations in Memory*, 13–60, Baltimore: Johns Hopkins Press.

Felman, S. and D. Laub (1992), *Testimony: Crisis of Witnessing in Literature, Psychoanalsyis and History*, New York: Routledge.

Festic, F. (2012), *Gender and Trauma: Interdisciplinary Dialogues*, Cambridge, UK: Cambridge Scholars Publishing.

Finlay, E. (2013), "On the Value of Anthropomorphism," *Southerly: Lyre/Liar*, 73 (2): 74–93.

First Footprints (2013), [TV program], ABC 1, Sydney, August 4.

Fletcher, J. (1999), "Introduction: Psychoanalysis and the Question of the Other," in J. Fletcher (ed.), *Essays on Otherness*, 1–51, J. Laplanche, London: Routledge.

Foucault, M. (1980), *The History of Sexuality, Vol. 1. An Introduction*, translated by R. Hurley, New York: Vintage.

Foucault, M. (2006), "The Incitement to Discourse," in A. Jaworski and N. Coupland (eds), *The Discourse Reader*, 491–98, London: Routledge.

Frank, A. (2012), "'There Is No Such Thing as Time,'" *Australian Popular Science*, September 19. Available online: http://www.popsci.com.au/science/there-is-no-such-thing-as-time,378327 (accessed February 3, 2016).

Frank, A. and E. Wilson (2012), "Response to Ruth Leys," *Critical Inquiry*, 38: 874.

Freud, S. (1917), "Mourning and Melancholia," *Standard Edition*, 14 (239): 1957–61.

Freud, S. (1922), *Beyond the Pleasure Principle*, translated by C. J. M Hubback, London, Vienna: International Psycho-Analytical.

Freud, S. (1939), *Moses and Monotheism*, London: The Hogarth Press.

Freud, S. (1974), in J. Strachey (ed.), *New Introductory Lectures on Psychoanalysis*, London: Hogarth Press.

Freud, S. (2011), *Beyond the Pleasure Principle*, Peterborough, ON: Broadview Editions.

Gallop, J. (1988), *Thinking Through the Body*, *Gender and Culture*, New York: Columbia University Press.

Ghitis, F. (2015), "How Is This Not WWIII?," CNN, November 25. Available online: http://edition.cnn.com/2015/11/24/opinions/ghitis-russia-jet-shot-down/ (accessed February 16, 2016).

Gibbs, A. (2001), "Contagious Feelings: Pauline Hanson and the Epidemiology of Affect," *Australian Humanities Review*, December. Available onlinle: http://australianhumanitiesreview.org/archive/Issue-December-2001/gibbs.html (accessed July 14, 2012).

Gibbs, A. (2005), "Fictocriticism, Affect, Mimesis: Engendering Differences," *Text* 9 (1). Available online: http://www.textjournal.com.au/april05/gibbs.htm (accessed March 1, 2016).

Gibbs, A. (2006), "Writing and Danger: The Intercorporeality of Affect," in T. Brady and N. Krauth (eds), *Creative Writing: Theory Beyond Practice*, 157–68, Teneriffe: Post Pressed.

Ginsberg, A. (1992), "Howl," in A. Charters (ed.), *The Penguin Book of the Beats*, 62–71, London: Penguin Books.

Glass, C. (2007), *Damaged*, London: Harper Element.

Gleeson-White, J. (2013), "Going Viral," *Sydney Review of Books*, August 23. Available online: http://sydneyreviewofbooks.com/going-viral/ (accessed September 5, 2013).

Greene, B. (2005), *The Fabric of the Cosmos: Space, Time, and the Texture of Reality*, New York: Vintage.

Gregg, M. and G. J. Seigworth, eds (2010), *The Affect Theory Reader*, Durham: Duke University Press.

Hall, S., ed. (1997), "Introduction," in *Representation: Cultural Representations and Signifying Practices*, 1–6, London, Sage.

Hanisch, C. (1970), "The Personal Is Political," in S. Firestone and A. Koedt (eds), *Notes From the Second Year: Women's Liberation, Major Writings of the Radical Feminists* (pamphlet), New York: Radical Feminists.

Hardt, M. (2007), "What Affects Are Good For," in P. T. Clough (ed.), *The Affective Turn: Theorizing the Social*, ix–xiii, Durham: Duke University Press.

Harlow, H. F. and S. J. Suomi (1971), "Social Recovery by Isolation-reared Monkeys," *Proceedings of the National Academy of Sciences of the United States of America*, 68 (7): 1534–38.

Harlow, H. F., E. Hansen, and B. Sealy (1962), "Mother-Infant Separation in Monkeys," *Journal of Child Psychology and Psychiatry*, 3 (3–4): 123–32.

Harlow, H. F., R. O. Dodsworth, and M. K. Harlow (1965), "Total Social Isolation in Monkeys," *Proceedings of the National Academy of Sciences*, 54 (1): 90–97.

Hasham, N. (2016), "These Children Are Among the Most Traumatised We Have Ever Seen," *The Sydney Morning Herald*, February 4. Available online: http://www.smh.com.au/federal-politics/political-news/these-children-are-among-the-most-traumatised-we-have-ever-seen-20160203-gml9dv.html?&utm_source=facebook&utm_medium=cpc&utm_campaign=social&eid=socialn%3Afac-14omn0012-optim-nnn%3Apaid-25062014-social_traffic-all-postprom-nnn-smh-o&campaign_code=nocode&promote_channel=social_facebook (accessed February 6, 2016).

Hedges, C. (2003), "What Every Person Should Know About War," *The New York Times*, July 6. Available online: http://www.nytimes.com/2003/07/06/books/chapters/0713-1st-hedges.html?pagewanted=all (accessed February 5, 2016).

Herman, J. (1997), *Trauma and Recovery: The Aftermath of Violence—from Domestic Abuse to Political Terror*, New York: Basic Books.

Hiroshima, Mon Amour (1959), [motion picture], Argos Films, Como Films, Daiei Studios, Pathé Entertainment.

Hirsch, M. (1997), *Family Frames: Photography, Narrative, and Postmemory*, Cambridge, MA: Harvard University Press.

Hirsch, M. (2008), "The Generation of Postmemory," *Poetics Today*, 29 (1): 103–28.

Hirsch, M. (2012), *The Generation of Postmemory: Writing and Visual Culture After the Holocaust*, New York: Columbia University Press.

Hong, M. K. (1992), “Introduction,” in M. Duras and B. Bray (ed. and trans.), *The Lover*, v–ix, New York: Harper Perennial.

hooks, b. (1990), “Marginality as Site of Resistance,” in R. Ferguson et al. (eds), *Out There: Marginalization and Contemporary Cultures*, 341–43, New York: New Museum of Contemporary Art.

Howarth, S. (2006), *Please Daddy, No: A Boy Betrayed*, London: Harper Element.

Huggins, J. (1998), *Sister Girl*, St Lucia: University of Queensland Press.

Institute for Critical Animal Studies, The, “About,” viewed February 6, 2014, <http:// www.criticalanimalstudies.org/about/ (accessed January 2, 2014).

Iraq Body Count (2016), Available online: https://www.iraqbodycount.org/ (accessed February 3, 2016).

Jacques Derrida and the Question of "The Animal" (2008), hiperf289, December 18. Available online: http://www.youtube.com/watch?v=Ry49Jr0TFjk.

Jones, A. R. (1981), “Writing the Body: Toward an Understanding of ‘L’écriture Feminine’,” *Feminist Studies*, 7 (2): 247–63.

Jordan, S. (2013), “Autofiction in the Feminine,” *French Studies*, LXVII (1): 76–84.

Jung, C. G. (1981), *The Archetypes and the Collective Unconscious. Vol. 9*, Princeton, NJ: Princeton University Press.

Kafka, F. (2001), *The Metamorphosis*, translated by I. Johnston, New York: Tribeca Books.

Kilby, J. and A. Rowland, eds (2014), *The Future of Testimony: Interdisciplinary Perspectives on Witnessing*, New York: Routledge.

Kristeva, J. (1984), *Revolution in Poetic Language*, New York: Columbia University Press.

Kristeva, J. (1987), “Talking About Polylogue,” in T. Moi (ed.), S. Hand (trans.) *French Feminist Thought: A Reader*, 110–17, Oxford: Basil Blackwell.

Kristeva, J. (2002), *Intimate Revolt: The Powers and Limits of Psychoanalysis*, translated by J. Herman, New York: Columbia University Press.

Lacan, J. (1977), *Ecrits: A Selection*, translated by A. Sherdian, New York: W. W. Norton & Co.

LaCapra, D. (1999), “Trauma, Absence, Loss,” *Critical Inquiry*, 25 (4): 696–727.

LaCapra, D. (2001), *Writing History, Writing Trauma*, Baltimore: Johns Hopkins University Press.

La Cruz, M. and H. M. Lloyd (2011), “Philosophy and the ‘Affective Turn’,” *Parrhesia*, 13: 1–13.

Laplanche, J. (1999), in J. Fletcher (ed.), *Essays on Otherness*, London: Routledge.

Lattwak, E. (2000), *Turbo-Capitalism: Winners and Losers in the Global Economy*, New York: PerfectBound.

Leane, J. (2015), “Historyless People,” in A. McGrath and M. A. Jebb (eds), *Long History, Deep Time: Deepening Histories of Place*, 151–62, ACT: Australian National University Press.

Levi, P. (1959), *If This Is a Man*, London: The Orion Press.

Leys, R. (2000), *Trauma: A Genealogy*, Chicago: The University of Chicago Press.

Leys, R. (2007), *From Guilt to Shame: Auschwitz and After*, Princeton, NJ: Princeton University Press.

Leys, R. (2011a), “The Turn to Affect: A Critique,” *Critical Inquiry*, 37 (3): 434–72.

Leys, R. (2011b), “Affect and Intention: A Reply to William E Connolly,”. *Critical Inquiry*, 37 (4): 799–805.

Leys, R. (2012), “Facts and Moods: Reply to My Critics,” *Critical Inquiry*, 38: 882–91.

Lo, H. Y. (2013), “Mapping Indigenous Language Across Australia,” *Australian Geographic*, August 22. Available online: http://www.australiangeographic.com.au/topics/history-culture/2013/08/mapping-indigenous-language-across-australia (accessed February 11, 2016).

Massumi, B. (1996), “The Autonomy of Affect,” in P. Patton (ed.), *Deleuze: A Critical Reader*, 217–39, London: Blackwell.

Massumi, B. (2002), *Parables for the Virtual: Movement, Affect, Sensation*, Durham: Duke University Press.

Mastroianni, B. (2015), “On a Pedestal,” *The Paris Review*, April 27. Available online: http://www.theparisreview.org/blog/2015/04/27/on-a-pedestal/ (accessed March 24, 2016).

McAfee, N. (2004), in R. Eagleston (ed.), *Julia Kristeva*, New York: Routledge.

McCourt, F. (1996), *Angela’s Ashes*, London: Harper Collins.

Meares, R. (2000), *Intimacy and Alienation: Memory, Trauma and Personal Being*, London: Routledge.

Millar, L. (2015), “Australia’s Asylum Seeker Policies Heavily Criticised at UN Human Rights Council Review,” *ABC News*, November 10. Available online: http://www.abc.net.au/news/2015-11-10/australias-asylum-policies-heavily-criticised-at-united-nations/6926032 (accessed February 3, 2016).

Mindframe: National Media Initiative (2016), “Aboriginal and Torres Strait Islander Australians.” Available online: http://himh.clients.squiz.net/mindframe/for-media/reporting-suicide/priority-population-groups/aboriginal-and-torres-strait-islander-australians (accessed March 24, 2016).

Moi, T. (1988), “Feminism, Postmodernism, and Style: Recent Feminist Criticism in the United States,” *Cultural Critique*, 9: 3–22.

Molloy, D. (2013), “Finding Hope in the Stories: Alexis Wright’s Carpentaria and the Carnivalesque Search for a New Order,” *Journal of the Association for the Study of Australian Literature*, 12 (3): 1–8.

Moreton-Robinson, A. (1999), "Unmasking Whiteness: A Goori Jonda's Look at Some Duggai Business," *Queensland Review*, 6: 1–7.

Morrison, T. (1987), *Beloved*, New York: Plume.

Morrison, T. (1998), "Playing in the Dark," in J. Rivkin and M. Ryan (eds), *Literary Theory: An Anthology*, 923–35, Boston, MA: Blackwell.

Murakami, H. (2000), *South of the Border, West of the Sun*, New York: Vintage.

Murakami, H. (2006), *Kafka on the Shore*, New York: Vintage.

Negri, A. (1990), *Control and Becoming: Gilles Deleuze in Conversation with Antonio Negri*. Available online: http://www.generation-online.org/p/fpdeleuze3.htm (accessed March 30, 2012).

Newman, M. (2015), "Australian Government Seeks to Block High Court Case on Offshore Detention Centers," *World Socialist Website*, October 19. Available online: https://www.wsws.org/en/articles/2015/10/19/aust-019.html (accessed February 4, 2016).

New York State Writers Institute (2011), "Hélène Cixous at the NYS Writers Institute in 2007," August 22. Available online: http://www.youtube.com/watch?v=evT0gGJ5Oms (accessed February 16, 2014).

Nietzsche, F. (1968), *The Will to Power*, edited by W. Kaufman, New York: Vintage.

Oliver, K. (1993), *Reading Kristeva: Unraveling the Double-bind*, Bloomington: Indiana University Press.

Orange, D. (1995), *Emotional Understanding: Studies in Psychoanalytic Epistemology*, New York: Guildford Press.

Pelzer, D. (2001), *A Child Called It*, London: Orion.

Perera, S. and J. Pugliese (2015), "Offshore Detention 'Black Sites' Open Door to Torture," *The Conversation*, August 26. Available online: http://theconversation.com/offshore-detention-black-sites-open-door-to-torture-46400 (accessed February 3, 2016).

Perez-Giz, G. (2015), "Are Space and Time an Illusion?," PBS *Space Time*, April 22. Available online: https://www.youtube.com/watch?v=YycAzdtUIko (accessed February 20, 2016).

Perlez, J. (2007), "Aboriginal Lit," *New York Times*, November 18. Available online: http://www.nytimes.com/2007/11/18/books/review/Perlez-t.html?pagewanted=all&_r=0 (accessed December 9, 2013).

Phys.org (2015), "NIST Team Proves 'Spooky Action at a Distance' is Real," November 12. Available online: http://phys.org/news/2015-11-nist-team-spooky-action-distance.html (accessed February 8, 2016).

Pilger, J. (2016), "A World War Has Begun. Break the Silence," *johnpilger.dom*, March 20. Available online: http://johnpilger.com/articles/a-world-war-has-begun-break-the-silence- (accessed March 27, 2016).

Potts, A. and J. Parry (2010), "Vegan Sexuality: Challenging Heteronormative Masculinity Through Meat-free Sex," *Feminism & Psychology*, 20 (1): 53–72.

Probyn, E. (2014), "Oceanic Ecologies" [conference presentation], June 19–21, Affective Habitus: New Environmental Histories of Botany, Zoology and Emotions, Canberra: Australian National University.

Rand, N. T. (1994a), "Introduction: Renewals of Psychoanalysis," in N. T. Rand (ed.), *The Shell and the Kernel: Renewals of Psychoanalysis*, 1–22, Chicago: University of Chicago Press.

Rand, N. T. (1994b), "Editor's Note on 'The Illness of Mourning and the Fantasy of the Exquisite Corpse'," in N. T. Rand (ed.), *The Shell and the Kernel: Renewals of Psychoanalysis*, 99–106, Chicago: University of Chicago Press.

Ravenscroft, A. (2010), "Dreaming of Others Carpentaria and Its Critics," *Cultural Studies Review*, 16 (2): 194–224.

Reconciliation Action Network (2008), "Aboriginal Child Abuse and the NT Intervention," June 29. Available online: http://reconciliaction.org.au/nsw/recent-issues/aboriginal-child-abuse-and-the-nt-intervention (accessed December 31).

Rich, A. (1976), *Of Woman Born: Motherhood as Experience and Institution*, New York: Norton.

Riding, A. (1995), "Testifying to the Ravages of Granddad's War," *The New York Times*, December 6. Available online: http://www.nytimes.com/1995/12/06/books/testifying-to-the-ravages-of-granddad-s-war.html?rref=collection%2Ftimestopic%2FBarker%2C%20Pat&action=click&contentCollection=timestopics&region=stream&module=stream_unit&version=latest&contentPlacement=10&pgtype=collection (accessed March 24, 1996).

Riley, D. (2005), *Impersonal Passion: Language as Affect*, Durham: Duke University Press.

Rilke, R. M. (2002), *Sonnets to Orpheus*, translated by S. Cohn, New York: Routledge.

Robson, K. (2004), *Writing Wounds: The Inscription of Trauma in Post-1968 French Women's Life-writing*, New York: Rodopi.

Said, E. (1978), *Orientalism*, New York: Pantheon Books.

Scarr, L. (2015), "Rosie Batty Says Domestic Violence Should be Seen as Akin to Terrorism," *The Guardian*, June 3. Available online: http://www.news.com.au/national/politics/rosie-batty-says-domestic-violence-should-be-seen-as-akin-to-terrorism/news-story/8f1472e3ad60549edda0115f1122d35d (accessed April 11, 2016).

Schlunke, K. (2004), "Dumb Places," *Balayi, Culture, Law and Colonialism*, 6: 72–81.

Schwab, G. (2006), "Writing Against Memory and Forgetting," *Literature and Medicine*, 25 (1): 95–121.

Schwab, G. (2010), *Haunting Legacies, Violent Histories and Transgenerational Trauma*, New York: Columbia University Press.

7.30 Report (2007), [TV program], ABC 1, Sydney, June 21.

7.30 Report (2016a), [TV program], ABC 1, Sydney, February 2. Available online: http://www.abc.net.au/7.30/content/2015/s4399153.htm (accessed February 3, 2016).

7.30 Report (2016b), [TV program], ABC 1, Sydney, February 3.

Shakespeare, W. (1604), *The Tragedy of Hamlet, Prince of Denmark*, Chapel Hill, NC, USA: Hayes Barton Press.

Sharp, A. and T. Arup (2009), "UN Says Aboriginal Health Conditions Worse Than Third World", *The Sydney Morning Herald*, December 5. Available online: http://www.smh.com.au/national/un-says-aboriginal-health-conditions-worse-than-third-world-20091204-kay8.html (accessed December 31, 2013).

Simpson, M. (2007), "If This Is a Man," *The Atlantic*, June. Available online: http://www.theatlantic.com/magazine/archive/2007/06/if-this-is-a-man/305897/ (accessed February 29, 2016).

Singer, P. W. (1975), *Animal Liberation*, New York: Harper Collins.

Singer, P. W. (2015), "This Is What WWIII Will Look Like," June 30. Available online: http://time.com/3934583/world-war-3/ (accessed February 16, 2016).

Smart, E. (1991), *By Grand Central Station I Sat Down and Wept*, London: Paladin.

Spiegelman, A. (1996), *The Complete Maus*, New York: Pantheon.

Spinoza de, B. (1996), *Ethics*, ed. and trans. E. Curley, London: Penguin Books.

Steffen, W., W. Broadgate, L. Deutsch, O. Gaffney, and C. Ludwig (2015), "The Trajectory of the Anthropocene: The Great Acceleration," *The Anthropocene Review*, 2 (1): 81–98.

Syson, I. (2007), "Uncertain Magic," *Overland*, 187: 85–86.

Taefi, N. (2009), "The Synthesis of Age and Gender: Intersectionality, International Human Rights Law and the Marginalisation of the Girl-child," *International Journal of Children's Rights*, 17: 345–76.

Tasso, T. (1820), *Gerusalemme Liberata*, translated by R. Zotti, Londra.

Tegmark, M. (2015), "Consciousness as a State of Matter," *Chaos, Solitons, and Fractals*, 76: 238–70.

Thrift, N. (2004), "Intensities of Feeling: Towards a Spatial Politics of Affect," *Geografiska Annaler: Series B, Human Geography*, 86 (1): 57–78.

Tomkins, S. (1963), *Affect Imagery Consciousness Vol II: The Negative Affects*, New York: Springer Publishing.

Tomkins, S. (1991), *Affect Imagery Consciousness Vol III: The Negative Affects: Anger and Fear*, New York: Springer Publishing.

Tomkins, S. (1995), *Shame and Its Sisters: A Silvan Tomkins Reader*, edited by A. Frank and E. S. Kosofsky, Durham: Duke University Press.

Torok, M. (1994), "The Illness of Mourning and the Fantasy of the Exquisite Corpse," in N. T. Rand (ed.), *The Shell and the Kernel: Renewals of Psychoanalysis*, 107–24, Chicago: University of Chicago Press.

United Nations Environmental Programme (2010), "Accessing the Environmental Impacts of Consumption and Production." Available online: http://www.unep.org/search.asp?q=Accessing+the+Environmental+Impacts+of+Consumption+and+Production&sa.x=0&sa.y=0&sa=go%21&cx=007059379654755265211%3Ajkngxjgnyii&cof=forid%3A11 (accessed February 20, 2016).

United Nations High Commissioner for Refugees (2016), "Syrian Regional Refugee Response," February. Available online: http://data.unhcr.org/syrianrefugees/regional.php (accessed February 3, 2016).

Valenti, J. (2015), "Worldwide Sexism Increases Suicide in Young Women," *The Guardian*, May 28. Available online: http://www.theguardian.com/commentisfree/2015/may/28/worldwide-sexism-increases-suicide-risk-in-young-women?CMP=share_btn_fb (accessed March 29, 2016).

van Alphen, E. (2006), "Second-generation Testimony, the Transmission of Trauma, and Postmemory," *Poetics Today*, 27: 473–88.

Watson, J. (2008), "Autographic Disclosures and Genealogies of Desire in Alison Bechdel's *Fun Home*," *Biography*, 31 (1): 27–58.

Webb, J. (2013), "Living Wound," *Australian Book Review*. Available online: https://www.australianbookreview.com.au/component/k2/105-abr-previews/1597-living-wound-the-swan-book (accessed December 20, 2013).

Wheeler Center, The (2013), "Alexis Wright: *The Swan Book*," [video recording], October 10. Available online: http://wheelercenter.com/videos/video/alexis-wright-the-swan-book/ (accessed December 30, 2013).

Wild, R. and P. Anderson (2007), *Ampe Akelyernemane Meke Mekarle: "Little Children are Sacred": Report of the Northern Territory Board of Inquiry Into the Protection of Aboriginal Children from Sexual Abuse 2007*, Northern Territory Board of Inquiry into the Protection of Aboriginal Children from Sexual Abuse, Darwin, NT: Department of the Chief Minister Office of Indigenous Policy.

Wilkie, M. (1997), *Bringing Them Home: Report of the National Inquiry into the Separation of Aboriginal and Torres Strait Islander Children from Their Families*. Human Rights and Equal Opportunity Commission, Sydney, N.S.W.

Wolfe, P. (1991), "On Being Woken Up: The Dreamtime in Anthropology and in Australian Settler Culture," *Comparative Studies in Society and History*, 33: 197–224.

Wolfreys, J. (2002), *Victorian Hauntings: Spectrality, Gothic, the Uncanny and Literature*, New York: Palgrave.
Wright, A. (1997a), *Grog War*, Broome, WA: Magabala Books.
Wright, A. (1997b), *Plains of Promise*, Brisbane: University of Queensland Press.
Wright, A. (2006), *Carpentaria*, Sydney: Giramondo.
Wright, A. (2007a), "On Writing *Carpentaria*," *Heat Magazine*, 13: 79–95.
Wright, A. (2007b), *Carpentaria* (B Format Edition), Australia: Tower Books.
Wright, A. (2013), *The Swan Book*, Sydney: Giramondo.

Index

CPSIA information can be obtained
at www.ICGtesting.com
Printed in the USA
LVHW080209250719
625298LV00005B/77/P

9 781501 349119